Palgrave Studies in Impact Finance

Series Editor
Mario La Torre, Department of Management, Sapienza University of Rome, Rome, Italy

The *Palgrave Studies in Impact Finance* series provides a valuable scientific 'hub' for researchers, professionals and policy makers involved in Impact finance and related topics. It includes studies in the social, political, environmental and ethical impact of finance, exploring all aspects of impact finance and socially responsible investment, including policy issues, financial instruments, markets and clients, standards, regulations and financial management, with a particular focus on impact investments and microfinance.

Titles feature the most recent empirical analysis with a theoretical approach, including up to date and innovative studies that cover issues which impact finance and society globally.

More information about this series at
http://www.palgrave.com/gp/series/14621

Živko Bergant

Accountancy and Social Responsibility

An Innovative New Approach to Accountancy Theory and Practice

palgrave
macmillan

Živko Bergant
College for Accountancy and Finance
Ljubljana, Slovenia

ISSN 2662-5105 ISSN 2662-5113 (electronic)
Palgrave Studies in Impact Finance
ISBN 978-3-030-77927-6 ISBN 978-3-030-77928-3 (eBook)
https://doi.org/10.1007/978-3-030-77928-3

Cover illustration: Denis Pobytov

This Palgrave Macmillan imprint is published by the registered company Springer Nature Switzerland AG
The registered company address is: Gewerbestrasse 11, 6330 Cham, Switzerland

To Sava, Katja, and Darko

Preface

The initial purpose of writing this work appeared as relatively modest: to determine the importance of accounting and find a place within the framework of the social responsibility. During the writing, it turned out that critical view is needed and quite a lot of notions and categories needed to be defined more precisely. Within these notions and concepts, particularly the difference between accounting and accountancy, the concept of comprehensive accountancy theory, the role of accountancy, the right to solidarity, the value-added law, the surplus value added, the surplus value-added statement, the personal balance sheet, the concept of comprehensive financial policy, the sustainable society, the sustainability triangle and the sustainability pyramid can be mentioned.

All of them have to be placed in a comprehensive accountancy and financial system. Therefore, a systemic approach was necessary, especially with the help of partial systems, which also proved to be a very convenient analytical tool.

Accountancy, as a base of information system required the definition of the main objective of business system. Through principles of social responsibility and sustainable future, it appeared that value added is the main information to be followed. It was based on general value-added law that worked in history and still continues to work in all societies.

On the above statements, the accountancy theory was based and positioned into sustainability triangle. Comparing to the starting aim, the work ended into unexpected findings about accountancy and its role in the relationship with social responsibility and sustainable society. It allows unsuspected further development of financial accounting, accountancy theory and practice, and promising connections with other social sciences. Last but not least, on this basis, starting points for important changes in the socio-economic system and for a step forward toward a humane society are given.

The above findings can be a source of pride and motive for both accounting professionals and practitioners, and a powerful motive for those driving social changes.

Of course, these findings also mean a huge responsibility, not only for the academic and political spheres, but also for each individual person who wants to get involved in a developing and modern society.

At the end, I would like to express much gratitude to my colleague Neven Borak Ph.D., who encouraged me during writing this book. Without his participation, this work would not be as it is now.

Ljubljana, Slovenia Živko Bergant

Contents

List of Figures

List of Tables

CHAPTER 1

Introduction

Most people know the concept of accounting, but under this term every one imagines something in its own way. At the same time, there are no completely uniform views even among experts on this important area.

The work is intended not only for accounting professionals, but also for managers and professionals in various organizations. In its own way, it touches on their activities from a business standpoint and from a personal perspective as well. The content of the present work is subordinated to this purpose.

The work is divided into 13 basic chapters, followed by appendices: References and Index. In order to follow the red thread, they will be briefly presented. At the end of each chapter, questions for discussion are offered. Their purpose is to draw attention to the important content of each chapter and to enable discussion of it as well. This is also the reason why no answers are offered.

After the introduction, Chapter 2 deals with definitions of accounting and accountancy with help of partial systems aspect. Some shortcomings of accounting theory are exposed. The accounting is described deeper through main process (from data to information) and through particular processes from different points of view. The connection between forecasting, planning and analyzing is depicted and emphasized.

Ž. Bergant, *Accountancy and Social Responsibility*,
Palgrave Studies in Impact Finance,
https://doi.org/10.1007/978-3-030-77928-3_1

Chapter 3 makes a distinction between creating information and the reporting process. It is discussed from managerial, informational, operational and quality aspects. Special attention is given to quality of reporting, including some general delusions in the interpretation of accounting information in the literature. The quality of reporting is defined as its usefulness, therefore through the efficiency and effectiveness of business decisions. Some delusions in financial analysis are exposed.

Chapter 4 introduces a role of risk in human activities and describes an origin and the creation of value added. A deeper definition of value added is given, its content and accounting calculations. Several explanations of value added are discussed, including its broader understanding.

Chapter 5 reveals a formulation of general value-added law (*VAL*) in society that is valid and works through entire human history. The economic and social characteristics of *VAL* are discussed. *VAL* presents a key starting point for further implementation in this book and for substantiation of accountancy theory. Guidance, structure and distribution of the value added are discussed. A surplus value added as a basis for its distribution among the stakeholders is defined. The relation between capital owners and employees is addressed as a crucial in thinking about social responsibility, especially regarding the distribution of the surplus value added.

Chapter 6 gives a structured proposal of accounting surplus value-added statement (*SVAS*), comparing it to the classic accounting income statement. *SVAS* includes information of creating and distributing surplus value added and presents a most important accounting statement. Some economic and financial aspects of surplus value added, including analysis of surplus value-added statement (together with operational and financial leverage), are discussed. The important point is that in the framework of surplus value added several traditional economic and financial approaches and models are not useful any more.

Chapter 7 discusses consequences of adopting the value-added principle to the management of organizations. A comprehensive management model on the value-added basis is offered. It is included in general principle of sustainable development. Cybernetic version of a model is given as well. It is connected with financial policy in the framework of value added regarding investment policy and solvency of an organization. A comprehensive model of financial policy on this basis is presented.

Chapter 8 deals with ethics on the basis of value-added law. It claims that there are not several types of ethics, but there is always only one: personal ethics. Therefore, business and professional ethics represent two partial systems of personal ethics. The aspects of accounting and management are discussed. The development of accounting and the development and the accounting department are shown. The development and characteristics of recent accounting theory are presented and shown its important shortcomings.

Chapter 9 offers starting points for accountancy theory as a basis for implementing an efficient accounting information system. The basic areas of the theory are principles and rules of accounting process, principles and rules of management in accountancy and finally accountancy system resources. A short critical discussion of the theory is given. All its weaknesses can be overbridged in the sustainable future perspective. The notion of sustainable future to the sustainable society is transformed. On this basis a comprehensive model of accountancy theory is offered. The fundamental criteria of good accountancy theory and its implementation stem from principles of social responsibility. The issues of social responsibility are discussed. Some critical remarks are given on recent achievements in this area. They have important impact on current accounting theory. The social responsibility is expanded to individual person and individual's accounting statements are offered from social responsibility point of view. Main factors of different people's behaving are found. Still, social responsibility is the main criteria for their behaving.

Chapter 10 finally finds the role and a position of accountancy (and information system as a whole) in relationship with social responsibility and sustainable future in a sustainability triangle and in a sustainable pyramid. It shows a needed harmony among these categories. Such position reflects all the importance of accountancy and accounting professionals and their impact on the events in the society.

Chapter 11 gives the summary of findings and the main point from previous chapters in order to facilitate red thread recognition.

Chapter 12 offers an idea of some possible duties to various carriers of development. Without their effort, there will be no changes in society.

INDEX at the end helps finding some important categories.

> If our life goal was to win a Nobel Prize,
> we would have studied medicine, physics,
> or economics instead of accounting. (Miller et al. 2002)

Reference

Miller, Paul B. W., Bahnson, R. Paul (2002). *Quality Financial Reporting*. New York: McGraw-Hill.

CHAPTER 2

Accounting and Accountancy

2.1 The Definition of Accountancy

Accountancy is often understood as a synonym of *accounting* (e.g. *CGAP* Glossary). Even a book can be found, titled as *Accountancy*, but subject of the book is only accounting (e.g. Hadi 2013). Inside the book, there is no word about accountancy (except in the preface).

More detailed definitions of accountancy can be found in Market Business News (*MBN* 2019): "Accountancy is an *information science* we use to gather, classify, and manipulate financial information. Not only companies, but also individuals, charities, and many other entities are familiar with accountancy." However, "Accounting is the *work or process* of keeping financial records. It is the systematic recording, reporting, and analysis of the financial activities (transactions) of a person, business, or organization. In business, it allows companies to analyze their financial performance" (*MBN* 2019).

Similar definitions have Radhakrishnan et al. (2017):

> Accountancy refers to *a systematic knowledge* of accounting. It explains 'why to do' and 'how to do' of various aspects of accounting. It tells why and how to prepare the books of accounts and how to summarize the accounting information and communicate it to the interested parties." However, "Accounting refers to the *actual process* of preparing

Ž. Bergant, *Accountancy and Social Responsibility*, Palgrave Studies in Impact Finance,
https://doi.org/10.1007/978-3-030-77928-3_2

and presenting the accounts. In other words, it is the art of putting the academic knowledge of accountancy into practice. (Radhakrishnan et al. 2017)

These examples show that *accountancy* has mainly a broader meaning that is related to information science, knowledge, profession, journals, subject in schools, auditing, "business language," etc. It represents an entire body of the theory and practice of accounting (Kohler in: Juthani and Mehta 2019).

Accounting however is predominantly reserved for naming the process. Therefore, the question is, what does accountancy mean in an organization. The next question is, what the criterion for proper accounting performance is. These questions deserve more attention in next chapters.

2.2 Accounting and Accountancy in an Organization

Considering accountancy as a broader concept comparing to accounting, first, we must define a content of accounting and accountancy on the level of an organization.

Most authors agree that accounting has now been raised to the level of an information system of a company (e.g. *AICPA* 2015). However, such an understanding is not consistent with accounting, which is defined as a mere process.

To clarify this inconsistency, the systemic approach (with partial systems)[1] is useful. On the highest level, an organization (or a business system) has three partial systems: the operational partial system, the information partial system and the managerial (decision-making) partial system. The position of accounting in information partial system is shown in Fig. 2.1.

Figure 2.1 has four main triangles showing four *information functions* of *each* information system:

[1] Partial system in accordance with the theory of systems is defined as the entire system is viewed only from a certain point of view (e.g. the skeleton, nervous system or blood circulation in the human body. Subsystems represent, for example: head, arm, leg, etc. Partial system therefore allows studying a system from a selected viewpoint. More in Knoflacher (2002, p. 121).

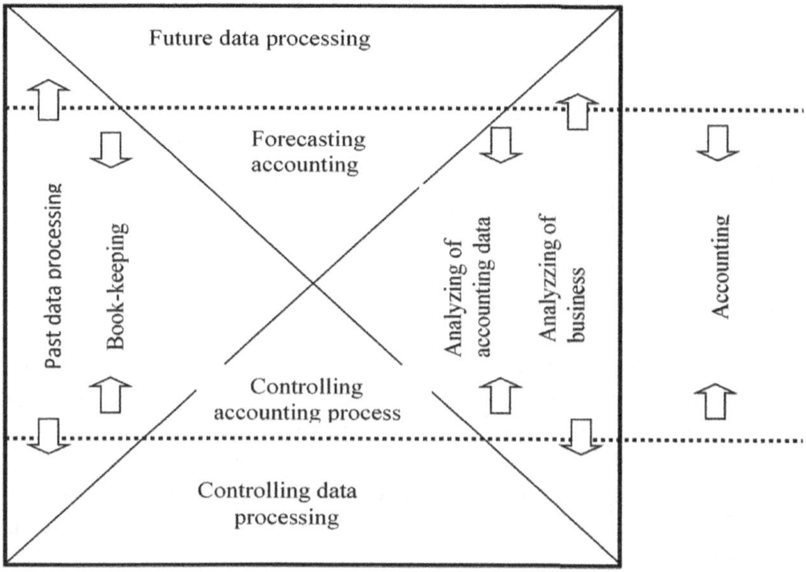

Fig. 2.1 Accounting as a part of information system (*Source* Adopted from Turk [1978, p. 76])

1. Past data processing
2. Future data processing
3. Controlling data processing
4. Analyzing data

The arrows in Fig. 2.1 show firstly, the broader scope of information function in an information system and secondly, the narrower scope of these functions in accounting. Obviously, the accounting that lies between bold lines has parts of all information functions. These parts are ***accounting information functions***:

1. *Book-keeping* as a part of past data processing
2. *Forecasting accounting data* as a part of future data processing
3. *Controlling accounting process* as a part of controlling data processing
4. *Analyzing of accounting data* as a part of data analyzing function

The approach shown above confirms the inextricably interwoven character of accounting in an organization that was already stressed by some authors (e.g. Roberts and Scapens 1985, p. 444; Hopwood 1987, p. 232). Namely, almost all employees are part of informational partial system and therefore they are part of accounting system as well. This confirms the justification for the use of partial systems.

We can now approach the definition of accountancy and its position in an organization. If accountancy is generally an information science (as defined in Sect. 2.1), what about accountancy on the level of a company and its information system?

We can find an answer to this question using a systemic approach and viewing the information system through partial systems. Therefore, a company's accountancy could be viewed through three partial systems: operational (execution) partial system, informational partial system and managerial partial system. They are shown in Fig. 2.2.

Operational partial system encompasses operating parts of accounting: book-keeping, forecasting, analyzing and operational controlling (internal controls).

Informational partial system of accounting system encompasses informing, respectively reporting (presentation, explanation, communication, display etc.), archiving data or information, and reporting about controlling.

These two partial systems are the subject and the elements of *accounting process* in an organization. Together with the management

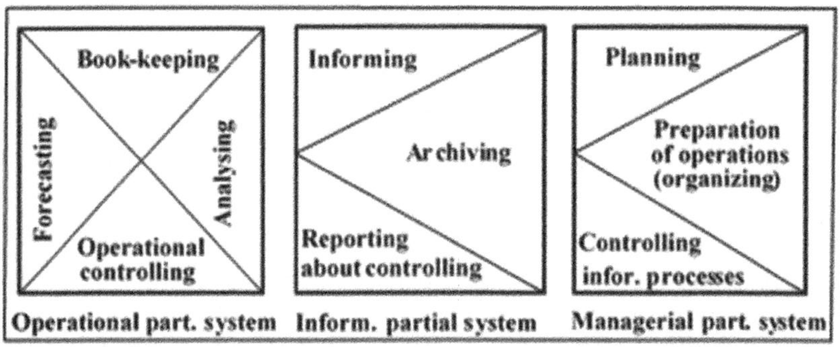

Fig. 2.2 Partial systems of accountancy in an organization (*Source* Own research)

partial system, they form ***accountancy*** as a whole concept in an organization. ***Accounting is therefore a subset of accountancy.***

The accounting process is governed by accounting standards and internal accounting rules. Management of the accounting process should be ruled by basic management principles, which are adjusted to accounting activities.

The head of accounting department is also a manager with all management responsibilities. Therefore, his tasks and their implementation are integral parts of accountancy as a whole. Such an understanding of accountancy implies the need to treat the accountancy management professionally as a specific subject of study. In doing so, adequate interdisciplinary approach is needed.

Management in accountancy comprises all the basic management functions: planning, organizing and controlling of accounting processes. It can be seen from Fig. 2.2 as well.

The ***information part*** of planning process in an organization is named ***forecasting***. Forecasting is one of information functions that provide information about future, which is based mainly on past trends and forecasted changes in the future. The head of accountancy in an organization is in charge for this process. In Fig. 2.2, forecasting of accounting data is therefore positioned in the information partial system.

Managerial part of accounting planning process is positioned in managerial partial system as a ***planning*** function, and results in a planned decisions. The plan of accounting activities includes a determination of information needed, the users of information, planned human resources and their development, fixed assets, intangible assets, information technology, etc., which are needed for an effective functioning of accounting process.

Plan of accounting activities is a "business plan" for an accounting information system. It should be approved by the management of an organization and therefore represents the goals to be achieved. Of course, it is not necessary to be a special document, but its content should be incorporated into business plan of the organization, as a whole. Such an approach is very important in promoting of accounting activities and the accounting profession inside an organization.

Information part (forecasting) and management part (decisions) of the planning process and their interactive operations form the entire planning process in the organization.

Differentiation between forecasting and planning (decisions for the future) is important to distinguish the responsibilities of organization's information officer (or manager of accountancy), which provides information, to the responsibilities of the manager of an organization (for providing decisions). At the same time, this differentiation enables one to understand close connectedness of both and their cooperation in the total planning process.

Another distinction is important: supervising the accounting process is the responsibility of the head of accounting, while supervising accountancy as a whole is the task of the manager of an organization.

In the above considerations, an accounting department in an organization is not mentioned, nor does it appear in Fig. 2.2. The accounting department is namely an organizational unit (it means it is a subsystem), therefore it appears in the organizational structure of an organization and not in the partial systems approach. Accounting department does not normally perform all accounting tasks in accordance with Fig. 2.2. In addition, it often also performs non-accounting tasks, especially in smaller organizations.

Non-accounting tasks are those, which do not belong to the information partial system, so they are not parts of the main information process (data ⇨ process ⇨ information). The basic criterion for the provision of such non-accounting tasks in an accounting department (and of course all its other activities) is rationality, i.e., lower costs with the same quality of service. Such a solution however is rational only *temporarily*, until circumstances change.

2.3 Accounting Theory and Its Shortcomings

Accounting theory has evolved throughout history. More about history of accounting theory can be found in Unegbu (2014). Recent accounting theory achieved the status that is best represented by the international accounting standards. These standards however are focused primarily to external reporting, which is mostly named as financial accounting. Internal reporting is treated in a number of professional studies, through other accounting disciplines (e.g. cost accounting and management accounting) and good accounting practices as well.

Such an accounting theory has at least four important drawbacks. Firstly, it treats accounting only as a process (e.g. Hendriksen 1965) and basic accounting principles (e.g. Smyth 2018). Therefore, it neglects the management aspect (management partial system) that is an integral part of accountancy, which is shown in Fig. 2.2. Secondly, it neglects the importance of connectedness of accounting with actual economic system, which dictates criteria and main information of business success. Thirdly, it neglects also the impact of accounting theory on socio-economic and political development. This effect is otherwise recognized, but the authors usually do not connect accounting theory closer to social responsibility aspects. Fourthly, the conceptual framework of accounting, as its theoretical base is still missing albeit it was emphasized already relatively early (e.g. Watts and Zimmerman 1979, p. 301; Hines 1989, p. 89; Montagna 1991, p. 94).

A special attention will be paid to these aspects and they will be a red line in the continuation of this work.

2.4 The Main Process of Accounting

In Sect. 2.1, accounting was defined as a process, so it's time to shed more light on it.

Information process in accounting can be treated from two points of view. Firstly as main information process and secondly as particular processes of different accounting operating functions (e.g. book-keeping, forecasting, analyzing and controlling).

The main information process (from data to information) has been already defined in the preceding chapter. Information is therefore an output from the information system. Unlike data, information contains "something more," it is useful to the user.

The usefulness of information must be understood differently from its expressive power, although they are in some way related. Without expressive power there is no information. The expressive power of information is defined as its explanatory power of a particular phenomenon.

The usefulness of information can be verified relatively quickly in practice. The information should *give the user a sense of danger or opportunity*. Unlike information, the data leave the user indifferent. In such a case the user did not get some feeling about danger or opportunity.

It is possible that the information designer provided very important information, but the user did not understand it. The user may have misunderstood it or did not even know what to do with it. From user's point of view, it was worthless information or even misinformation.

Such a communication noise can be the result of insufficient level of user's knowledge or of inappropriately (unclearly) provided (presented) information.

Therefore, it is in principle the responsibility of the information designer to check whether or not the user has received the appropriate information.

The above considerations can be illustrated schematically as a process of changing data into information mode, as shown in Fig. 2.3.

Data is the basic raw material (e.g. iron), which is processed by the information designer (e.g. the blacksmith) with his or her analytical skills (in our case, forging knowledge). In this way, the information designer creates "potential information." The blacksmith produces a pair of tongs and the information designer (the analyst) provides a specific indicator.

Firstly, there is a need to find out why this indicator is not yet final information yet, since it is only potential information. The reason is that

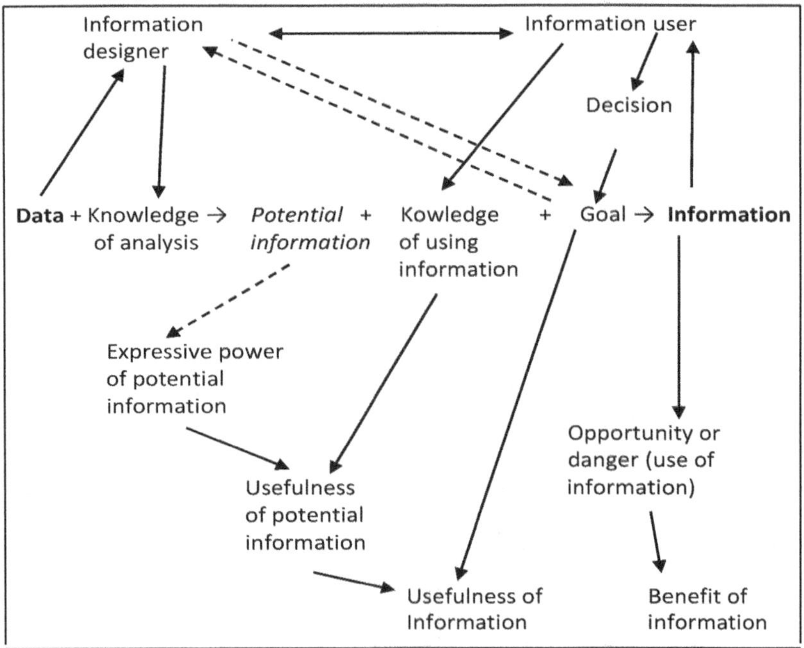

Fig. 2.3 Process from data to an information (*Source* Own research)

its use requires some knowledge of the user, just as it is necessary to know how to use the tongs. Potential information therefore has a certain expressive power (dashed line), which is usually defined and explored by the business analysis as a profession. The expressive power of potential information is a kind of "potential utility," which the tongs also have, since they can be ergonomically shaped, solid, easily open and close and the like. There are also different ways to explain a particular indicator in principle. Also, the tongs can be used in different ways.

Similarly, potential information obtains its actual usefulness only from the user, who understands and can use that information. However, usability is still not a sufficient condition for potential information to become useful, just as the knowledge of the use of tongs does not mean that they are useful. Indeed, tongs are only useful if the user actually needs them for a particular job, that is, when the purpose of use is defined. Similarly, information (indicator) is useful when it gives the user a sense of opportunity or danger regarding a particular (intended or already implemented) business decision. The purpose of the information comes from the type of business decision of the user of the information. The designer of the information is supposed to be aware of this fact. The two-way arrow in Fig. 2.3 shows the link, which must be established between the designer and the user of the information. This communication is important because the decision purpose is crucial for the proper design of the information and thus for its expressive power. The user informs the information designer about the purpose of the business decision, and the designer proposes a goal of analysis as a criterion of this basis. This is illustrated by the dashed lines in Fig. 2.3. The well-known purpose of business decision-making is therefore the final condition for potential information to become useful information.

It follows from the above that information is, as a rule, the result of an appropriate cooperation between the designer and the user of the information. This is also their shared responsibility. This means that when interacting with the information designer according to Fig. 2.3, the user is an integral part of the information system or information process, since without it there is no proper output from the information system. This is an important finding that means a significant and direct impact of users on the efficiency and effectiveness, which makes a quality of the information system.

From Fig. 2.3 we can therefore summarize the following relations that explain the meaning and the content of each category:

Data	+	Knowledge of analysis	=	Potential information
Expressive power of potential information	+	Knowledge of using information	=	Usability of potential information
Usability of potential information	+	Purpose of using information	=	Utility of information
Utility of information	+	Use of information	=	Benefit of information

As a rule, the information alone is not sufficient for a variety of reasons to decide the user's business. The latter must have adequate managerial knowledge and ability (not least to include the decision maker's intuition and vision) for the final judgment of business decision-making, as shown by the following relation:

Information + Management judgment = Decision.

2.5 Particular Processes of Accounting

It is reasonable to treat individual processes in accounting according to their functions, which are shown in Fig. 2.1. These processes may also be studied in light of the partial systems. Such an approach is illustrated in Table 2.1.

Before addressing the individual processes, it is useful to define some starting points:

a. Table 2.1 covers all accounting tasks within an organization.
b. As mentioned in the commentary on Fig. 2.2, not all tasks are performed in the accounting department.

Table 2.1 Partial systems of accounting functions

Points of view	*Book-keeping*	*Forecasting*	*Analyzing*	*Controlling*
Operational aspect				
Informational aspect				
Managerial aspect				

Source Own research

c. Table 2.1 can be a guide to assessing whether all types of tasks are performed, regardless of their location within the organization.
d. Using Table 2.1, it is possible to identify the responsible holders of individual tasks.
e. The main reason for approaching individual accounting processes is the organizational view and the need for clearly defined responsibilities.

Below, the process within each accounting functions will be discussed.

In principle, *the book-keeping process* is illustrated in Fig. 2.4.

Figure 2.4 shows the book-keeping process through three partial systems. The involvement of accounting management at all points of this process shows dashed lines.

Each of the displayed points of book-keeping process can be deeply examined (e.g. book-keeping processes in cost accounting), but this is beyond the scope of this book.

Next process, *forecasting in accounting*, will be examined. The main output of this process is short- or long-term forecasting accounting statements. The process is illustrated in Fig. 2.5.

Figure 2.5 shows the accounting forecasting process through three partial systems. The involvement of accounting management at all points of this process is illustrated by dashed lines. Each of the displayed points of forecasting process needs to be deeply examined on lower levels (organization units, projects, business areas, etc.), but this is beyond the scope of this book.

Like past data, predicted data are also subject for analyzing. The main output from accounting analysis[2] is information. In principle, the *process of accounting analysis* is shown in Fig. 2.6.

Figure 2.6 shows all three aspects of analysis and also involvement of accounting management through all the points of this process.

The main *areas* of accounting analysis are efficiency, effectiveness and solvency of an organization. The main approach of accounting analysis is analyzing past changes and planned changes of company's operations.

[2] Analysis of accounting data.

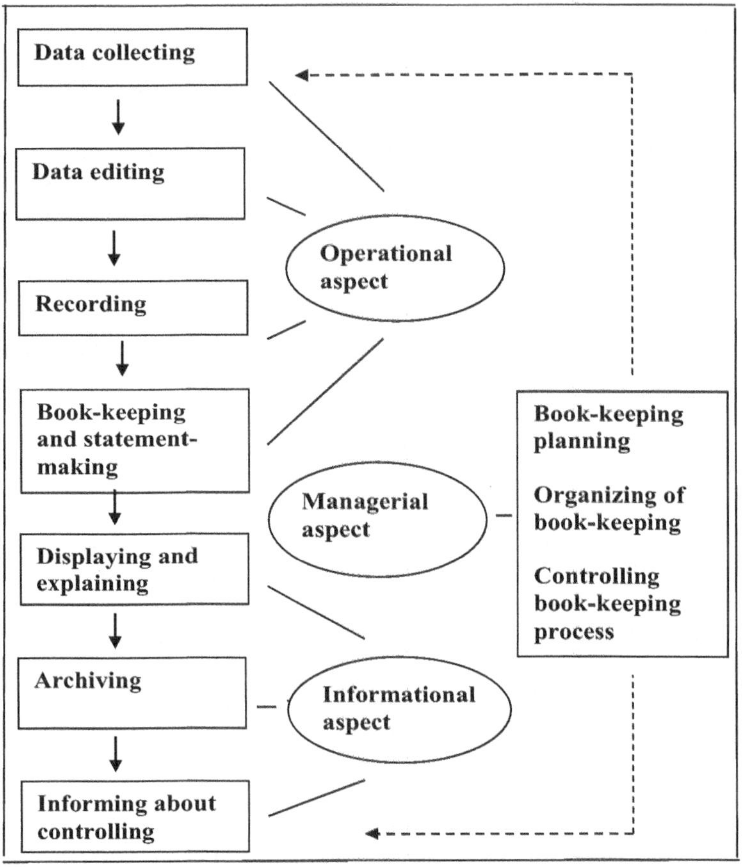

Fig. 2.4 Book-keeping process (*Source* Own research)

Such an analysis uses basic analytic tools as deviations from planned items, business flows[3] and ratios.[4]

The process of analysis is closely linked to the processes of forecasting and decision-making. These links are in principle shown in Fig. 2.7.

[3] Business flow is any change of company's assets or its obligations.

[4] Ratio is an indicator, expressed in relation (fraction, index etc.).

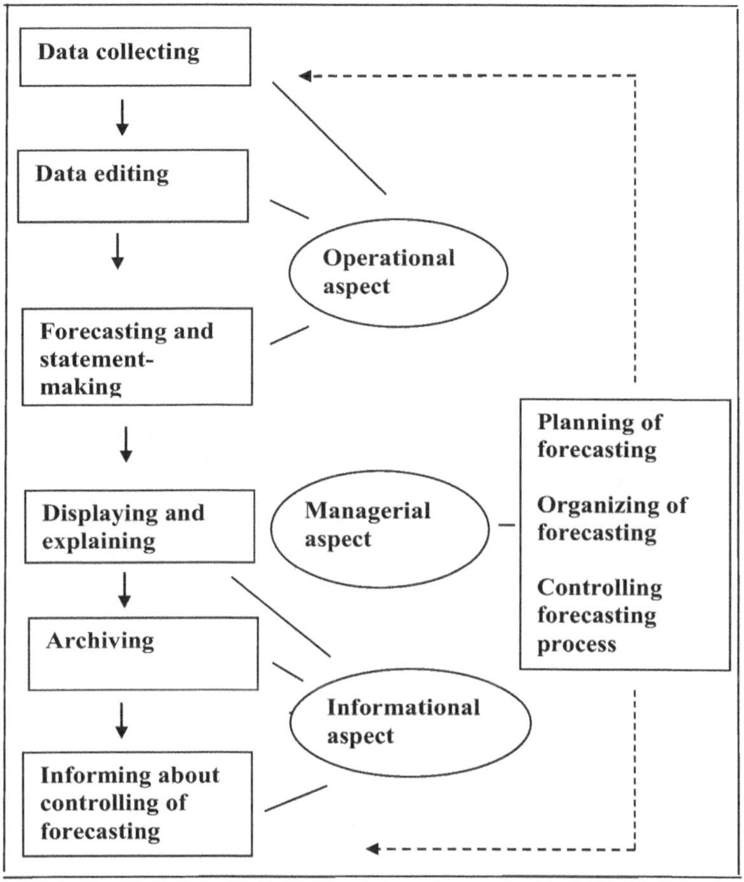

Fig. 2.5 Accounting forecasting process (*Source* Own research)

Figure 2.7 shows the involvement of all three types of input data in the forecasting process (analysis of the past and the environment, as well as projected business decisions). In the Fig. 2.7, marked with a dotted line, the process of planning, which ends with the plan, takes place.

The accounting forecasting holder can be an accountant if there is no special planning and analytical service, organized within the company. Such a department is usually the coordinator of the overall planning process within the company. Planners are heads of core business functions

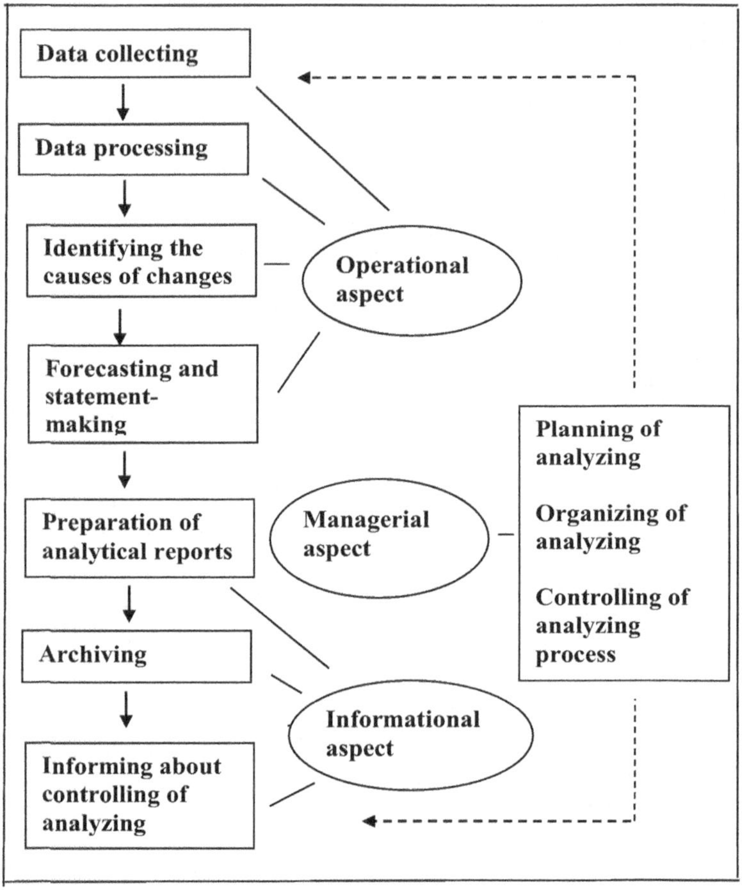

Fig. 2.6 Process of analyzing accounting data (*Source* Own research)

or heads of responsibility in the matrix organization of the company, each for their own area of work. The final plan is adopted by the management and the competent authorities of the organization.

The next basic process in accounting is *controlling in accounting*. It means determining the correctness and elimination of irregularities in accounting data and information in the framework of book-keeping, accounting forecasting and accounting analysis. It therefore applies to all parts of accounting. It is aimed at achieving the financial objectives

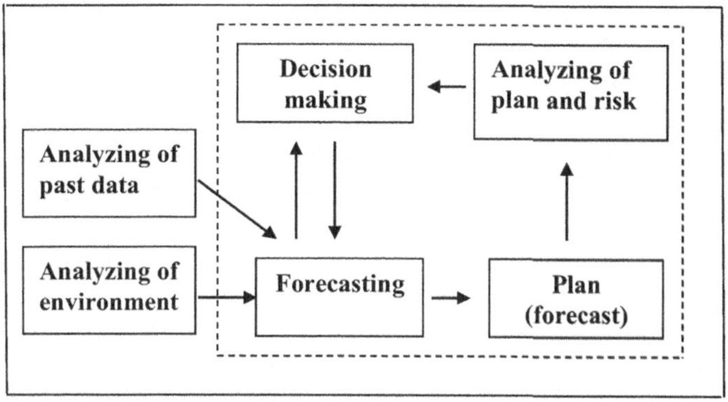

Fig. 2.7 Linking forecasting, planning and analyzing (*Source* Own research)

(compliance with accounting policies and procedures, safeguarding of assets, the preparation of reliable financial reports and business compliance with internal and external regularity trial).

Controlling in accounting is one of the accounting functions, which means that it is a professional (rather than formal) responsibility of the accounting manager.

In substance, controlling in accounting covers the following areas:

1. Controlling the authentication of business events:
   (a) Pre-execution control
   (b) Post-execution control
2. Controlling the reality of business transactions
   (a) Controls on receipt of goods or services and controls on acceptance of obligations
   (b) Post-receipt controls or post-commitment controls
   (c) Monitoring the security of the assets of the organization
3. Monitoring the compliance with the economic financial regulations, which is limited mainly to book-keeping, financial statements, financial reports and tax and insolvency legislation.

In the process of assets transformation and obligations transformation, there must be an internal control system whereby each worker in the next phase controls the worker from the previous phase (the principle of liability relief). Otherwise, there is a greater risk that book-keeping data reflects the true position or business processes. The responsibility for controlling in accounting therefore extends to all organizational units (and to their heads) where the data is generated, processed or stored. This is reflected in the requirements and norms regarding the design of forms, methods, and degree of accuracy, delivery time and the like.

It follows that controlling in accounting is not only controlling of the book-keeping activity within an accounting department, but also controlling of the operating activities of an entity that can be carried out using accounting documents. This implies a fundamental organizational principle of separating the execution of transactions from the records of this work.

Based on the above considerations, we can conclude that controlling in accounting has mostly a character of internal control.

Like other information functions, controlling in accounting extends over the entire operations of the company; it is therefore a partial system.

Controlling in accounting must be distinguished from the *control of accounting*, which is the responsibility of top management. It is mainly conducted through external auditing and internal audit department and it is not the subject of this book.

The position of controlling in accounting is shown in Fig. 2.8.

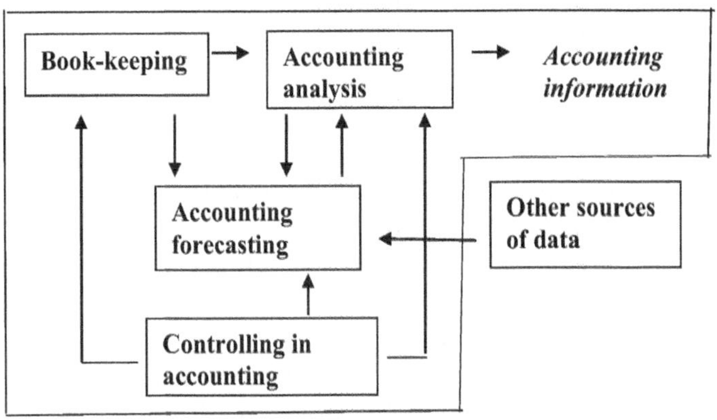

Fig. 2.8 Position of controlling in accounting (*Source* Own research)

The start of accounting information process is book-keeping process, giving "material" to analyze and for forecasting as well. All three processes are subject to accounting control. The final stage of the accounting process is analyzing, which provides accounting information. In the intermediate stages, analysis also provides data for forecasting process.

Of course, it does not mean that the analysis process cannot be started without prior book-keeping, since the analysis can only be based on planned data. Therefore, data for forecasting does not provide only book-keeping, but other sources of data are also necessary. For instance, information on contracts already concluded, planned business decisions, etc. As a rule, accounting information for decision-making contains forecasting information as well.

From the above discussion of individual information processes, it can be concluded that, despite the great differences in content between them, they are linked to all organizational units of the company, making it impossible to organize them as independent organizational units. So, each of them is a partial information system. Therefore, we cannot organize the entire information system in one organizational unit. The above findings are important for the proper organization of accounting processes within an organization.

Questions for Discussion

2-1 What is the difference between accounting and accountancy?
2-2 How do you see this difference on the level of an organization?
2-3 How would you explain the concept of a partial system?
2-4 What are the main functions of each information system?
2-5 Explain accounting information functions.
2-6 How would you explain the interwoven character of accounting in an organization?
2-7 Explain the partial systems of the accountancy.
2-8 Why is accounting a subset of accountancy?
2-9 Explain the role of the head of accounting department.
2-10 What should be the content of the accounting plan in an organization?
2-11 How do you differentiate forecasting and planning?

2-12 Why the accounting department cannot perform all accounting tasks in an organization?
2-13 How do you differentiate accounting and non-accounting tasks?
2-14 What shortcomings of a recent accounting theory could you find out?
2-15 What is the main information process in accounting?
2-16 What do you understand with the usefulness of information?
2-17 Who is responsible for the usefulness of information?
2-18 Is there any difference between the expressive power of potential information and its usefulness?
2-19 Explain some particular processes of accounting.
2-20 How do you explain the connections between forecasting, planning and analyzing?
2-21 How would you explain the controlling process in accounting?
2-22 Is there any difference between controlling in accounting and the control of accounting?

References

AICPA (2015). *Introduction to Accounting*. American Institute of certified Accountants. (Retrieved: December, 2019). http://www.ncert.nic.in/ncerts/l/keac101.pdf.

Hadi, U. Noor. (2013). *Comprehensive Guide & Key to Modern Accountancy*. Peshavar: Nadeem Trade Center. (Retrieved: December, 2019). https://www.researchgate.net/publication/280597660_Comprehensive_Guide_Key_to_Modern_Accountancy.

Hendriksen, Eldon (1965). *Accounting Theory*. Homewood: Richard D. Irwin, Inc.

Hines, D. Ruth (1989). Financial Accounting Knowledge, Conceptual Framework Projects and the Social Construction of the Accounting Profession. *Accounting & Auditing Journal*, Vol. 2, No. 2.

Hopwood, G. Anthony (1987). The Archaeology of Accounting Systems. *Accounting, Organizations and Society*, Vol. 12, No. 3, pp. 207–234.

Juthani, Toral, Urvi Mehta. Book. Keeping & Accountancy. STD. XI. Mumbai: Target Publications Pvt. Ltd. (Retrieved: December, 2019). https://www.targetpublications.org/download/11-commerce/std-11-book-keeping-and-accountancy.pdf.

Knoflacher, Markus (2002). *A Conceptual Model for Integrated Assessment.* Seibersdorf: Austrian Research Center. (Retrieved: May, 2020). https://pdfs.semanticscholar.org/3c56/6be91c590506c382e14a280ed92a6cd84e8a.pdf?_ga=2.104776320.1440620216.1588506548-1321762634.1587388447.

MBN—Market Business News. Accounting—Definition and Meaning. (Retrieved: October. 2019). https://marketbusinessnews.com/financial-glossary/accounting-definition-meaning/.

Montagna, Paul (1991). Accounting Elites and Accounting Theory. *Accounting, Organizations and Society*, Vol. 16, No. 1, pp. 93–99.

Radhakrishnan, G. T., Kumaran, T. S. S., Moorthy, T. N., Rama, N. (2017). *Accountancy.* Government of Tamil Nadu, India, Tamilnadu Textbook and Educational Services Corporation, Chennai, 2017. (Retrieved: December, 2019). https://www.academia.edu/34412465/ACCOUNTANCY_HigHer_SeCONdArY_FirST_YeAr.

Roberts, John, Scapens, Robert (1985). Accounting Systems and Systems of Accountability – Understanding Accounting Practices in Their Organisational Contexts. *Accounting, Organizations and Society*, Vol. 10, No. 4. pp. 443–456.

Smyth, Danielle (2018). What Are the Basic Accounting Theories? (Retrieved: January. 2020). https://bizfluent.com/about-5121481-basic-accounting-theories.html.

Turk, Ivan (1978). *Podatki in informacije v poslovnem sistemu.* (In Slovene). Ljubljana: ZRFS.

Unegbu, O. Angus (2014). Theories of Accounting: Evolution & Developments, Income-Determination and Diversities in Use. *Research Journal of Finance and Accounting*, Vol. 5, No. 19, 2014. (Retrieved: January, 2020). https://arxiv.org/abs/1411.4633.

Watts, L. Ross, Zimmerman, L. Jerold (1979). The Demand for and Supply of Accounting Theories. *The Accounting Review*, Vol. 54, No. 2, pp. 273–305.

CHAPTER 3

Accounting and Reporting

3.1 Introduction

Reporting is to be understood separately from the creating of information. Creating information is the last stage of the process of analyzing. Figure 2.2 in Sect. 2.2 shows that the analysis is part of the operational partial system. Reporting (informing) at the same picture is part of an informational partial system of the accountancy. This difference is very important because it separates the process of information creation from the reporting process.

The above statement differs significantly from the approach followed by International Accounting Standards Board, which treats financial reporting as an integral part of the accounting conceptual framework (*IFRS* 2018). In this way, the boundary between creating of information and reporting is blurred. This prevents effective and comprehensive improvement of the quality of financial reporting. The direct consequence is a lack of trust in accounting information. The expression of this is also reproach, that "the major rationale for undertaking conceptual framework projects was not functional or technical, but was a *strategic maneuvre* for providing legitimacy to standard setting boards and the accounting profession" (Hines 1989, p. 89). This statement will be discussed in the last sections.

Ž. Bergant, *Accountancy and Social Responsibility*,
Palgrave Studies in Impact Finance,
https://doi.org/10.1007/978-3-030-77928-3_3

The process of *creating* the information namely requires above all analytical skills. The *reporting* process, however, requires mainly the skills to explain, show and communicate. On this basis, we can distinguish also the respective responsibilities of the heads of these two processes. This distinction can be compared to the difference between production and sales function within the organization.

Reporting is therefore one of the information functions of any information system. It is a process of communication between information providers and its users in all possible forms and methods. It transmits information to its users.

Reporting can be considered in particular through the following important aspects:

1. Managerial aspect of reporting
2. Informational aspect of reporting
3. Operational aspect of reporting
4. Quality of reporting

In the following text we will further discuss these four aspects.

3.2 Managerial Aspect of Reporting

Managerial aspect of reporting encompasses decision-making and coordination about:

planning short-term and long-term reporting
organization of reporting
controlling reporting processes
ethics of reporting.

The plan of reporting should take into account in particular the purpose of reporting to individual users, their interests and needs, as well as their knowledge.

With short-term reporting planning, in the annual plan the methods and providers of periodic reporting and the corresponding dynamics are defined. In addition, there is also planning of particular reporting, which is more complex (in terms of importance, time, scope, assets, etc.).

Long-term reporting planning covers reporting that is of a continuous, periodic nature for each type of user across different levels of decision-making process. In this context, in particular, the basic modes of transmission of information, messages and notifications, the reporting agents and their responsibilities should be defined.

The final output of a reporting planning is a plan that provides appropriate presentation and clarification of information for different types of users across different decision-making levels. At the same time, it is the goal and criterion for reporting performance. Such a plan must be consistent with the plan of accounting process, which identifies key information.

The reporting planning coordinator may be the head of accounting or another designated person with the participation of major users of information. The final reporting plan is adopted by the organization's management.

Organizing of reporting encompasses mainly:

1. The definition of the responsibilities of individual information providers.
2. The definition of ways or paths and dynamics of information.
3. The provision of adequate means of disseminating information, in particular information and communication technology.
4. The appropriate education and training providers and users of information.

Monitoring of reporting should also be planned and its effectiveness is based on the feedback. The control bearer is the information coordinator within the reporting system or the head of accounting.

Reporting ethics must be ensured, which requires a reduction in subjectivity to an acceptable extent. Continuous prevention of "communication noise" and unilateral or lack of information is needed. The information must be subordinate to the interests of the organization as a whole and not to be discounted by any other pressure. Reporting responsibility is professional and moral. It is fully covered by the concept of professional diligence.

3.3 Informational Aspect of Reporting

Informational aspect of reporting encompasses decision-making and coordination about:

1. Reporting on information process in organization
2. Analysis of reporting quality
3. Monitoring of reporting
4. Archiving and storing information documentation.

Reporting about reporting process is a form of feedback on the achievement of information goals and is the basis for analyzing the reporting process. Information rapporteurs are information providers and the recipient of the report is the head of the information system (often the head of accounting). In the event that the accounting manager is also the provider of the information, it is important that he obtain the feedback on his reporting on the basis of which he can analyze his reporting and improve it accordingly.

The reporting quality analysis encompasses mainly:

- usefulness of information
- user's satisfaction
- intelligibility of submission, which requires submission in a language, understood by the recipient of the information
- relevance achieved
- appropriateness of the scope of information
- flexibility of information (for multiple users)
- efficiency and relevance of the use of information and communication technology.

Monitoring of reporting is aimed to improve the reporting process and to prevent false, harmful or biased information.

3.4 Operational Aspect of Reporting

From an operational aspect of reporting some elements must be defined, e.g. types of information,[1] informant, and the way of communication, type of information transmission path, the recipient and the user of information.

The reporting process should be adequate in terms of preparation, dynamics, resources (technical aspect) and persuasion (substantive aspect).

In order to provide information, it is important to define in particular the responsibility of information providers, information tasks (purpose), mode of reporting, extent of reporting and possible affiliation with the information designer.

The information provider is responsible for the true and fair presentation of the information but he is not responsible for the consequences of the business decision of the decision maker. It is therefore important that the user of the information is aware of the potential risks. The information provider must also contribute to this awareness. Therefore, it is often necessary interdisciplinary collaboration involved.

The importance of the feedback and how it works can be compared to after-revenues activities in the marketing field. Therefore, an important aspect of the user's education is encompassed within this framework, which enables a quick and correct understanding of the information received. At the same time, such training also aims at raising users' needs for improved and/or new information. It could be said to influence the development of a "market" for its information services. This is also the role of the head of accounting.

3.5 Quality of Reporting

3.5.1 Introduction

The quality of reporting in principle depends on the quality in three main areas. The first one is the quality of information, the second one is the quality of the information system and the third one is the quality of communication with users.

[1] Even though the principal financial statements are defined by accounting standards, there is a sufficient scope for specifying them.

Examining the quality of information means to the study of the process of analyzing rather than reporting. However, the quality of information is a prerequisite for the quality of reporting. It will therefore be addressed in this context.

A fundamental criterion for the *quality of information* is its *usefulness*. American Institute of Certified Auditors requires as a prerequisite for quality greater benefit information in relation to its costs (*AICPA*, adapted by Gleam and Delaney 1989, p. 680).

What is surprising is the lack of self-criticism of accountants and analysts regarding the usefulness of the information they produce.[2] This was already noted by Lynch: "Let's end to prepare useless information, let's support the decision" (Lynch 1994, p. 38).

In addition, the academic sphere plays an important role in this, especially by constantly repeating some key mistakes in explaining certain accounting indicators. Therefore, most analysts in practice repeat these errors. For illustration, some of them will be shown in the next section.

The basic path to useful information is shown in Fig. 2.3 in Sect. 2.1. Since the full usefulness of the information requires user's involvement, the expressive power of the potential information must first be addressed.

The Fig. 2.3 shows that the expressive power of information depends on the quality of data and knowledge of the analyst.

The quality of accounting data has been the subject of many studies, so there will be no discussion of this aspect in this section. In contrast, the expressive power of accounting information is still an important area of development, both in theory and in practice. Especially, this is important because of the presence of errors in the contemporary theory of financial analysis, financial statements and consequently also in business finance.

Mistakes and misinterpretations of accounting data and information have an important impact, both on practice in organizations and on the decline in confidence in the accounting profession and its usefulness. This is especially true due to constant repetition of the same mistakes in professional literature.

Some of such examples have no place in a social responsible accounting theory and practice. Therefore, they will be discussed in next section.

[2] The possible (but common) excuse that decision-makers do not require different (better) information or are satisfied, is not deserving serious consideration.

3.5.2 Some Delusions in Financial Analysis

3.5.2.1 Delusions, Related to Net Working Capital

The most common definition of net working capital (*NWC*) is the difference between short-term assets (*STA*) and short-term liabilities (*STL*) (e.g. Arnold 1998, p. 543):

$$NWC = STA - STL. \tag{3.1}$$

The disadvantage of such a definition is the fact that it is purely computational and not substantive. The usual result of this is reflected in the wrong opinion that "components (content) of net working capital are: inventories, trade receivables, marketable securities, cash, less current liabilities" (e.g. Arnold 1998, p. 543; Brigham et al. 1999, p. 595 and 596; O'Reagan 2002).

Many authors forget that net working capital cannot be influenced by short-term categories, although it can be calculated from them. Such a direct link between current assets and working capital, of course, does not exist. This would mean a switch of cause and effect, which is completely unacceptable in the analysis.

Such an error is generated due to neglecting of the fact that net working capital can be calculated also as the difference between the long-term sources (*LTS*) and long-term assets (*LTA*).

$$NWC = LTS - LTA. \tag{3.2}$$

The Eq. 3.2 can be found already in Rao (1987, p. 517). The neglecting of the above equation enables the wrong belief that net working capital can be changed by changing current assets or current liabilities. This is still wrongly repeated by some authors (e.g. Arnold 1998, p. 563 or Smart et al. 2004, p. 268).

Independent variables that affect the change in net working capital are just on the right side of the Eq. 3.2 and the dependent variable is to the left side of this equation. Net working capital is therefore part of ***long-term financing*** of organization. Therefore, only equity and/or long-term debt can be actual components of net working capital.

The structure of net working capital indicates its higher or lower quality. The important difference is, for example, if net working capital consists only of long-term debt or only equity. This structure has an important impact on company's solvency risk. Failure to consider this fact leads to a number of erroneous explanations, but also misleads decision-makers in business malicious actions.

3.5.2.2 Delusions About Statement of Cash Flow

The next common mistake is misinterpretation of the statement of cash flow. Unfortunately, even international accounting standards (*IAS 7* 2008, p. 18) recommend the direct method to report cash flow from operating activities as better information against the indirect method (*IAS 7* 2008, p. 19).

This is somewhat reminiscent of the scholastic debate over whether the income statement has greater expressive power than the cash flow statement. At that time, Donleavy critically compared such discussions with those of greater utility of the left or right shoe (Donleavy 1994, p. 162).

When comparing direct and indirect method of cash flow statement, the first question is, whether they are comparable at all. Two financial categories are in principle comparable only if they have exactly the same purpose.

Furthermore, it should be noted that it is possible to calculate each accounting category for at least two (but usually more) methods. Each of these methods does not demonstrate cause and effect relationship between categories, although the calculation result is the same. Therefore, due to the different method of calculating a category, as a rule, its expressive power changes, and its purpose changes as well. Such categories (information or indicators) are then not comparable.

It will be shown later that the direct method of calculating cash flow does not reflect a causal relationship, while the indirect method allows it. In contrast, the direct method provides some more information related to the organization's current liquidity than the indirect method. Both methods are therefore complementary, but not exclusive.

The recommendation of the international accounting standards is therefore incorrect and misleading. Even Miller and Bahnson make the same mistake when they favor the use of the direct method in reporting cash flow from operating activities over the indirect method (Miller and Bahnson 2002, p. 87).

Fortunately, it is very likely that the direct method will not be largely extended in practice, since its costs (taking into account the available information technology) and in the thoughts of managers today usually exceeds its expressive power.

3.5.2.3 Delusions About Liquidity Ratios

Important errors are related to the interpretation of liquidity ratios (current ratio, quick ratio and cash ratio). Many authors treat these indicators as important information about a company's solvency (e.g. Pinches 1994, p. 640; Brigham et al. 1999, p. 62). The expressive power of these indicators is by no means sufficient to explain the evolution of a company's liquidity or solvency.[3] The consequence is usually insufficient assessment of the solvency of the company and its credit rating in practice. This is especially important in several empirical researches, where the current ratio is often misused as a liquidity indicator of an organization.

So-called liquidity ratios are usually explained by comparing the numerator and the denominator (e.g. Friedlob and Schleifer 2003, p. 75) because the indicator computationally represents a fraction. This approach assumes that the counter (directly proportional) and the denominator (inversely proportional) affect the indicator. Such an assumption in the case of these ratios is completely wrong. The equations, by which these indicators are usually calculated, do not reflect a causal relationship.

Bierman, for example, stated that the company can achieve a higher current ratio because of surplus inventories (Bierman and Drebin 1978, p. 360). However, due to an increase in inventories, current ratio (CR) decreases rather than increases. We see that such inadequate explanation dates back for at least 30 years. A similar slip occurs even to Brigham, who believes that a low current ratio may indicate a small stock (Brigham et al. 1999, p. 62). Samuels et al. (1995, p. 56) wrongly suggests reducing the too high current ratio by reducing inventories and trade receivables, since such measures increase the ratio rather than decrease it.

This is due to the fact that only the following equation represents the causal effect relationship for current ratio (CR):

$$CR = \frac{1}{1 - \frac{NWC}{STA}} \tag{3.3}$$

[3] Although we may differentiate between these concepts in financial theory, we will not deal with this here. Both terms in principle explain the organization's ability to settle its liabilities.

The Eq. 3.3 shows that *CR* depends only on net working capital (in proportional way) and is inversely proportional on short-term assets (*STA*). Current ratio therefore depends on the ratio $K = NWC/STA$, which shows a part of short-term assets, which are long-term financed (by *NWC*). Moreover, *CR* is another form of indicator *K*: $(CR - 1)/CR$. This is the maximum expressive power of *CR*.

The value of 2 for the current ratio and a value of 1 for the quick ratio, which is still recommended by several professional authors is completely without theoretical basis (e.g. Westwick 1989, p. 178).

Wrong explanation of liquidity ratios can be found unfortunately also in many contemporary authors (e.g. McLure 2004, p. 375; O'Hare 2013, p. 41; Nuhu 2014, p. 109), that these ratios explain very inadequately. They proceed from the wrong assumption that short-term assets or receivables with cash involved "cover" short-term liabilities. For the same reasons as in the current ratio, this approach in case of quick ratio is not appropriate. The maximum expressive power of quick ratio is the monitoring of short-term financial intermediary position (net short-term debt or net short-term claim) and the relationship between inventories and net working capital.

3.5.2.4 *The Absence of a Theory About Capital Adequacy Assessment of Organizations*

An important shortcoming of contemporary financial analysis theory is a lack of an assumption of net working capital that is needed for safe operations regarding company's solvency. This is a consequence of a lack of common understanding of permanent current assets. It is important issue, because they represent long-term engaged money, so permanent current assets should be in principle long-term financed. This principle, however, is widely accepted in the context of feasibility studies about investment in fixed assets.

Some research suggests that the best approximation of permanent current assets is the difference between spontaneous short-term receivables with inventories included and spontaneous short-term payables (Bergant 2019, p. 4). Such an approach is of course the first approximation, because it is without an estimate of other risks in operations of an organization. They require additional reserve of long-term financing, on or off-balance sheet.

An estimate of permanent current assets also means an estimate of the working capital needed, which, as a rule, is not equal to the actual working capital. Larger or smaller difference between the two indicates a better or worse capital adequacy of the organization and thus lower or higher insolvency risk.

3.5.2.5 *Delusions About Operating Cash Flow*

The cash flow statement prepared in accordance with accounting standards has two disadvantages:

1. Does not separate short-term and long-term cash flows, which are important for monitoring the solvency of an organization.
2. Does not show the causes of changes in the cash balance.

Therefore, it does not serve its primary purpose that is, reporting on changes in the liquidity or solvency of an organization. Likewise, an otherwise well-known *operating cash flow* does not serve sufficiently in managing the insolvency risk of the organization. Even more, cash flow statement ***is not and it cannot be*** a basis for assessing future cash flow of an organization though "financial analysts seek to prognosticate the risk attached to a firm's future cash flows" (Miller and Bahnson 2002, p. 103).

This weakness has been already noted by Sumner: "We can misunderstand and wrongly explain operating cash flow if we do not separate its two basic components: the part that comes from the profitability of the company and the other part that comes from the financing of the company" (Sumner 1988, p. 530).

After all, the main cause of changing cash balance in the organization still remains unknown. The solution is simple, considering the capital adequacy of the organization. This is in principle indicated by the following equation[4]:

$$\Delta\, Cash = \Delta\, NWC_{act} - \Delta\, NWC_{need} + \Delta\, NSTFD \qquad (3.4)$$

The Eq. 3.4 shows that changes of cash balance depend on changes in capital adequacy (the difference between net working capital actual and net working capital needed) and net short-term financial debt (the difference between short-term financial investments and short-term financial obligations). Any change in capital adequacy therefore directly affects

[4] More about this equation in Bergant and Manohin (2020).

the increase or decrease of cash, and thus the solvency of the organization. This also means that ***future cash flow cannot be estimated without anticipated changes in the organization's capital adequacy.***

Given that the difference between actual and required working capital ($NWC_{act} - NWC_{need}$) represents a surplus or deficit of working capital ($OBK_{surplus}$ or OBK_{def}), Eq. 3.4 can also be used for the quickest assessment of the capital adequacy of an organization (Bergant and Manohin 2020):

$$NWC_{def} = STFD - STFI - Cash. \tag{3.5}$$

In accordance with Eq. 3.5, *NWC* deficit can be calculated by short-term financial debts (*STFD*), short-term financial investments (*STFI*) and cash, which includes also cash equivalents. When the result of Eq. 3.5 is negative, the company has *NWC* surplus. The weakness of Eq. 3.5 is that it does not show the causal relationship, however, it allows for continuous monitoring the changes of capital adequacy. The assumption of Eq. 3.5 is that the organization settles its business obligations within normal periods. Otherwise, it is necessary to adapt accordingly the data of *STFD*.

3.5.3 Quality of Information System

The quality of accounting information system includes more than just the quality of potential information in the reporting process. Accounting information system has a direct impact on the quality of reporting, not only by the usefulness of the information, but also by its relevance and reliability (AICPA 2015).

These characteristics can be achieved with the quality and proper functioning of all components (hardware, software, liveware, orgware, netware and dataware), which represent the capacity of each information system. There are several models for measuring the quality of information system (e.g. Al-Hudhaif 2010), an interesting one is also Cohen's model that is discussed in Idowu and Louche (2011, p. 240). Further discussion is out of scope of this book.

Proper management of all the components of an accounting information system is the content of management in accounting, which will be discussed later.

3.5.4 *Quality of Reporting*

The quality of reporting means its efficiency and effectiveness. It depends on many factors on the side of reporting provider and on the information user's side as well.

Factors which impact reporting quality on the information provider's side:

1. Knowledge about:
    a. Analyzing (knowledge of relevant indicators, their expressive power and methods of analysis)
    b. Information formulation
    c. Formulating appropriate guidelines or proposals
2. Ability to communicate (both in defining the analysis criteria, as well as in the information process).
3. Ability to empathy with the recipients of information (understanding of their interests).
4. Characteristics and character of reporting provider (reporter, head of accountancy or analyst).

The first point is discussed in more detail in the accounting professional-related literature. Some critical points were exposed in Sect. 3.5.2. The points two and three will be presented below. The fourth point will not be discussed, because it goes beyond the purpose of the paper.

Business communication is a process aimed at realizing business goals. Therefore, we can talk about the communication model shown in Fig. 3.1

Figure 3.1 shows that the communication process is not complete until the analyst receives feedback (in any form) about the effect of the user (a feeling of opportunity or danger). The user should not be left indifferent. The feedback is shown in Fig. 3.1 with dashed lines. The full line of feedback shows the user's initiatives, which suggest the reporter (or analyst) to develop additional information.

The central dashed lines in Fig. 3.1 show another important process that is giving initiatives and training for the user. It is necessary to continuously study the needs of users and give initiatives to create new or different, better quality information.

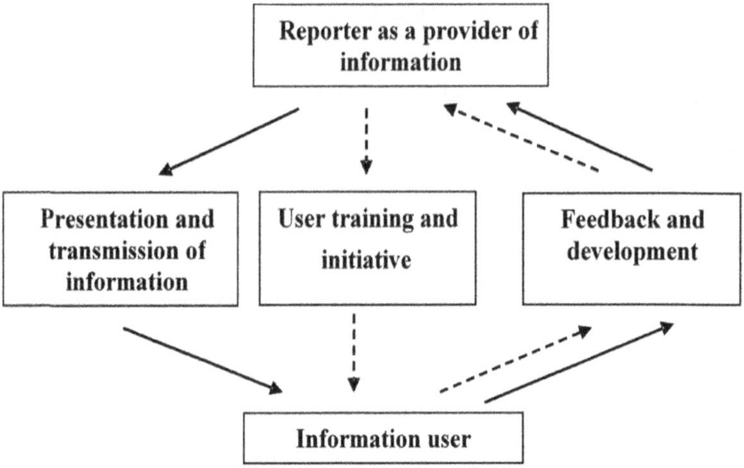

Fig. 3.1 Business communication model (*Source* Own research)

Constant training of users, in order to better understand the information, and thereby raising awareness of the need for new information is needed as well.

Both contribute to the quality of communication and to the development of the information system as a whole.

Of course, Fig. 3.1 does not show the whole process from information to business decision, which is important for the success of information. Therefore, we must also consider a further part of process, where user's information is included in business decisions. An impact of reporting on the decision-making process must be discussed.

The efficiency of communication is not ideal, due to a number of factors. These are as a rule not only on the provider's side, but also on the user's side. The ultimate effect of these factors is the user's interest or motivation for business decision-making. The user's response to the information received is the emerging form of this interest. On this basis, the user makes the business decisions.

It is therefore important to determine how and why this interest emerges. A more detailed reporting process that runs from the reporter to the user is shown in Fig. 3.2. With its help, some important considerations could be found.

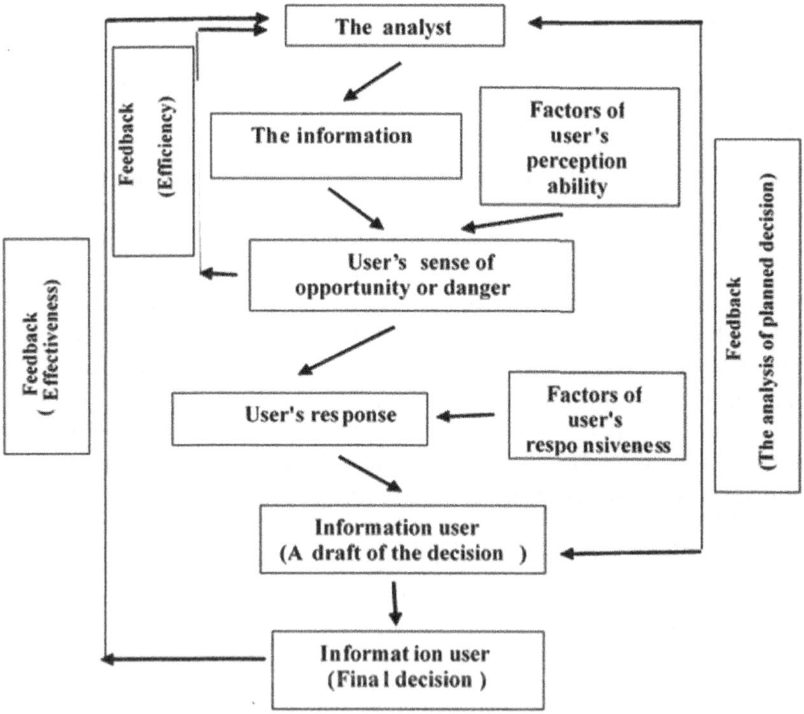

Fig. 3.2 Process from information to business decision (*Source* Own research [Bergant 2021, p. 4])

For a reporter, the success to create a feeling of danger or opportunity for the user is important. Information about such excited feeling is information about the efficiency of the reporting process. It is often called a communication effect. Of course, the reporting is less efficient, if the reporter spends more time to excite the feeling. It is therefore a question of whether the reporter (analyst) has acted in the right way.

It may happen that the user's response is not the same as the reporter anticipates. It usually means that the user does not see the significance of the danger or opportunity, or that his sense of risk or opportunity is different than estimated by the analyst. In such a case the efficiency of reporting cannot be viewed as satisfactory one. The reporter (analyst) should consider the causes of an unexpected user's response or "noise in communication." Obviously, a deeper empathy is needed to understand it.

At first, it is important to consider factors that influence the user's *perception ability* to understand information. Several factors form the ability of the user to accept an appropriate sense of risk and its weight. The ability to perceive information, of course, changes over time, even under the influence of these factors.

Figure 3.2 shows that the efficiency of the reporting (the ratio between the excited feeling and the received information) does not depend solely on the information provided by the analyst, but also on numerous factors that influence the user's ability to objectively understand the situation. This fact is therefore the first condition the analyst has to consider at presenting and explaining information.

It is obvious that the analyst will need a different portion of time or effort in the same objective circumstances (in a case of the same information but for the different user) in order to excite an appropriate sense of opportunity or danger.

The efficiency of the information process therefore varies depending on *risk perception ability* of the individual user. Several factors influence the response of the user to the feeling of risk or opportunity. They will be briefly discussed in Sect. 9.8.

User's response is reflected in his expressed interest in making a business decision. Figure 3.2 shows that it is affected by the perceived sense of danger or opportunity, as well as many other factors that we have listed above as an example.

The analyst's empathy toward the information user, which is the basic precondition for successful communication, means taking into account as many factors as possible in a given situation and appropriately adjusting the form and content of the information in order to maximize its efficiency.

In the continuation of the reporting process, the user forms a business decision in accordance with interest and based on analyst's proposals. This is shown in Fig. 3.2 as well.

It is useful for the user to consider the intended decision in the draft together with the analyst, as shown in the feedback in Fig. 3.2. In this way, the user can get additional information about the possible consequences of the intended decision.

The final decision therefore means feedback to the analyst about the *effectiveness* of reporting, which is also shown in Fig. 3.2. This shows whether or not the user was motivated also for the right things and, not just for the right path.

The ultimate goal of the reporting process is therefore the efficiency and effectiveness of a business decision. At the same time, this represents an adequate approach to the *quality of the reporting process.*

We need to raise this awareness in order to understand and act socially responsibly.

3.5.5 Quality of External Reporting

In the previous section, mainly internal reporting was discussed. Comparing to it, external reporting has some other characteristics:

1. External information users are often unknown, except those to whom an organization is legally or contractually obliged to report.
2. The form and minimum content of reports is more or less governed by laws or standards.
3. External reporting is usually the responsibility of only one person, for internal reporting it does not apply.
4. External reporting is usually the responsibility of only one person, for internal reporting, it is not mandatory, because the informers and users are positioned at numerous levels of organization.
5. Internal reporting should usually give more fresh and up-to-date information.
6. The extent and diversity of internal reporting are generally higher.
7. Internal reporting gives greater emphasis on non-accounting information.
8. The most important difference is that internal reporting is usually focused on relatively known areas of business decisions, however deciding orientation of external users is left to them. This results in the fact that, as a rule, the organization does not receive a direct feedback. As a rule, the feedback is indirect, as it is usually manifested as a changed behavior of users.

However, there is also an important link between external and internal reporting: quality of internal reporting is a prerequisite for the quality of external reporting.

The last feature of external reporting (in point 8) implies that its efficiency and effectiveness (i.e. the quality) depend on the *degree of reduction of user's uncertainty*. On this basis comes a conclusion that the quality of external reporting does not depend on its compliance with laws and standards. They, as a rule, do not meet the information needs of external users that are mostly creditors and investors (Miller and Bahnson 2002, p. 43). Their fundamental need is to minimize the uncertainty about the organization's future operations. Reducing uncertainty has the effect of reducing expected returns and, consequently, it is lowering the price of capital in the market and vice versa (Miller and Bahnson 2002, p. 8).

Superficiality or even misinterpretation of data increases the uncertainty of users of information; in particular, it gives rise to the following thinking:

1. Management underestimates the role and the influence of users.
2. Management is not capable of proper analysis and does not know enough the actual financial situation of the organization.
3. Management is afraid and refuses to disclose all relevant facts.
4. Management is not aware of its social responsibility.

Each of the above options contributes to increasing the uncertainty of users of information.

The quality of external reporting depends on several different factors. The fundamental precondition is of course the knowledge of financial categories' expressive power and adequate use of analytic tools as it is the case with internal reporting. This area has been briefly discussed in Sect. 3.5.2.

Other impacts on quality of external reporting are primarily:

1. Recognition of the importance of the information needs of external users, particularly creditors and investors.
2. The extent and quality of the information provided is a key to better external reporting. In doing so, it is a mistake to think about the minimum information required, based on accounting standards. The latter is not sufficient for the desired reduction in the uncertainty of users. Additional voluntary disclosures are of a paramount importance for improving the quality of external reporting (Miller and Bahnson 2002, p. 130 and 223).

3. Audit as an essential component of the financial reporting process should go over minimum requirements of disclosure and help the organization to achieve higher trust of external information users. "They can do a great deal to add real value to the statements" (Miller and Bahnson 2002, p. 24 and 217).
4. Development of professional financial analysis and also academic education that should be focused on improvement of the quality of financial reporting.
5. Recognizing that contributing to the quality of internal and external reporting is an essential component of the socially responsible behavior of all parties involved in these processes.

In 1997, Merton Miller was asked: "Why it seems that virtually all managers do not comprehend that they face higher capital costs when they fail to reduce uncertainty, as much they could by providing more information?" The answer without hesitation was: "because you, accounting professors, have never taught them" (Miller and Bahnson 2002, p. 94). Unfortunately, it can be said that this is not the only shortcoming of today's curricula of accounting.

Miller and Bahnson offer a basic recipe for quality reporting policy: "Tell the truth, the whole truth and nothing but the truth" (Miller and Bahnson 2002, p. 136). It is difficult to dispute this principle regarding external reporting, where creditors and investors are the main users of information.

However, the process in Fig. 3.2 in previous section indicates user's response that influences the final business decision as an important factor. Reporting that does not take this fact into account would be difficult to qualify as quality reporting. This, of course, does not in any way diminish the importance and the need for true information. In order to take into account the response of the user, information must be appropriately communicated.

3.6 Reporting and Decision-Making

In the previous chapter, the main path from feeling the danger to take a decision was explained. Innumerable factors impact a particular decision. It seems logical that the result of these impacts reflects in numerable possible forms of behaving and also in different decisions.

Behaving and taking decision is therefore a final response and reflects also a final user's interest in the process that is shown in Fig. 3.2.

Among other approaches, the interest of the user can be studied also through four main aspects of the response: reasonable (economical), emotional (psychological), social (sociological) and spontaneous (biological). These four types of manifestations of response will be discussed in Sect. 9.8.

Based on the above considerations, we can conclude that in the behavior of an individual person, as a rule, we must distinguish all four aspects. Otherwise, we are incapable of empathy and understanding people. Even more, we must recognize, how easy is to misread people and how deceptive the first impression can be.

Financial reporting must therefore take into account the various possible responses of information users, understand them and must be adapted to them. The fundamental question is what is to be achieved through such adjustment. Therefore, a criterion for assessing the appropriateness of behavior and decision-making is needed.

The correct, though principled, answer is only one: the response should be consistent with the social responsibility of the user of the information, because people behave differently also from the aspect of social responsibility. The quality of reporting therefore depends also on whether we can make decisions as socially responsible decision-makers. Accounting reporting is therefore not and should not be neutral, regarding social responsibility.

In the above discussion, we did not deal with the decision-making process itself, which requires a different approach. We have limited ourselves to showing the important role of both participants in the information process, that is, the role of analysts or information providers and information users. Without their cooperation, we can't guarantee the quality of the information process.

The basic condition for a good information process is the cooperation and trust between the user and the analyst, for which they are both interested. However, this depends to a large extent on the analyst's empathy toward the information user.

Of course, trust also depends on the decision-making process in a community (e.g. technocratic or democratic one). In distrust and soulless discipline, information is different, as in cooperation, understanding and creativity. However, there are neither totally technocratic nor fully democratic organizations—the reality is in the middle, the boundaries vary according to circumstances. The analyst has to adapt to them.

Many feedback loops in the process from the risk to the performance of an individual show the cybernetic character of the model in Fig. 4.1 in Sect. 4.2, which also provides answers to the starting points of the questions asked. The common denominator of all responses is the risk that the individual person feels and his (or her) response to this feeling. It is the fundamental reason for the difference in the functioning and behaving of people.

The model in previous Fig. 3.2 offers also a basic judgment (criteria) of the adequacy of the behavior and functioning of the individual person. It is the contribution to social well-being or value added in the broadest sense, regardless of the currently environment. This means that this criterion is always the most important one, despite the possible current partial or short-term interests of the individual person or organization.

The model provides an understanding of today's reality, which, under the influence of the neoliberalism, puts us in the face of difficultly solvable problems, such as inequality of people, wars, migrations, dangerous threats to the environment, which pose ever-greater risks for the existence of humanity. Moreover, the model redirects traditional ethics from a religious goodness of people, which is an ideological and idealistic delusion, to the ethics that is incorporated in the socially responsible behavior.

Figure 3.2 gives a theoretical overall basis and shows the role of policy at all levels and types of organization (starting from the state) in promoting the criteria of the social responsibility and thus at achieving appropriate behaving and decision-making. Social responsibility becomes the main and general criterion for adequate decisions of organizations.

Such a conclusion requires additional study, particularly about the content, criteria and measurement of social responsibility, which is a generally recognized precondition for a sustainable development. This discussion will be provided in next chapters.

Questions for Discussion

3-1 Explain the difference between creating information and reporting.
3-2 Explain the managerial aspect of reporting.
3-3 Explain the informational aspect of reporting.

3-4 Explain the operational aspect of reporting.
3-5 How do you understand the quality of information?
3-6 What changes impact the net working capital?
3-7 What is the quality of net working capital?
3-8 What is the difference between the direct and indirect method of cash flow reporting?
3-9 What does it mean if the current ratio is equal to 1.5?
3-10 What does it mean if the quick ratio is 1.2?
3-11 What do you understand by the capital adequacy of a company?
3-12 What is the shortest way to assess the capital adequacy of the company?
3-13 What are factors that impact the quality of reporting from information provider's side?
3-14 What are factors that impact the quality of reporting from information user's side?
3-15 How do you differentiate the efficiency and effectiveness of the reporting process?
3-16 What are main possible responses of information user?

References

AICPA (2015). *Introduction to Accounting*. American Institute of certified Accountants. (Retrieved: December, 2019). http://www.ncert.nic.in/ncerts/l/keac101.pdf.

Al-Hudhaif, A. Sulaiman (2010). Measuring Quality of Information System Services in Manufacturing Organizations in Riyadh. *JKAU*, Vol. 24, No 1, pp. 24–171. (Retrieved: April, 2020). https://www.kau.edu.sa/Files/320/Researches/55327_25670.pdf.

Arnold, Glen (1998). *Corporate Financial Management*. London: Pitman Publishing.

Bergant, Živko (2019). A New Approach to the Capital Adequacy Assessment of Companies. *Journal of Accounting and Management*, Vol. 9, No. 1, pp. 1–14. (Retrieved: March, 2020). https://hrcak.srce.hr/file/327727.

Bergant, Živko, Manohin, Igor (2020). Methods for an Accounting Estimation of Company's Capital Adequacy. Poreč: International conference: Accounting and management. June, 2020.

Bergant, Živko (2021). Accountancy Information System for Sustainable Future. *International Journal of Latest Research in Humanities and Social Science (IJLRHSS)*, Vol. 4, No. 1, pp. 01–07.

Bierman H. Jr., Drebin R. A. (1978). *Financial Accounting*. 3rd Edition. Philadelphia: W. B. Saunders Company.

Brigham, F. Eugene, Gapenski, C. Louis, Daves, R. Phillip (1999). *Intermediate Financial Management*. 6th Edition. Orlando: The Dryden Press.

Donleavy, D. Gabriel (1994). *Cash Flow Accounting*. London: Routlege.

Friedlob, T. George, Schleifer, Lydia L. F. (2003). *Essentials of Financial Analysis*. New York: Wiley.

Gleim, N. Irvin, Delaney, R. Patrick (1989). *CPA Examination Review*, Vol. 1. 16th Edition. New York: Wiley.

Hines, D. Ruth (1989). Financial Accounting Knowledge, Conceptual Framework Projects and the Social Construction of the Accounting Profession. *Accounting & Auditing Journal*, Vol. 2, No. 2.

Idowu, O. Samuel, Louche, Céline, Edit. (2011). *Theory and Practice of Corporate Social Responsibility*. Heidelberg: Springer.

IAS-International Accounting Standard 7. EU Commission (2008). (Retrieved: March, 2020). https://eur-lex.europa.eu/legal-content/EN/TXT/PDF/?uri=CELEX :02008R1126–20200101&qid=1408602215971&from=EN.

IFRS—International Accounting Standards Board (2018). *Conceptual Framework for Financial Reporting*. (Retrieved: June, 2020). https://www.ifrs.org/-/media/project/conceptual-framework/fact-sheet-project-summary-and-feedback-statement/conceptual-framework-project-summary.pdf.

Lynch, David (1994). *Quality in Finance Function*. London: Kogan Page.

McLure, B. (2004). *The Small Business Handbook*. Melbourne: Bas Publishing.

Miller, B. W., Paul, Bahnson, R. Paul (2002). *Quality Financial Reporting*. New York: McGraw-Hill.

Nuhu, Mohammed (2014). Role of Ratio Analysis in Business Decisions: A Case Study NBC Maiduguri Plant. *Journal of Educational and Social Research*, Vol. 4, No. 3, pp. 105–118.

O'Hare, J. (2013). *Analyzing Financial Statements for Non-Specialists*. New York: Routledge.

O'Reagan, P. (2002). *Financial Information Analysis*. London: Wiley.

Rao, K. S. Ramesh (1987). *Financial Management*. London: MacMillan Publishing Company.

Samuels, M. J., Wilkes, F. M., Brayshaw, R. E. (1995). *Management of Company Finance*. London: Chapman & Hall.

Sumner, N. Levine (1988). *The Financial Analyst's Handbook*. Homewood, IL: Dow Jones Irwin.

Smart, B. S., Megginson, W. L., Gitman, L. J. (2004). *Corporate Finance*. Mason, OH: Thomson, South-Western.

Westwick, C. A. (1989). *How to Use Management Ratios*. 2nd Edition. Aldershot: A Grower Workbook.

CHAPTER 4

Risk and Its Social Aspect

4.1 Human Work as the Response to Risk

Figures 3.1 and 3.2 have one important red thread, namely the risk. Obviously, the entire human life is under the pressure of risk for existence in a broadest sense.

A sense of threat to existence is *the origin of basic human needs,* which were studied by numerous authors (e.g. Galtung 1978). Adequate safeness is simply a prerequisite to meet these needs. The need of subsistence is on the top of the total system of human needs (Max-Neef 1991, p. 17).

Risks are threatening humankind since time immemorial. The risk can be managed only by working. Already the first human species had to find food and get dressed in cold times.

Not all risks can be eliminated. Furthermore, a fundamental feature of the need for security is that it is in principle never satisfied. Therefore, we must constantly establish appropriate reserves, which means the need for constant work. The exception is, of course, the case where we gain reserve at the expense of another person, working for us (e.g. the exploitation of slaves or other workers).

The need for the existence of human being was simply transformed into the need to work. It means that *the right to work is equivalent to the right to exist.* For those who cannot work or do not have enough work,

Ž. Bergant, *Accountancy and Social Responsibility*,
Palgrave Studies in Impact Finance,
https://doi.org/10.1007/978-3-030-77928-3_4

their right to work is transformed into *a right to solidarity*. Violation of this right denies their right to exist.

The supreme guardian of the existence of people and thus also for their work is (or should be) the state in which people are joined together for their own protection.

A discussion of person's instinctive response to threat can go into Darwinism and into a struggle for one's existence that neglects the interests of a broader society. Emotions in response to threat can also be positive or negative in this regard. Negative responses can be controlled only by mind and rationality, which again reflects in working.

4.2 Creation of Value Added

Human being can create more goods than they are currently needed. This surplus means a risk reduction reserve and is called *value added* because it has a direct impact on increasing the welfare of the people. A part of value added is available also for investment to increase work efficiency and again for increase human welfare.

In this context, human curiosity and desire for knowledge are paramount. Both are reflected in three fundamental areas of study. Namely, people practically and theoretically study and research:

1. Through orientation to environment, natural sciences, technical and information sciences were developed.
2. Through orientation to human himself, philosophical, psychological and medical sciences were developed.
3. Through orientation to the human role in the social environment, social and anthropological sciences were developed.

Throughout these processes of developing knowledge, people are also focused on the arts and entertainment that, due to the relaxation of the spirit that has a developmental impact on knowledge in general.

The fundamental benefit of studying and researching is to increase people's knowledge, innovation and ability to cope with all kinds of risks and thus increase the security of the whole society.

Harnessing the knowledge increases the efficiency of human labor (including eliminating barriers to its functioning), thereby directly increasing the value added. Thus, on the one hand, the reserve can be increased to facilitate risk management (e.g. retained earnings in the company) and, on the other hand, the standard of living may be increased (e.g. in the form of higher recognized labor costs and rewards).

Of course, knowledge can be misused (and indeed it is often abused) for narrower interests, indicating a lack of social responsibility. The wise use of knowledge is crucial for sustainable development of society.

Knowledge is therefore the common denominator of all kinds of work that is the only way to risk management. Also, the experience is only accumulated and emotionally valued knowledge. Above considerations are illustrated in Fig. 4.1.

Figure 4.1 shows in particular:

1. The need for security arises from a sense of risk, and from it all other human needs.

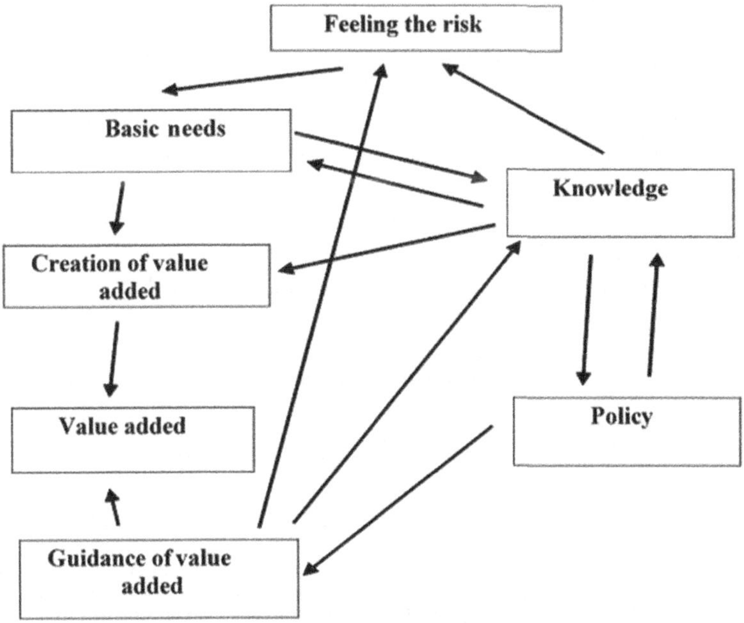

Fig. 4.1 Creation and guidance of value added (*Source* Own research)

2. The need for security forces human being to work, which is his basic activity, and thus to create added value, but also to increase his knowledge and skills.
3. The use of knowledge through development, innovation and better organization increases the efficiency of value creation.
4. Increasing knowledge has the effect of improving the sense of risk, but at the same time it can increase the risk of misuse of knowledge (e.g. atomic bomb, cyber-attacks).
5. Increasing knowledge also has the effect of increasing needs.
6. The guidance of value added is strongly influenced by policy in the broadest sense with balancing the needs and interests of stakeholders at all levels and in all organizational processes and all forms of organizations.
7. Policy is directly influenced by the volume of added value created. At the same time the policy impacts the creation of knowledge and the guidance of value added.
8. Part of the added value is channeled directly to develop knowledge and art, which further influences the formulation of value-added policy.
9. Appropriate guidance of added value increases reserves, allowing better risk management and reducing the sense of risk.

Figure 4.1 shows the close links between risk and work, added value and knowledge, which a sound policy should take into account.

The model in Fig. 4.1 can be simplified as shown in Fig. 4.2.

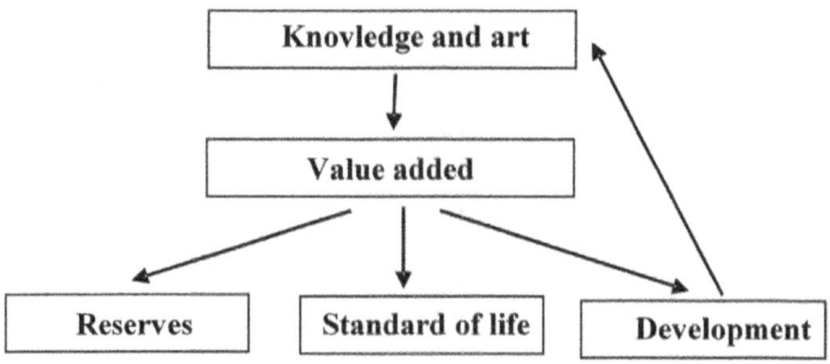

Fig. 4.2 Fundamental feedback (*Source* Own research)

Figure 4.2 summarizes that by using knowledge at work (every work uses knowledge) value added is created, which is available for:

- increasing reserves to facilitate risk management (or to increase the safeness)
- improving living standards
- developing knowledge and art to increase added value

The latter represents the fundamental feedback loop of the model, which is shown in more detail (though still relatively abstract) also in the previous Fig. 4.2.

It is also important to note that all the work done is not translated into added value, since energy is first used to reduce the internal entropy of the system. Only potential surplus is value added. The higher the entropy of the system, the lower the added value.

The efficiency (utilization) of the work invested in the organizational system is illustrated by the following principle form:

$$\text{Efficiency} = \frac{\text{Work Input} - \text{Entropy}}{\text{Invested work}} = \frac{\text{Value Added}}{\text{Invested work}}$$

The form above shows that the utilization of the work invested in managing the risks of the organizational system depends significantly on the energy required to overcome the entropic forces in the system. If they are stronger, the energy input is not sufficient to create added value. Value added becomes negative and leads to a system breakdown.

Based on the form above, we can define the source of added value more precisely, as *the excess of the effect of the work invested in managing the risks over the work necessary to control the entropy of the system.*

The amount of work required to overcome the entropic forces in a system depends on its *quality*, which is a complex category and is defined by three components (Kukoleča 1972, p. 37):

1. Achieving the goal
2. Orderliness (constitution)
3. Operating efficiency.

The model shown in Fig. 7.1, including the above comments, confirms that value added has not and also cannot have only accounting content. It is therefore important to examine this content in more detail.

4.3 Basic Definition of Value Added

Value added is used in many contexts. As a term, it expresses the newly created value and in principle means the difference between an input and an output in the business or operation of an organization. This is, therefore, the difference between the revenues value of the business effects and the costs (material and services) incurred in creating those effects. This definition already derives its importance, since only the newly created value contributes to the achievement of the economic goals of the whole society and to the satisfaction of its needs.

In principle, value added can be monitored at the level of:

- individual persons
- single product or service (unit value added)
- organizational units
- companies and associations
- states or national economies.

At all levels above is possible to treat value added for tax purpose (*VAT*), but it is out of scope of this work and will not be discussed further. The main focus will be on value added at the community and organization level (information aspect). Therefore, the accounting definition of value added will be discussed in the first place.

In terms of content, value added is the newly created value in the business of an organization. From calculation point of view in accounting, it is a difference between the sum of all revenues and all expenses, except:

- salaries and reimbursements to employees within operating expenses (labor costs)
- interest and other compensation attributable to lenders and other creditors
- taxes, excise duties and levies (in the following text: taxes).

The newly created value is created by the work of employees and the cooperation of investors of capital and/or financiers. This finding is the basic starting point for calculating value added and for explaining it and applying to the business decisions of the company. Among them the distribution of value added is of the utmost importance that will be studied in an especial section.

4.4 Information Content of Value Added

The previous section shows the importance of value added as information. It shows the achievement of the joint efforts of management, employees, equity investors and creditors, who jointly form a cooperative group. Value added thus provides a basis for measuring the overall effectiveness of the business. Of course, each of the stakeholders perceives added value in a different way, as it should also be consistent with their specific goals.

Value added adds a new dimension to financial accounting and financial reporting. Value added answers to the question: whose income is measured. This provides a direct link to the fairness of the distribution of value added and of the social responsibility of the association (Mandal and Goswami 2008, p. 103).

Value added reflects the social utility of an organization and is a prerequisite for its long-term survival. Its existence is possible in the short-term without profit, but the survival of the organization is not possible without long-term value creation.

Profit is a term in the classical theory of the firm that is discussed by numerous authors (e.g. Crossan 2004, p. 1; Kraaijenbrink and Spender 2011) where the main objective is profit maximization for owners. On the contrary, value added characterizes the theory that takes into account the interest of multiple stakeholders.

The absence of profit does not mean that the organization does not contribute to social well-being. Despite the loss, the organization can have positive value added. This only means that the share of other stakeholders in value added is greater than the loss. In such a case, owners lost the capital partly at the expense of other stakeholders in the company (employees, banks and the state). The organization nonetheless contributed to the greater prosperity of the country. This does not mean, however, that losing business is socially responsible. On the contrary, "the most socially irresponsible are the losers".

If the company does not add value, it improperly consumes the elements of the business processes. Therefore, value added is an important category of management accounting and an indispensable part of socially responsible accounting in terms of corporate performance.

Some authors even consider that "value added optimization is more important than profit optimization". Therefore, it is important to consider added value as a benchmark when drawing up organizations' business plans. They further believe that value allocation could be an appropriate criterion for resource allocation (e.g. Mandal and Goswami 2008, p. 102).

From this point of view, "salaries to employees are just as important as the payment of dividends" (Donleavy 1994, p. 398). Consistently, value-added measures the impact of the operations on the organization and is therefore more important than the profit and loss account (Donleavy, ibid.), since it represents a stakeholders' repayment for their involvement in the business. In this way, profit can only be understood as one of the operating expenses (Ianniello 2010, p. 372) and taxes as an expense, necessary to maintain an adequate economic and social environment.

From information point of view, value added has some advantages and disadvantages. The main advantages are:

1. The value added means newly created value and offers a broader view of the economic contribution of the organization than profit.
2. The value-added information expands the population of interested users and improves communication with them (Aruwa 2008, p. 9).
3. The value-added information can contribute to improving the organizational atmosphere of the company, especially with regard to positive changes in employee behavior.
4. The value added can play an important role in the motivation system of the organization as a whole.
5. The employees' share in the value added can be an important argument that workers are not exploited.
6. The state's share in the value added is important information for the environment, especially in times of crisis.
7. The value added is important information about the achievements of the organization and is also related to its social responsibility.
8. The value added is an important category in planning operations of organizations, especially in deciding on the effectiveness of long-term investments envisaged.

9. Value-added indicators are an important part of information about business performance, but also an integral part of a system of key warning signs of a possible crisis.
10. Value-added indicators are an appropriate way for comparing business achievements between organizations.
11. The value added indicates the contribution of the organization to the state's *GDP*.
12. Value-added-based ratios are interpreted as more indicative and predictive of the strength of the company than conventional ratios (Kaur 2020).
13. Better measuring the size and importance of companies (Kaur, ibid.).

The main disadvantages of information of value added are:

1. The added value can be misleading in identifying the factors that create new value. For example, the state is not involved in business decisions and its share does not depend on its contribution, but especially on tax bases. Similarly, the bank is involved, although it does not deal with the specifics of its clients' operations. Furthermore, new value creation factors do not include suppliers, especially strategic partners.
2. The growth of value added may be misleading in the event of a decrease in some of its other components.
3. In the event of a business loss, it is difficult to speak of value at first glance, as this is contrary to owner's logic.
4. In highlighting the value added could be unduly neglected category of profit.
5. An important disadvantage of the value added is a possibility to use different methods in the calculation, which limits its comparability between organizations.
6. Focusing solely on maximizing the value added can also lead to inappropriate business decisions (the same effect is in solely maximizing profit).
7. The compilation of a value-added statement entails additional costs, but as a rule, these are less than the potential benefit of new information.

The value-added properties listed above mean that the information on which it is based must be carefully used, which applies also to all other financial information.

4.5 Accounting Calculation of Value Added

There are two options for estimating value added from accounting data:

1. Depreciation (*Dep*) is included in the added value
2. Depreciation (*Dep*) is not included in the value-added statement

In the first case, we calculate ***gross value added*** and in the second case we calculate ***net value added***. Both options have their advantages and disadvantages from information point of view. However, the calculation of net value added is more coherent and consistent with the principle that all costs are deducted.

Both gross value added (*GVA*) and net value added (*NVA*) could be calculated through two methods:

$$NVA = GVA - Dep = TR - CMS - Dep \tag{4.1}$$

$$NVA = LC + EBIT \tag{4.2}$$

Equation 4.1 shows the ***subtracting method***, where the costs of materials and services (*CMS*) and depreciation are subtracted from total revenues (*TR*).

Equation 4.2 shows the ***additive method***, where labor costs (*LC*) are added to *EBIT* (earnings before interest and taxes).

The principle of value-added calculation shown above has many variations in practice. In doing so, even credit rating companies also differ.

4.6 Broader Understanding of Value Added

Accounting aspect of the value added is limited by the traditional accounting data. Therefore, it is in contrast to the wider, economic and social content of value added, which was presented in Sect. 5.2

The first improvement of the expressive power of the value added is ***expanded added value***. Mook suggests a model *EVAS* (***expanded value-added statement***), which takes into account also some non-accounting data (Mook 2003, 2007). An important example is voluntary work (e.g. Mook et al. 2003; Mook and Quarter 2004; Eller 2013).

In principle, such an approach is supported by the European Union Directive (EU 2003, point 14b), which also recommends the use of non-accounting indicators in order to better understand the achievements of the association.

Broadly, we can talk about "total net value added" (*TNVA*). It is made up of three dimensions that imply three social values: economic, environmental and social (Business Dictionary 2015).

All of the mentioned improvements are still not covering the entire content of the broadest term of value added, because they do not contain the effects of working and human activities that we do not measure or are immeasurable in practice of accounting.

We do not measure the many effects of work that are necessary for a normal human life. Let's look for example at the effects of the work of a spouse who is not employed anywhere. We can clearly distinguish her classic housework from participating in creating the right climate and emotions in the family. Climate emotion cannot be measured. We only value them when they are gone. The same is true of the husband, of course.

Similar, in organizations for example, we do not measure work, spent on improving organizational climate and emotional intelligence of employees.

All types of work that are socially recognized have one thing in common: they help to manage risks. Their effect is therefore a creation of the value added.

From above considerations, it is clear that there are different aspects about net value added and they therefore enable its different definitions or explanations. Some of them can be summarized as follows:

1. The estimation through subtracting method.
2. The estimation through additive method.
3. The new created value.
4. Expanded value added.
5. The value added is an expression and a result of work that is oriented to manage risk.
6. Value added is an expression and a result of all forms past and current work.

7. The excess of the effect of the work invested in managing the risks over the work necessary to compensate the fixed costs of labor and control the entropy of the system.
8. The value added is the value that does not diminish social welfare, although it is completely spent (otherwise it would not have been added).

The first two definitions are computational and derived from accounting data. The first definition expresses creating, and the second expresses distribution of value added. Their weakness in expressive power is caused by accounting origins.

The third definition emphasizes its content, the social dimension and its contribution to the welfare of society as a whole.

The fourth definition estimates value added in principle, more broadly and includes also non-accounting information.

The third and fourth definitions, therefore, emphasize the value-added information content rather than the computational assessment.

The fifth definition stems from an economic point of view, as it indicates the work as the origin of the added value.

The sixth definition expresses the economic aspect in another way, defining in more detail the forms of work submitted.

The seventh definition comes from a consistent understanding of the fifth definition from organization's point of view.

The eighth definition comes from a consistent understanding of the third definition from social and economic point of view. Although it appears to be the most general definition, it is substantially the most precise one. The value added therefore includes also human emotions[1] that impact on creating the well-being of society.[2] Even more, with such an understanding of value added, the original goal of work (the existence of human) is transformed into the objective of leisure time and non-remunerating activities[3] that reflect the quality of life in its broadest sense. This means that the content of the value added cannot be exhausted solely from an accounting, financial and economic point of view. It also

[1] More about pleasure and pain in Bentham (1780).

[2] More about well-being and its measuring in Stiglitz et al. (2018).

[3] Leisure time and non-remunerating activities are an important measure of advancing post capitalism (Mason 2019).

extends into other social sciences, such as sociology, psychology, philosophy anthropology and ecology. The value added should therefore be considered interdisciplinary.

The importance of value added is obviously not diminished with many definitions, but requires more detailed consideration, which will be done in the following sections.

Questions for Discussion

4-1 What is the basic human need?
4-2 What is the main human activity to manage the risk?
4-3 How value added is created and what is its source?
4-4 Discuss the connection between profit and value added.
4-5 Discuss the value added as a basis of measuring effectiveness of the business.
4-6 Discuss advantages and disadvantages of value added as information.
4-7 What are accounting methods for value-added calculation?
4-8 What is the broader meaning of value added?
4-9 What are possible different definitions or explanations of value added and which is its most general definition?

References

Aruwa, A. S. Suleiman (2008). The Worth of Disclosures in the Value-added statements and Pattern of Value Added Distribution. *Journal of Finance and Accounting Research*, No 1/2009. (Retrieved: April, 2020). http://www.academia.edu/222418/THE_WORTH_OF_DISCLOSURES_IN_THE_VALUE_ADDED_STATEMENT_AND_PATTERN_OF_VALUE_ADDED_DISTRIBUTION.

Bentham, Jeremy (1780). *An Introduction to the Principles of Morals and Legislation*. (Retrieved: December, 2018). http://www.utilitarianphilosophy.com/jeremybentham.eng.html.

Business Dictionary (2015). *Total Net Value*. (Retrieved: January, 2016). http://www.businessdictionary.com/definition/total-net-value-added-TNVA.html.

Crossan, Kenny (2004). The Theory of the Firm and Alternative Theories of Firm Behaviour: A Critique. *International Journal of Applied Institutional Governance*, Vol. 1, No 1. (Retrieved: April, 2020). http://www.managementjournals.com/journals/ig/vol1/21-1-1-2.pdf.

Donleavy, D. Gabriel (1994). *Cash Flow Accounting*. London: Routlege.

Eller, Helene (2013). Volunteers within an Organizational Context-One Term Is Not Enough. *Journal of Business and Economics,* Vol.4, No. 9, pp. 895–904.
EU (2003). *Directive EU2003/51.* (Retrieved: January, 2016). http://www.kapitalmarktrecht-im-internet.eu/en/Areas%20of%20Law/Company_Law/European_Law/9033/Directive_2003_51_EG.htm.
Galtung, Johan (1978). The Basic Needs Approach. (Retrieved: May, 2020). https://www.transcend.org/galtung/papers/The%20Basic%20Needs%20Approach.pdf.
Ianniello, Giuseppe (2010). *The Voluntary Disclosure of the Value-Added Statement in Annual Reports of Italian Listed Companies.* (Retrieved: March, 2016). http://www.agriculturejournals.cz/publicFiles/25300.pdf.
Kaur, Prabhjot (2020). Value-Added Statement (VAS). (Retrieved: April, 2020). http://www.yourarticlelibrary.com/accounting/financial-reporting/value-added-statement-vas/57379.
Kraaijenbrink, Jeroen, Spender, J. C. (2011). *Theories of the Firm and Their Value Creation Assumptions.* 31st Strategic Management Society international Conference. (Retrieved: May, 2020). https://www.researchgate.net/publication/42243920_The_Resource-Based_View_A_Review_and_Assessment_of_Its_Critiques.
Kukoleća, Stevan (1972). *Osnovi teorije organizacionih Sistema. Fundamental Theory of Organizational Systems.* (In Slovene). Beograd: privredno finansijski vodič.
Mandal Niranjan, Goswami, Suvarun (2008). Value-Added Statement (VAS) – A Critical Analysis. *Great Lakes Herald*, No. 2 (2008). (Retrieved: May, 2015). http://www.greatlakes.edu.in/pdf/Herald/Vol2/Value%20Added%20Statement%20-%20A%20Critical%20Analysis.pdf.
Mason, Paul (2019). Time for Postcapitalism. (Retrieved: may, 2020). https://www.socialeurope.eu/time-for-postcapitalism.
Max-Neef, A. Manfred (1991). *Human Scale Development: Conception, Application and Further Reflections.* New York: The Apex Press.
Mook, L. Ingrid (2003). *A Social Accounting Framework for Cooperatives: The Expanded Value-added statement.* (Retrieved: January, 2016). http://www.ace.coop/portals/0/institute/03/mook.pdf.
Mook, L. Ingrid (2007). *The Expanded Value-Added Statement.* Doctoral dissertation, University of Toronto. (Retrieved: January, 2016). http://home.oise.utoronto.ca/~lschugurensky/Mook_Thesis.pdf.
Mook, L. Ingrid, Quarter, Jack (2004). *Estimating and Reporting the Value of Volunteer Contributions.* (Retrieved: May, 2016). http://sectorsource.ca/sites/default/files/resources/files/Quarter_Estimating_Reporting_Final.pdf.
Mook L. Ingrid, Richmond, B. Jane, Quarter, Jack (2003). Calculating the Value of Volunteer Contributions for Financial Statements. *The Philanthropist*, Vol. 18, No. 1, pp. 71–83.
Stiglitz, E. Joseph, Fitoussi, Jean-Paul, Durand, Martine (2018). *For Good Measure: Advancing Research on Well-being Metrics Beyond GDP.* Paris: *OECD* Publishing.

CHAPTER 5

Law on Value Added

5.1 Formulating (Reveiling) the Law

The fundamental starting points are:

1. The basic goal or the desire of human being is its existence, which arises from the instinct aimed at self-preservation, and from this, the human basic needs and interests arise.
2. This is the reason why a person wants to ensure adequate safeness. For this purpose people create various organizational systems. The component of the operation of each organizational system is the risk.
3. Combining people into organizational system, in a way that each person which operates within it, contributes to a common goal.
4. Where the value added (in the broadest sense) is not (or no longer) the common goal of the participants, a system is in the process of decay.
5. Participants shall manage the risk in accordance with their respective interests within the limits of the objective possibilities and within the limits set by the environment.
6. In the case of legal or contractual regulation of the mutual relations between the participants in the organizational system, there will inevitably be a re-allocation of risk.

Ž. Bergant, *Accountancy and Social Responsibility*,
Palgrave Studies in Impact Finance,
https://doi.org/10.1007/978-3-030-77928-3_5

7. The fundamental interest of all participants in the organizational system is the acquisition of a share in the value added proportionally to their contribution to managing the risk.
8. If the interests of the participants are adequately met (and the narrow and short-term interests of individuals do not prevail), the organizational system is in balance.
9. The occurrence of a disproportion between the accepted risk and the yield, attributable to an individual participant, results in the creation of entropy, increases bad forces and their power in the system.
10. The strengthening of entropy forces threatens the sustainable development of the organizational system.
11. The basic conditions for the effective participation of participants are the appropriate level of knowledge or competence and appropriate information system with an appropriate communication process involved.
12. The inclusion of a greater number of actors in the functioning of the system (in particular in terms of decision-making) can be dysfunctional and inefficient; therefore, solutions are needed in order to use appropriate methods for their creative cooperation and effective monitoring system.
13. Participants in the organizational system are responsible for ensuring the existence and sustainable development of the system, if its sustainable orientation is accepted jointly.

On the basis of the above starting points, we define ***the general law of creating and guiding value added*** (hereinafter: value-added law), which includes two aspects:

1. Value added is the net outcome of the organizational system in managing the risk inherent to the system and belonging to risk holders in proportion to their contributions to the functioning of the organizational system (***the aspect of creating value added***).
2. The disproportionately high or disproportionately low participation of individual risk carriers in the value added (according to their work contribution) increases the entropy of the organizational system and threatens the realization of its sustainable development (***the aspect of value-added guidance***).

The value-added law is *a general law* because of its validation in *all* socio-economic systems (past, present and future), which are oriented toward sustainable development and all human associations, including families.[1] *It is valid and operates also for only two people and through entire human history. The value-added law operates regardless of the wishes or activities of the people and regardless of the normative organization of the organizational system or its environment. It is, therefore, totally independent of the human will.*

Because of different economic and political environments and different types of organization (relations between people) or associations, the manifestations of value-added law are different. *In the environment with huge disproportions in distribution of value added, there also discontent and even huge riots are present.*

The value-added law has two important, complementary characteristics, namely:

1. *Creation*, because the labor (contribution in the form of investments or personal co-operation) in risk management is the only source of the value added.
2. *Guidance*, which includes the fundamental principles of distribution of value added.

First of all, two important categories of the law need to be clarified: the net outcome and the contribution to the functioning of the organizational system.

The *net* outcome within the definition of this law should be understood in the broadest sense, from qualitative, accounting and broad value estimates to the satisfaction of the participants. The estimation of the net result therefore depends on the type of organizational system (e.g. household, society, institution, non-profit organization, economic community, municipality, state, humanity as a whole).

The important word is "net" because it means the difference between the outcome (recognized by users or market certified) and the estimated costs of operating the system, which are: *basic* labor costs, consumption of natural assets or the cost of their replacement, and costs of environmental conservation associated with the outcome.

[1] Neither partners in the family usually wants to be exploited.

The basic labor costs mean only compensation for partly wasting work force (like depreciation of fixed assets). They do not represent a newly created value, so they are not a part of value added. They also do not represent the total wages, which belong to workers. This important issue will be discussed later.

The same approach applies to the opportunity cost of capital, which does not represent a part of value added and also does not represent total participation, which belongs to owners of capital.

The contributions to the functioning of the organizational system should be understood in the broadest sense, i.e. in all possible forms (e.g. materialized work, real and monetary inputs, knowledge, and of course, current physical and intellectual work, including guarantees and opportunity costs or losses of individual participants). All carriers of contributions should be treated as stakeholders of the organizational system and therefore as participants in the distribution of value added.

On the basis of the value-added law we understand the entropy of organizational systems mainly as a consequence of the inequality between participants' contributions and their participations in the distribution of the value added. The inequality is devastating because it works against cooperation and mutual trust, which is necessary in the context of interdependence and interconnectedness of humankind. If equality is not assured, this is reflected also in crisis situations and their consequences. In today's life and even in the human history, there are numerous pieces of evidence for such a finding. Johnson claims: "The crisis of social democracy is also the crisis of equality" (Johnson 2019). A significant consequence of inequality is also reflected today in strong migration flows (Pierleoni 2018, p. 123).

It is important that we are aware that the balance of the organizational system (or minimum entropy) at the same time also means the position of its minimum stability as the balance is constantly collapsing. Therefore, there is a constant need for risk management and the effect of "invested effort" is reflected in the value added that is confirmed on the market or by users in the broadest sense.

The value-added law in its own way shows the shortcomings of various theories of a firm, including contract theory, which treats relationships between stakeholders only as a kind of contractual relationship.

An individual who contributes in any way to the added value and thus to the well-being of society has a sense of utility that is of utmost importance as it gives him or her the pleasure of working and acquiring knowledge in the broadest sense.

The value-added law clearly shows that there is not an accurate, otherwise commonly stated thought: "there is no profit without risk" (e.g. Kállay 2002, p. 42). Correct is: "there is no value added without risk".

5.2 Economic and Social Aspects of the Value-Added Law

Value-added law in terms of political economy contains in particular the following:

1. The claim that only basic need for existence and the sense of being threatened instigate the interests that underlie human action. The needs that are the starting point of political economy[2] do not arise on their own.
2. The answer to why the work is transformed into value added. It is about managing risk to ensure adequate safeness, which is not considered by other different theories of value.[3]
3. The distinction of value added in "capital income and labor income" (Piketty 2014) proves to be "artificial," as their common denominator is work.
4. The conclusion that private property is no longer important and represents only one form of contribution to risk management within the organization. The main issue is more about the equivalence of labor in relation to capital, which is directly in contrast to the existing capitalist thinking.
5. Justification of the equality of all stakeholders in the organization with regard to their contribution to risk management.
6. The equality as a fundamental ethical category, which is not only the result of some subjective thinking about ethics or moral norms (e.g. honesty). The ethics is an objectively inseparable component of the value-added law due to the interdependence of people in a society as a system. "Ethics is not only a matter of convenience,

[2] The term "political economy" reflects its political, moral and normative range (Piketty 2014, p. 742).

[3] For example, Marx considered only "productive labor".

but a condition of survival in society" (Coutinho de Arruda and Rok 2016, p. 3).

7. Breaching the principle of equality is not only "unfair," it is contrary to the value-added law. It works despite that someone denies the moral norm. That is reflected in increasing entropy of the system.
8. The principle of ethics which is not only because it contributes to the good name of the organization and to better effects in the long run, as justified by most authors. The value-added law demonstrates that the conduct, contrary to ethical standards, increases entropy and deteriorates performance of each company, until its collapse.
9. The justification that value added is the most important long-term goal, because only through the proper risk management can be ensured the sustainable development and existence of organization and of humanity as a whole.
10. Enabling proper social collusion and regulation through a common denominator of different stakeholder interests.
11. Simple and understandable policy that is consistent with the slogan: "to each according to his merits," which allows to reduce the huge inequality within wages.
12. The possibility of further development of theoretical and practical solutions for the creation and guidance of value added.
13. The proof of the correct finding that disregarding the interests of all stakeholders is in direct contradiction with the fundamental orientations of social responsibility.

From the above bases can be stated that in strict compliance with the value-added law, some assumptions of the model of economic value added (Economic Value Added—*EVA*) are no longer acceptable This model assumes that the entire net profit belongs to capital as capitalist bears the risk of the business. In this way, the minimum yield (based on the price of invested capital by *CAPM* model) that keeps the value of the capital invested is required.

The *CAPM* model also includes a risk assessment of this return. Such a requirement is in direct violation of the law of value added, since it omits the fact that the employees also take the risk. Therefore, for example, the retained profit, attributable to owners in the actual capitalist systems, according the value-added law belongs to all stakeholders in proportion to their contribution to risk management. They can give up their share in the value added only temporarily until when they decide to pay out.

The above findings substantially alter also the purpose, content and tools of traditional business analysis that will be discussed later.

Obviously, the value-added law requires changes not only in the tax system and economic legislation, but also in socio-economic system, legal system, politics and culture. It goes beyond the purpose of this work, because due to the great variety of changes requires also thorough theoretical and empirical treatment.

5.3 Guidance of Value Added

The guidance of the value added encompasses the policy of scheduling of the value added created and its distribution among stakeholders. The further discussion on the added value will be in a framework of accounting categories and focuses on the context of business operations.

The starting point is the basic principle that the value added belongs to all those who bear the risk or contribute to the risk management in the organization, that is to the stakeholders. This means that stakeholders need to be divided to governors and non-governors in this regard.[4]

Non-governors carry a smaller portion of the organization's risk. Their common feature is that they are affected by better or worse performance of the organization, but they cannot directly impact business decisions. However, they have different ways to control the business operations.

Stakeholders as non-governors are especially:

1. Creditors who are entitled to interest and compensation for services. Someone could argue that banks do not bear the risk, because the interest is a contractual obligation. Therefore, in most countries, the interest payments are independent of the performance of the organization. Such legislation is a fundamental source of the trap of borrowing, as debt becomes a systemic risk over time and one of the root causes of crises.[5] At the same time, without economic

[4] There are, of course, several possible classifications of stakeholders (e.g. Groenendijk 2003, p. 57).

[5] More about a trap of borrowing in Bajo, Roelants (2015, pp. 119–126).

justification it favors the lender in comparison with other stakeholders in the participation in the value added. Considering the value-added law, it means an embedded instrument of instability. Despite the regulations and collaterals, banks are exposed to *credit risk,* as there are many cases of debt write-offs due to insolvency of organizations. There are also other lending options, such as project finance or Islamic banking arrangements. These options also indicate the justification for treating banks in the stakeholder group, non-governors. Especially due to the fact that banks in their own way control business borrowers and thus partly also impact on business decisions.

2. The state to which taxes belong. The tax system, which considers interest as a deduction item from the tax base of the companies, is an additional motivation for borrowing (tax shield), but without economic justification. It is therefore an authoritative redistribution of risk in the business of the company. At the same time, this implies an unequal burden on value added stakeholder's participation. Such an arrangement is therefore an additional built-in instrument of instability.

   Nevertheless, *the state also carries the risk*, as there are many cases of tax write-offs due to the insolvency of organizations. Additionally, the state has a huge impact on performance of organizations. Partly through control function, but much more through adopting its economic policy. The importance of the state decisions is even increased in times of corona virus crisis (Mazzucato 2020).
3. Shareholders and portfolio investors who are entitled to dividends but are inactive owners of financial capital (small shareholders). They bear the risk depending on organization success, but with relatively small impact on business decisions or control.

Stakeholders in the role of governors are those, which in addition to carrying risk, also contribute to risk management. These include employees, shareholders (owners of active financial capital) and the management, but may also include others (e.g. the strategic business partners who contractually assume part of the risk of loss from participation in joint operations).

The differentiation of stakeholders between internal and external ones is also possible, but is neither useful for the definition of the value added, nor for guidance and distribution of the value added.

Given that only the stakeholders in the role of governors, through their decisions or their influence, directly manage the risk, they should have the right to decide on its allocation or retaining. Such an approach is obviously in conflict with the law in force in many countries, which would obviously have to change. For example, it is not economically possible to justify the right to decide on dividends for shareholders who are not actively involved in risk management.[6]

The role of employees is important in this group, either through workers' ownership or through the trade union or its bodies. Employee engagement, especially on a co-ownership basis, has already been addressed by many studies (e.g. Dethier and Defourny 2015).

Obviously, the above division of stakeholders into governors and non-governors cannot be permanent, as it changes over time with the development of co-governance. At the same time, this also presents one of the motives for development of co-governance, which should therefore not be too rigidly administratively limited. This should be reflected when allocating the value added in a particular organization.

5.4 The Value-Added Structure

Based on the definition of stakeholders in previous section, we can further define the value-added structure. The starting point is the principle structure:

$$NVA = LC + I + T + Div + RVA \tag{5.1}$$

According to the Eq. 5.1, net value added in principle includes costs of labor (*LC*), interest (*I*), taxes (*T*), dividends (*Div*) and retained part of value added (*RVA*).

Due to the net approach, the labor cost (*LC*) in Eq. 5.1 should be separated into:

1. Consumption of labor (*CLC*), which in economic terms entails constant operating costs and is similar to depreciation of fixed assets. According to the eighth definition of the value added in Sect. 6.4,

[6] In such a situation, short-term interests at the expense of sustainable development are clearly possible.

these costs should not be included in net value added. Like depreciation these costs also should not be taxed. They can be defined as a "minimal wage" which is equal amount for all employees.[7] Setting a minimum wage in this sense is predominantly arbitrary (similar to maximum depreciation rates) and depends on a number of factors, which we will not address here.

2. Variable portion of employee's participation (*EP*), which in principle depends on classic wage system criteria and on the effectiveness of the company as a whole.

We will not discuss the criterion of the division of labor costs in the above way, since it requires broader social consensus and is expected to result in negotiations between employers and the trade union on the basis of relevant legal norms.

However, it should be emphasized that treating all labor costs as costs of doing business means that labor is not considered as one of the basic productive factors, since labor costs in the existing legal order constitutes the costs of labor "procured on the market" as for example raw material (Gostiša 2014, p. 209).

The minimum wage category in point 1 could play an important role:

1. Employers would not be able to take advantage of a better bargaining position, vis-à-vis workers for longer than a certain limit (Piketty 2014, p. 391).
2. The equality of minimum wages (with the exception of the difficulty of work) would have the effect of changing the perceptions of the role of employees in the company, especially from a social point of view.
3. The tax exemption of minimum wage could have a beneficial impact on employment in the company.
4. The minimum wage should become a part of the fixed costs in calculating the break-even point from the point of view of the value added, which enables the formation of additional information about the business of the company from an economic point of view.

[7] It could differ only according to difficult and health related conditions of work of particular employee.

5. The minimum wage could become an indispensable element in the planning of the company's operations.
6. The minimum wage may become a starting point to implement universal basic income. In the last two years, the Finnish experiment has yielded encouraging results regarding the possible implementation of universal basic income (Van Parijs 2020). The discussion in *EU* is possible again because of the COVID-19 crisis (e.g. Neves and Merrill 2020).

The participation of owners of capital (Div) in Eq. 5.1 should be separated into:

1. The opportunity cost of capital owners (OCC), which, from an economic point of view, represents fixed costs of doing business. They have the role similar to minimum wages and should be negotiated as well. In this context, it should be recognized that the injection of capital into the business also contributes to the risks management in the organization (in particular, the risks related to the solvency of the entity).
2. The variable part of owners' participation (*OPC*) depends in principle on the performance of the organization. It belongs to them due to the direct management and innovation or the actual implementation of corporate governance, which means their ongoing contribution to risk management.

The definition of the criteria for the above separation depends on broad social consensus, which should be properly regulated (but not explicitly stated) by the legal order of the state.

The retained (unpaid) value added (*RVA*) in Eq. 5.1 should also be separated into:

1. The part of retained value added that would belong to employees (*RDVE*) upon payment.
2. The part of the retained value added that would belong to the owners of the equity (*RDVO*) upon payment.

The definition of the criteria about separation parts of retained value added should be consistent with pre-agreed starting points, which define the relationship between the amounts of rewards to the active owner of the capital and the amounts of salaries of other employees. In principle, it does not bother that all employees (or only a part of them) are also (co)owners of the organization at the same time, which, of course, must be duly taken into account.

The subsequent payment of retained value added is therefore possible, in principle, in a proportionate share of the two stakeholder groups, since a different decision would be contrary to the fundamental principle of the value-added law, unless, of course, all shareholders agree to such a payment.

Based on the above implementation, it is clear that traditional theories of dividend policy do not take into account the law of value added. They are primarily based on the assumption that dividend policy affects the market value of company's shares and thus also to the owners' income. From a value-added point of view, this is a wrong judgment, particularly when measured from too short-term point of view. This is probably also one of the reasons that the existing empirical research into the impact of different dividend policies does not provide unambiguous findings.

The short-term perspective, which does not consider the value added as an expression of sustainable development, most probably does not lead to the most favorable (optimal) decisions. Therefore, it is not surprising to find that modern financial theory has not yet found an answer regarding the optimal dividend policy. This topic will be discussed later.

Considering the above starting points, the structure of the net value added should be as follow:

$$NVA = CLC + EP + I + T + OCC + OPC + RDVE + RDVO \tag{5.2}$$

It could be noticed that only two categories: i.e. taxes (T) and interest (I) remained the same as in Eq. 5.1.

Inclusion of taxes in net value added is justified by the fact that the state also carries business risks, since in many cases it has to write off its tax receivables. In addition, the state significantly influences business conditions, the tax base and the tax rate. The state should therefore be aware of its role as a stakeholder in organizations, since it is directly interested in obtaining taxes. This interest gives the state *the right and duty* to adequately respond[8] to potential loss, generated in each organization, as loss reduces the tax base and the added value at the national level, thereby also social welfare. Obviously, losing should not be a problem just for equity owners in an organization.[9]

Interest is an added value component according to the explanations in Sect. 8.1.

Given the fact that the CLC and OCC represent fixed costs, by definition, does not belong to the otherwise traditional calculation of value added. Subtracting them gives a new category, namely ***the surplus value added*** (*SVA*). Its structure is shown in Eq. 5.3.

$$SVA = EP + OPC + I + T + RDVE + RDVO \tag{5.3}$$

The Eq. 5.3 shows that the surplus value added (*SVA*) consists of:

- participation of employees (*EP*).
- participation of capital owners (*OPC*).
- participation of creditors (*I*).
- participation of the state (*T*).
- retained *SVA* that belongs to employees (*RDVE*).
- retained *SVA* that belongs to capital owners (*RDVO*).

The surplus value added defined in Eq. 5.3 has some important advantages over the traditional value-added category, namely:

1. It means a consistent derivation of the substantive definition of added value in Sect. 6.4.
2. It means the value that is (or is intended to be) shared.
3. It is the basis for equal treatment of all stakeholders, thus eliminating the inequality of labor and capital in the existing socio-economic system.

[8] The state responds to the occurrence of insolvency of the organization, as a rule only, through establishing insolvency legislation. As a rule, this is too late and shows insufficiently response of the state as a stakeholder. At the same time it means also insufficient social responsibility of the state.

[9] A similar case of social irresponsibility of the state is when it does not take action against owners who behave irresponsibly towards their property (e.g. real estate) and let it go bankrupt, thereby reducing the value of the social assets.

4. It eliminates the misrepresentation and virtual fairness regarding the employee's involvement in value added.
5. It represents the only real source of payment for the work and contribution in risk management in the organization.
6. It represents a more exact category, compared to other known categories, for example, newly created value and profit.
7. It replaces the category of profit as a fundamental objective of the organization's business.

Equation 5.3 does not take into account the so-called entrepreneurial annuity, which is a substitute for the founders of the association for the entrepreneurial idea and investment initiative. Such a motivational instrument is undoubtedly economically important for the development of the economy and society as a whole. It is not displayed in Eq. 5.3 because it should be limited by a fixed term, since even the legal protection of patents and licenses is limited to a maximum of twenty years or even less.

According to the explanations above, Eq. 5.2 in Sect. 4.5 should be understood only from the perspective of the existing legal order, since there is no room for profit as a separate category in surplus value added.

This can be seen from Eq. 5.4 that is only a different notation of Eq. 5.3.

$$SVA = LC + EBIT - CLC - OCC \tag{5.4}$$

Equation 5.4 shows only a computational link between surplus value added (SVA) and profit from operations. Profit becomes, in fact, a secondary category in terms of the sharing of surplus value added. Its usefulness can only be seen in analytical information as a basis for individual business decisions and calculations with the aim of increasing business efficiency and maximizing surplus added value.

According to the above, we can conclude that the value-added law, which is defined in Sect. 5.1, is, from a substantive point of view, actually *the law of creating and guiding the surplus value added.* However, in the following we will continue to refer briefly only to the "value-added law."

5.5 The Distribution of the Surplus Value Added

Despite the principled equality of stakeholders in participating in the surplus value added (or precisely because of this), its distribution must take into account different circumstances that also lead to different criteria of division.

These circumstances are in particular:

- legal status of stakeholders;
- stakeholder's relationship in risk management;
- need to follow the basic principles of stakeholder's motivation;
- need to further develop the efficiency and reliability of the operations;
- need to achieve the desired triple bottom line (Elkington et al., 1998) for social responsibility and sustainable development of the company.

Due to the necessity of different criteria, the allocation of the surplus value added to stakeholders in accordance with its principle structure in Eq. 5.3 (Sect. 5.3) should be carried out in successive stages, in the appropriate order. Therefore, we can talk about *the process of the surplus value-added distribution*, which in principle covers the following procedures:

1. Determination of stakeholder's participation in accordance with applicable regulations (e.g. tax regulations).
2. Determination of stakeholder's participation in accordance with accepted contracts or agreements (e.g. interest obligations).
3. Determination of the required amount of retained surplus value added in accordance with the development business plan, which must also take into account the capital adequacy of the organization.
4. Determination of the amount of wages (labor income) in the planned appropriate (agreed) amount (with management included in accordance with the adopted internal rules). This amount is allocated in accordance with the adopted wage rules.
5. Determination of the amount of the surplus value added for capital owners in accordance with the defined dividend policy, adopted by active capital owners together with union representatives.
6. Determination of any residual surplus value added that could be further distributed among employees and management as a reward for successful business.
7. Determination of the share of employees and capital owners in retained surplus value added.

The most sensitive parts of the above process are undoubtedly points 3, 4 and 5. The order shown is principled, but in practice depends on the ratio of power between management, active owners and employees. Therefore, the criteria used to determine their participation may also be different.

From the point of view of sustainable development, it is of primary importance to define the retained surplus value added, which is related both to development opportunities and to the long-term borrowing capacity of the organization.

The decision to do so is undoubtedly linked to an appropriate wage policy and to the overall motivation system within the organization, which must also to be development-oriented.

The decision to pay out dividends is normally due to the determination of development investment and the amount of wages.

The process of distributing the surplus added value is principled, but it enables to implement concrete solutions in accordance with the added-value law, that is, with the equality of stakeholders while ensuring the sustainable development of the organization.

Summary sources of payments to employees are as follows:

1. Minimum wages, taking into account difficult working conditions.
2. Basic salaries and compensations according to the general act of the organization (in which, as a rule, the variable part of the salary according to the individual's contribution is also taken into account).
3. Reward from the residual surplus value added, after elimination of the retained amount of the surplus value added (in this context, there is also an opportunity for rewards to be paid to management given the business success of the company).

The owners of the capital receive:

1. Compensation for the opportunity cost of capital.
2. Dividends in accordance with the defined dividend policy with regard to the surplus value added achieved.

Questions for Discussion

5-1 Discuss the starting points of the value-added law.
5-2 What are the two main characteristics (aspects) of value-added law?
5-3 The value-added law has a characteristic: *general*? Why?
5-4 Explain the independence of the value-added law, regarding human will?
5-5 Who are stakeholders of the organization?
5-6 Why the inequality between stakeholders impacts the entropy of a business system?
5-7 Discuss the thesis that the work is transformed into value added.
5-8 What is the basis of the equality between the stakeholders?
5-9 Discuss ethical norms (e.g. fairness and honesty) as a component of the value-added law.
5-10 Discuss the traditional thinking about the purpose of business.
5-11 How can stakeholders be classified?
5-12 Discuss the rationale that the state should be treated as companies' stakeholder.
5-13 Discuss the rationale that the creditors should be treated as companies' stakeholders.
5-14 Discuss the minimum wage category as an assessment of consumption of labor force.
5-15 Discuss the opportunity cost of capital owners.
5-16 How should the retained value added be separated?
5-17 What is a definition and structure of surplus value added?
5-18 Discuss the process of the distribution of the surplus value added.
5-19 What are the sources of payments to capital owners?
5-20 What are the sources of payments to employees?

References

Bajo, C. Sanchez, Roelants, bruno (2015). *Kapital in past zadovževanja*. Capital and the Trap of Borrowing (In Slovene). Ljubljana: Modrijan.

Coutinho de Arruda Maria Cecilia, Rok, Boleslaw (2016). *Ethics and Responsibilities*. In: Understanding Ethics and Responsibilities in a Globalizing World.

(Retrieved: February, 2021). https://www.academia.edu/21950107/Economic_Inequality_as_an_Obstacle_to_Development?auto=download&email_work_card=download-paper.

Dethier, Fanny, Defourny, Jacques (2015). *The Effects of Workers' Participation in Governance, Ownership and Profit on the Economic Performance of Worker Cooperatives.* (Retrieved: January, 2017). https://orbi.ulg.ac.be/bitstream/2268/194594/3/Article%20SCOP.engl.final.150621.pdf.

Elkington, John, Hailes, Julia, Makower, Joel (1998). *Triple Bottom Line.* Appendix 11. (Retrieved: April, 2020). http://archive.babymilkaction.org/pdfs/spinpdfs/appendices/triplebl.pdf.

Gostiša, Mato (2014). *Teorija ekonomske demokracije kot nove sistemske eeping kapitalizma.* The Theory of Economic Democracy as a New Paradigm of the Capitalist System (In Slovene). Kranj: ŠCID.

Groenendijk, Lisa (2003). *Planning and Management Tools.* In: Enschede: The International Institute for Geo-Information Science and Earth. (Retrieved: May, 2020). https://webapps.itc.utwente.nl/librarywww/papers_2003/tech_rep/groenendijk.pdf.

Johnson, Carol (2019). Is the Crisis of Social Democracy a Crisis of Equality? https://www.socialeurope.eu/crisis-of-equality.

Kállay, Bálazs (2002). Ktheory of the Firm. *Economics & Sociology,* Vol 5, No 1, pp. 39–50.

Mazzucato, Mariana (2020). *Capitalism's Triple Crisis.* Social Europe. (Retrieved: April, 2020). https://www.socialeurope.eu/capitalisms-triple-crisis.

Neves, Catarina, Merrill, Roberto (2020). *Encouraging European Solidarity: An Unconditional Basic Income.* Social Europe. (Retrieved: may, 2020). https://www.socialeurope.eu/encouraging-european-solidarity-an-unconditional-basic-income.

Pierleoni, M. Rita (2018). The Analysis of Inequalities: The Review of Economic Approach and Policies. *Journal of Business and Economics,* Vol 9, No 2, pp. 123–136.

Piketty, Thomas (2014). *Capital in the Twenty-First Century.* USA : Amazon.

Van Parijs, Phillippe (2020). Finland 's Final Verdict. (Retrieved: May, 2020). https://www.socialeurope.eu/basic-income-positive-results-from-finland.

CHAPTER 6

Value-Added Statement

6.1 A Short History of the Value-Added Statement

The theoretical starting points for value added were already given by Petty in the seventeenth century, when he considered the national income (Petty 1690) and laid the foundations for a working theory of value. His work was continued by Adam Smith, David Ricardo and Karl Marx.

Statistical estimates of social income in the *USA* (ICA 2014, point 1.1) and France (Haller and Stolowy 1999, p. 2) date back to the eighteenth century. The use of value added in the United States began in 1790 (Van Staden 2000, p. 2).

Value added was widely used in the world as an indicator of the economic development of a country, i.e. at the level of national economies at the beginning of the nineteenth century. After the Second World War, the United Nations developed a standardized calculation of national income, thereby facilitating comparisons between countries (Haller and Stolowy 1999, p. 2). With certain amendments, this method of calculating the economic performance of countries in the world is still used today.

Value added therefore has a purely macroeconomic origin. One of the first authors to propose the use of a company's performance test

Ž. Bergant, *Accountancy and Social Responsibility*,
Palgrave Studies in Impact Finance,
https://doi.org/10.1007/978-3-030-77928-3_6

was Suojanen (1954, p. 395), who referred to the US Department of Commerce's definition of value added in 1974. He proposed a value-added statement and considered it important information, not only at the company level but also at the level of its individual activities. The larger companies (conglomerates) are in fact dealing with several activities (ibid., pp. 396–397).

A broader awareness of the added value at the enterprise level occurred in 1975 in the *UK*, with the report of the Committee on Accounting Standards (Accounting Standard Steering Committee—*ASSC*), entitled The Corporate Report.

In this report, the value-added statement (*VAS*) is seen as "the most direct way of putting profit into an appropriate perspective in terms of the combined efforts of capital, management and employees" (ASSC 1975, point 6.7). Further, a possible calculation is shown by corresponding items in the value-added statement, which is intended to be a "useful measurement of the performance and performance of the enterprise" (ASSC 1975, point 6.10).

The same document foresees an even greater relevance and role of the future value-added statement (ASSC 1975, point 7.4). The Committee notes that existing accounting practices do not meet all the needs of users of information, and therefore recommends that additional financial statements (most notably the value-added statement) should be used in order to further develop social accounting in a going concern (ASSC 1975, point 8.10).

Based on these recommendations, corporate value-added reporting has expanded relatively quickly in many countries, such as the Netherlands, France, Germany, Denmark, Switzerland, Italy, Australia, South Africa, India, Singapore, (e.g. Mandal and Goswami 2008, p. 103; Singh 2013, p. 2) although on a voluntary basis.

Pong and Mitchell consider this a rare case in history that companies have voluntarily published a new financial statement (Pong and Mitchell 2014, p. 5). Many banks have also joined in the publication of the value-added statement (Donleavy 2015, p. 322).

The publication of the value-added statement was also supported by the profession of the time:"*VAS* has become an indispensable part of corporate social reporting" (Reichmann and Lange 1981, p. 17). Morley estimated that *VAS* was gaining even more popularity and expected that soon all major UK companies would include *VAS* in their reports (Morley 1979, p. 629).

Further development of financial reporting showed that expectations were too high at that time. The volume of publishing value-added accounts peaked in the *UK* in 1980 and then it started to decline. The decline in the publication of value-added statements also in other countries has been noted by many authors (Van Staden 2000, p. 3). There has also been a significant decrease in the value-added research (Van Staden, ibid.).

The causes of this decline, the authors without exception, found in the changing social and economic circumstances, where the focus is on social and environmental role of companies decreased significantly, as well as the role of trade unions (e.g. Pong and Mitchell 2014, pp. 5–8; Van Staden 2000, p. 5; Ianniello 2010, p. 368). In empirical research, this has been reflected in reduced user's interest in value-added information (Pong and Mitchell 2014, p. 18).

This trend was followed also by international accounting standards. In 1997, they recommended the value-added statement as "an additional statement if management believes that it will contribute to business decisions," but with amendments in 2004, this recommendation was omitted. Thus, *even today*, the International Financial Reporting Standards only refer to a value-added statement *as one of the possible* additional financial statements, but are not subject to *IFRS* (IFRS 2018, paragraph 14). The same text was adopted by the European Union (EU 2008, *IAS* 1, point 10).

The rise and fall of *VAS* popularity over the period is a good example of how the socio-economic environment affects accounting (Pong and Mitchell, ibid.). The notion that "accounting has its own particular social and political dimension is confirmed, since accounting policies directly benefit some groups in society and neglect others" (Cooper and Sherer 1984, p. 208). In any case, it should be borne in mind that the value-added statement also has "conflicting content, which has always been considered a hot political issue" (Haller and Stolowy 1999, p. 5).

In spite of all this, in the world today, the usefulness of the value-added statement is recognized in practice of numerous firms. Many of them include it in their annual reports (e.g.: Volkswagen Group 2017; Barloworld Limited 2017; Netcare Limited 2017; Blue Label Telecoms 2018; Migros Group 2018; Unilever Nigeria Plc 2018; OANDO Plc 2018; Singtel 2019). As a rule, international corporations publish a value–added statement in the context of concern for the local environment and its long-term development.

VAS is not limited only to the companies but it is also published by financial institutions, banks and insurance companies (e.g. First national Bank Ghana 2018; Centenary Bank 2018).

The frequency of use of the value-added statement varies from country to country. A survey of 211 published financial statements for the fiscal periods 2003 of Italian listed companies shows that the publication of the value-added statement is the marginal phenomenon (Ianniello 2010). The study reveals that about 81 (38.39%) companies out of 211 have disclosed value-added information in the annual report, while as only as 3 (1.42%) companies publish *VAS* as a separate statement. American and Canadian companies have not published value-added statements at all.

The value-added statement is widespread, especially in India, South Africa and China, where large corporations in particular want to prove their social responsibility (Fang and Zhu 2013). Many Latin American companies also add value-added statements to their annual reports (Perera and Zicari 2012, pp. 490–492).

In Bangladesh, for example, 45% of all publicly listed organizations publish also a value-added statement. Among them, are as many as 93% of banks, 55% of other financial institutions and 42% of insurance companies (Islam 2019, p. 13).

One particular example is Brazil, which in 2007 introduced a value-added statement in its accounting standards as a mandatory component of external reporting (Machado et al. 2016, p. 4). Empirical research in this country confirms the hypothesis that *VAS* contains crucial information for capital markets (Machado et al. 2016, p. 11). This is justified by the fact that *VAS* provides broader information than a profit and loss account and that the capital markets take into account the corporate social responsibility (Machado, ibid.). Value-added statement is subject to audit as well (e.g. Grupo Carrefour Brasil 2020).

Value-added statement reporting is mandatory for listed companies on the stock exchange also in Nigeria (Donleavy 2015, p. 322; Aruwa 2008, p. 1).

How to explain the resurgence of the value-added statements in corporate reporting practices? Undoubtedly, we can explain it in the same way as its fall: social and political conditions are changing. Generally, "the future of the value-added statement as additional information or basic information about a firm's achievements is linked to the development of the political, social and economic environment" (Ianniello 2010, p. 371). In its own way, this was also confirmed by the fact that in the

United States and Canada is not an appropriate atmosphere for wider enforcement of reporting on value added (Ríahi-Belkaoui 2010, 27).

However, the above interpretation should not be understood too narrowly. Accounting is not just unilaterally depending on the environment, but it also affects the return. "The added value not only represents the team as a collaborative team, but also has a positive effect on the harmony of this collaboration. Thus, the value-added statement can open up the community to the general public and seek to meet the information needs of different stakeholders" (Ianniello 2010).

The uneven development and use of the value-added statement across countries and organizations is therefore evident. However, the above explanation of the situation is probably a bit too narrow. Accounting (with the added-value statement included) really depends on the socio-economic environment, but account also influences the environment as a feedback. However, this impact is not equally strong in all environments. This means that the causes could be on both sides.

The socio-environmental impacts are different in different countries, due to their historical and political development, and especially because of their different economic system. But even between capitalist countries, there are huge differences, mostly due to their different stage of development.

Van Staden cites the case of the Republic of South Africa. There, the socio-economic environment is different mainly for the following reasons (Van Staden 2000, p. 6):

1. The country is developing.
2. There are strong unions and legislation that protects workers.
3. The country is in an economic transition following its political transition to democracy.
4. Companies are trying to overcome the consequences of racial discrimination and want to show themselves in a better social orientation.
5. Companies, among the first in the world, have a high difference between the highest and lowest wages and are under pressure to reduce this difference.
6. Companies are trying to show the importance of their role in society.

On the other hand, the influence of the accounting profession is also not uniform due to different theoretical perspectives. For example, Friedman argues that "corporate social responsibility is to increase profits" and points out that social spending can have a negative impact on investors (Friedman 1970). Others argue that investors will reward a company that is socially oriented, through investments despite the risk of lower yields (Van Staden 2000, p. 9). Empirical research shows that trade unions did not see a special quality in such information, which was explained also by the technical and substantive shortcomings of the value-added statement (Van Staden 2001, p. 12).

Probably due to the above disagreements, there is a significant expectation gap between the principal reasons for the publication of *VAS* and the actual use of this information. There may be several reasons for such weak theoretical background. The main three of them seem to be:

1. There is a lack of critical analysis of the empirical findings about the usefulness of the value-added statement (*VAS*).
2. There is a lack of a comprehensive theoretical assessment of the expressive power of the value added as information.
3. Insufficient theoretical assessment of the fundamental expressive power of *VAS* has a negative impact on the development of the social and social environment, and thus on users' expectations as well.

Ad 1)

In empirical research, there are several shortcomings, in particular the following:

1. Not all *VAS* users are taken into account, since active owners, management and supervisory authorities are completely omitted from the findings in the surveys as internal users of the information.
2. There is no research on the use of the value added in deciding the business of an organization. For example, how can management use value-added information in its business decisions and not just gain a reputation in the environment?
3. An important emphasis in research is on the trade unions, which are supposed to represent employees. In this way, they become intermediaries in the flow of information, which for many reasons increases

the possibility of a communication noise. The potential for this noise is compounded by the fact that analyzes for trade unions are mostly carried out by external organizations, but mostly do not take into account the information about the value added, as noted by Van Staden (2001, 10).

4. There is too little reliable research in relation to the importance of *VAS* as a basis for decision-making for other stakeholders.
5. Research is focused on *VAS*, which is not standardized, so there are differences in individual associations, which affects different perceptions of users.
6. In principle, it could be questioned any conclusion of a study that claims that users in some information see no benefits. Perhaps they were not enough, or have been wrongly informed.[1]
7. If someone does not like the particular information, it does not mean that the information is not useful. It could even be the opposite. The medicine can also be bitter.

An important critical view of empiricism is also offered in Miller and Bahnson (2002, p. 138). This does not, of course, mean that empirical research is in principle questionable, but we must critically evaluate it.

Ad 2)

While the authors emphasize corporate social responsibility and sustainable development, the profession is not yet unified in emphasizing the added value as the basic accounting information on sustainable development. This is particularly evidenced by the shy treatment of *VAS* in accounting standards.

Empirical research shows that trade unions did not see a special quality in such information, which was also explained by the technical and substantive shortcomings of the value-added statement (Van Staden 2001, p. 12).

[1] At the first glance, it would make sense for decision-makers with high accounting skills to make greater use of value-added information. Research in the US proves the opposite. The author sees the reason mainly because a high accounting knowledge is the result of a traditional study that assumes the firm's profit orientation and does not take into account the company's orientation toward sustainable development (Riah-Belkaoui 2010, p. 128).

Due to the consideration of the value-added statement as ***additional*** information, empirical research loses the basic criterion for its usefulness, as only the interests of shareholders are often taken into account.

Dealing with the expressive power of some information, without considering its underlying purpose, is similar to treating the usefulness of a boat in terms of driving on the road. An inadequately defined purpose of the information leads to incorrect user's expectations. Dealing with the expressive power of some information without considering its underlying purpose is similar to treating the usefulness of a boat in terms of driving on the road.

It is therefore not surprising that many studies have concluded that value added does not have a statistically significant effect on cash flow from operating activities (e.g. Khoshkhoo et al. 2013, p. 2930).

It should also be borne in mind that the same criterion for the same research might be appropriate in one environment (country) and not in another, because the information users understand it differently, due to different, historical and developmental paths. This may be one of the important reasons why empirical research in one country indicates a statistically significant correlation of value-added information, with the movement of a firm's value in the capital market (e.g. Donleavy 2015, p. 325). In another country, no such links have been identified (e.g. Van Staden 2000, p. 11).

Ad 3)

The development of accountancy really depends on the development of information needs. Of course, the question is whether they are properly defined or recognized. If a man does not feel thirsty, he will die. In such a case, he should be persuaded to drink. Each profession (science) has a similar role to play with its influence on social and political development. The relationship between the accountancy and the society therefore can be fatal if not treated from a long-term perspective.

The value-added statement provides information that, from an accounting point of view, accompanies a firm's orientation toward sustainable development, although other non-accounting information is also relevant here. From this point of view, there are, in principle, no adversaries in the profession, but its influence in the environment is still significantly too small due to the shyness of its treatment.

Accounting theory has already made significant progress by treating accounting in interactivity with society and the environment, but it still should do an effort in treating the entire society as a system with a common goal: well-being of people. It cannot do this because the whole society has not yet identified itself with the principles of sustainable development in the broadest sense. Therefore, some consider that the further development of the value-added statement, as important information about the achievements of the organization's business depends on further social and political development (Ianniello 2010, 377).

Nevertheless, we can agree with the statement that "in the face of growing importance of: social responsibility, green accounting, pollution disclosures and of focus on integrated reporting, it is time to rethink value-added reporting" (Donleavy 2015, p. 316).

The academic sphere plays an important role in how quickly information about value added is more widely recognized and used (Donleavy 2015, p. 329). It is rational to believe that this role is important in particular in:

1. Promoting sustainable development as a long-term goal of the associations.
2. Developing and promoting socially responsible accounting and quality reporting.
3. Developing curricula in educational institutions.
4. Eliminating the weaknesses of the value-added statement (especially through appropriate standardization).
5. Supplementing the value-added statement with additional, including non-accounting information.
6. Developing the analysis of the added value and expressive power of information on its basis.
7. Reduction of distrust in the value-added statement, which may be also the result of voluntary reporting by organizations.[2]
8. Promoting value-added reporting as an important means of communication of each organization with its stakeholders and the environment.
9. Improving the collaboration of scientists and experts worldwide.[3]

[2] The distrust of *VAS* information as a result of voluntary decisions by management companies is cited by Van Staden (2000, p. 9) and Donleavy (2015, p. 327).

[3] Perera and Zicari (2012, p. 487) argue that the citing among researchers is very regionally limited.

The value-added concept is useful in the context of large companies that influence large sections of society and have a general economic and social importance besides the limited interests of shareholders (Kaur 2020).

6.2 The Purpose of the Value-Added Statement

Suojanen is probably the first author, who suggested the preparation of the value-added statement as a supplementary statement to the balance sheet and income statement (Suojanen 1954, p. 396). He justified it with a different view of the company, where, besides the owners, several stakeholders participate in the business, which are also responsible for the company's achievements (Suojanen 1954, p. 398). After him, many authors argued for the rationality of preparing *VAS*.

Among the basic reasons for the development of *VAS* are many users of value-added information, both at the macro level and at the level of individual public and private entities, for example:

1. Government (taxes and budgetary finances, statistics, planning and monitoring of economic growth and well-being of society, local authorities).
2. Management of the organization (information to decide on sustainable development, to balance interests and stakeholder's engagement, and to achieve long-term goals, information about efficiency and effectiveness of the organization).
3. Business partners interested in long-term business cooperation.
4. Competitors and potential acquirers (information related to the development and the value of the company).
5. Potential investors (information on the possible movement of the market value of the share and the development prospects of the company).
6. Lenders (information on reducing credit risk).
7. Trade unions (information to evaluate the effects of employees' work and the opportunities for rewards or employment).
8. Employees for better motivation (value added is the simplest way of understanding organization's success).
9. Analysts, consultants, journalists, economists, researchers, credit rating agencies.

10. The general public (individual customers, individual interest groups, political parties, environmental associations, regional and sectoral associations).

Another important reason for introducing *VAS* comes from the nature of the organization's goals. Namely, it changes the attention from the owners to other stakeholders of the company who are also responsible for its business (Riahi-Belkaoui 2010, p. 18). Related to this, *VAS's* intention is to fulfill the duty of management for interested users to provide more information than they can obtain from the income statement and balance sheet (Singh, 2013, 1).

Another role of *VAS* is the impact on changes in society in general, where the labor takes on a stronger role (e.g. through trade unions) and requires a fairer distribution of the value created (Riahi-Belkaoui 2010, p. 18). In doing so, *VAS* provides an information basis for creating a balanced business policy, with the participation of all stakeholders and with the aim of sustainable development of an organization.

Objectives of *VAS* are arising from the role of companies in society, that is, in relation to the stakeholders who want to be informed how the company does its business according to their individual financial goals.

At the same time, *VAS* shows the economic and financial position of the organization in relation to the environment, especially to customers and suppliers (Reichmann and Lange 1981, p. 17). This indicates the important role of *VAS* in the connection between the economic and social dimension of the business of each organization.

VAS is defined as a statement that shows the income of the company as a whole and its division among the contributing factors (Mandal and Goswami 2008, p. 102). In this way, *VAS* gives a comprehensive picture of the generation and the use of value added. It is generally considered as a broader basis for measuring an entity's performance in relation to traditional criteria based on a traditional accounting system. *VAS* represents an important part of the social reporting of a company (Prasad 2015, p. 3). Last but not least, *VAS* is "an important means of communication" (Aruwa 2008, p. 9).

On the basis of the above, we are not surprised to find the latest research showing that value added is significantly one of the key indicators of sustainable business development and thus an integral part of integrated reporting (e.g. Oshika and Saka 2015, p. 14).[4]

Due to the close link between corporates social responsibility and sustainable development, some authors use the term sustainability reporting as a synonym for social responsibility (e.g. Van Staden et al. 2013, 21).

Some empirical studies also confirm that *VAS* provides relevant information in the context of socially responsible accounting, especially in developing countries (Perera and Zicari 2012, p. 485). Some authors give particular emphasis on the impact of *VAS* on accelerating the development of socially responsible reporting (e.g. Perera and Zicari 2012, p. 487).

This confirms the definition of value-added flow as information from a long-term perspective. At the same time, we can explain why some research based on erroneously (short-term) set criteria has not found reliable confirmation of the usefulness of this information to some users (e.g. Van Staden 2000).

In this way, *VAS* becomes a kind of synthesis of the ***technocratic design*** of the organization, where are the primary interests of the owners and founders and the ***humanistic design***, where is important the community of interests of external and internal participants (individuals, groups and the public).

6.3 The Principal Content of the Value-Added Statement

The principal content of the value-added statement covers both the creation of added value and its distribution to key stakeholders.

The basic model is presented as a separate financial statement in the form of a balance sheet in Table 6.1, where the value added created is equal to the allocated value added. The principal content of the *VAS* is therefore well known, but it differs in details in different countries and also in different companies.

[4] The survey was conducted on the basis of data from Japanese companies that have survived 100 years and more.

Table 6.1 Basic model of the value-added statement

Creating value added	*Distributing value added*
Revenues (Total revenue)	Employees
– Costs of materials and services	Taxes
Created gross value added	Creditors
– Depreciation	Society and environment
Created net value added (*NVA*)	Capital owners
	Retained profit
	Distributed net value added

Source Own research

Because *VAS* is not standardized, differences are mainly due to different social and political backgrounds (Perera and Zicari 2012, p. 487), which supports the view that the accounting profession is a constantly evolving social phenomenon.

Obviously, we have the ability and (due to different users) also the need for more types of value-added statements. Therefore, the orderliness of the various *VAS* models or their classification (typology) is useful both for the further study and for practical application.

The most important criteria for the typology of information are their purpose and content. From these two perspectives, models of value-added statements (*VAS*), can be classified into four types, as shown in Table 6.2.

Table 6.2 shows four types of standardized *VAS* for external reporting and four types of non-standardized *VAS* for internal reporting. Internal users require more detailed information, which the company can adapt to their needs. So, it is talking about a *customized VAS*.

Profit and non-profit activities are separated for both types of reporting because of significant differences in the core objectives of the activity that require different information. A significant contribution for non-profit organization reporting was offered by Baba et al. (2015, pp. 1–22).

The expanded *VAS* is also shown separately because it (as opposed to basic) contains also non-accounting information.

Undoubtedly, standardizing *VAS* would be a significant step forward, in particular in regard to the greater usefulness and wider use of this statement.

Table 6.2 Typology of value-added statements, regarding their purpose

The purpose		*The content*	
		Basic VAS	*Expanded VAS*
External reporting	Profit industry	Standardized VAS	Standardized expanded VAS
	Non-profit industry	Standardized *VAS*	Standardized expanded *VAS*
Internal reporting	Profit industry	Adapted *VAS*	Adapted and expanded *VAS*
	Non-profit industry	Adapted *VAS*	Adapted and expanded *VAS*

Source Own research

A number of authors have identified the inappropriateness of value-added statements between organizations as a significant weakness that diminishes their expressive power and also complicates the empirical research (e.g. McLeay 1983, p. 54). Therefore, they emphasize *VAS* standardization as a prerequisite for the continued development of sustainable reporting (e.g. Arangies et al. 2008). At the same time, some authors emphasize that value-added statements should be audited as well (e.g. Van Staden et al. 2013, p. 22).

The next step in standardizing the basic *VAS* requires the additional effort in defining non-accounting value-added information for external reporting. This means producing a ***standardized extended*** *VAS,* enriched with information not provided by traditional accounting. This need is also indicated by some authors (e.g. Mook 2007, p. 104).

Table 6.2 envisages different users, which have different purposes for using *VAS*. This leads to different types of *VAS* as a result of adapting their expressive power to the needs of individual users.

Each of these four types of *VAS* in Table 6.2 can therefore be broken down into different kinds of *VAS*, following two basic criteria: the type of users and the primary purpose of decision-making. This is shown in principle in Table 6.3.

Table 6.3 can be used for making various kinds of *VAS* for each of the *VAS* types defined in Table 6.2.

Table 6.3 Kinds of value-added statements

Users	*Purpose of decision making*
xxx	xxxxx

Source Own research

Designing different kinds of *VAS* and information based on them is primarily the responsibility of business analysts. This requires a proper refinement of the internal reporting system within each organization, especially in terms of content, orderliness and reporting methods.

Various kinds of *VAS* have been developed in different industries (e.g. in manufacturing, agriculture, cooperatives, non-profit associations) (Stanton et al. 1992 and Perrot 2006).

In practice, different types of *VAS* have also been developed across countries, as a result of the particularities of their accounting and methodologies in measuring value added (McLeay 1983, p. 54).

6.4 Surplus Value-Added Statement

Taking into account the purpose of the value-added statement in the previous section and the principle definition of the distribution of the surplus value added (*SVA*) in Sect. 5.5, it is logical to define the surplus value-added statement (*SVAS*).

In creating a surplus value-added statement particularly the following starting points should be considered:

1. The statement should be useful for a wider circle of interested people or organizations.
2. The statement should be useful for creating indicators and improving the organizational climate.
3. The costs of products and services sold include minimum wages as an expression of the consumption of labor in the business.
4. The costs of products and services sold include the opportunity cost of invested financial capital.
5. The category gross *SVA* is not meaningful in comparing gross value added as a general known category, therefore it is not shown in the statement.

6. The statement should show the way of creating (sources) of surplus added value (*SVA*) and its distribution.
7. The most important starting point for *SVAS* is the equality of stakeholders in participating in surplus value added, consistently with their contribution to risk management. It means that both ***stakeholders as non-governors*** and ***stakeholders in the role of governors*** (Sect. 5.3) should be included.

For the illustration of the surplus value-added statement (*SVAS*) and its comparison with profit & loss statement (*P &L*) in the Table 6.4, the following assumptions are made:

1. There are 100 employees.
2. Minimum wage per capita is € 800.00.
3. Total capital is € 5.000.00,000.
4. Opportunity cost of capital is 2, 5%.
5. Profit tax is 15%.
6. Retained profit is allocated to employees and active owners in the ratio between the amount of rewards to active owners and the amount of salaries of other employees (the assumption of the agreement is one to two).
7. For the sake of simplification, we assume that all employees are active co-governors.
8. For the sake of simplification, we did not differentiate between gross and net amounts of remuneration (the difference is, in principle, the state's participation in surplus added value).

In the Table 6.4, the surplus added value was allocated to:

1. Non-active (non-governing) stakeholders. They carry a small part of the risk and their common feature is that they cannot directly influence the business decisions, but have a possibility to control the operations.
2. Governing (active) stakeholders who, in addition to bearing the risk, also contribute to risk management.

Table 6.4 shows in particular:

Table 6.4 Income statement (P&L) comparing surplus added-value statement (in € 1,000)

	ITEMS	*P&L*	*SAVS*
	A. GENERATING PROFIT AND *SVA*		
1	Revenues	9,100	9,100
2	Material costs	4,900	4,900
3	Amortization and depreciation	1,280	1,280
4	Labor costs	1,900	
5	Financing costs	400	
6	Costs of minimal wages		80
7	Opportunity cost of equity		125
8	*Profit*	*1,008*	
9	*Added value* (4 + 5 + 8)		*3,308*
10	***Surplus value*** added (9 – 6 – 7)		3,103
	B. DISTRIBUTION OF PROFIT AND *SVA*		
11	Tax	151	
12	Net profit (8 – 11)	857	
13	Net profit for dividends	525	
14	Net profit for management awards	32	
15	Retained net profit	300	
16	*SVA* for financiers (interest) *I*		400
17	*SVA* for non-active shareholders dividends		400
18	*SVA* for the state (taxes) *T*		151
19	*SVA for non-active stakeholders* (16 + 17 + 18)		*951*
20	*SVA* for employees		1,820
21	*SVA* for management awards		32
22	Retained *SVA* for employees		200
23	Retained *SVA* for active shareholders		100
24	*SVA for active stakeholders* (20 + 21 + 22 + 23)		*2.152*
25	**Surplus value added** (19 + 24) = 10		3,103

Source Own research

1. Value added (€ 3,308) is significantly higher than profit (€ 1,008), as it also includes labor costs (€ 1,900) and financing costs (€ 400).
2. Surplus value added (€ 3,103) is equal to added value, reduced by minimum wages (€ 80) and capital costs (€ 400).
3. After deduction of dividends, taxes and rewards to management, the net profit of € 300 remains retained.
4. Surplus value added is allocated to non-active (€ 951) and to active stakeholders (€ 2,152).

5. The largest portion of surplus value added is distributed to employees (€ 1,820), which is the result of the assumption of their active participation. Otherwise, this part would of course be lower for the amount that would be shown among non-active stakeholders.
6. Retained earnings belong both to employees and to active owners in the assumed (agreed) proportion.

In accordance with the idea of the extended value added, a broader aspect of the surplus value added could be defined (e.g. Mook 2007), which is important for presenting of achievements from the social responsibility aspect. Therefore, this part should be included in the notes to the statement of the surplus value added. These explanations would play the similar role as the explanations to the income statement.

From the comparison between the two statements in Table 6.4, we can summarize in particular the following:

1. *SVAS* (together with explanations) takes into account the equality of stakeholders in accordance with the added-value law and contributes to the disclosure of the corporate social responsibility, orientated to sustainable development.
2. *SVAS* does not mean only a different view of the organization's income statement, but it also shows that profit is not basic piece of information about the operations from the social responsibility point of view, and in terms of sustainable development. Profit as a category in *SVAS* simply does not exist anymore.[5]
3. *SVAS* takes over a leading role before the income statement. Therefore, it can no longer be regarded as only complementary information to the income statement.
4. *SVAS* is a useful basis for analyzing the efficiency and effectiveness of the operations, since the surplus added value replaces the profit as the underlying organization's goal.
5. *SVAS* is an important piece of information, especially for stakeholders of the organization who carry the risk of operations.

[5] This is consistent with the findings of many authors who demand a shift of organization's goal from shareholder's value to stakeholder value (e.g. Brennan 2008).

6. *SVAS* can be an important piece of information for investors and business partners, especially in terms of long-term and stable operations.
7. *SVAS* is also an important piece of information for wider public, especially in terms of social responsibility. In particular, information of the distribution of surplus added value is important.
8. Table 6.4 shows the connectivity of the surplus added value with the income statement, which is otherwise completely unnecessary for the preparation of *SVAS*.
9. This does not mean that P&L would not be prepared. It still contains (in terms of a different view of business) useful supplementary information. This is particularly true for a transitional period until value added is widely implemented.
10. *SVAS* should become an integral part of an integral reporting.

SAVS has some disadvantages, in particular the following ones:

1. In a comparative assessment (benchmarking) or within an activity, comparability is difficult, if there are differences in starting points for determining the minimum wage or assessing the opportunity costs of the financial capital.
2. For the same reasons, *SAVS* may be less suitable for statistical processing at the state level and for comparisons between different countries.

Problems with comparability can be solved satisfactorily with an appropriate standardized statement, which will undoubtedly be the subject of development over a longer period of time in the future.

6.5 Analysis on the Basis of Value-Added Statement

Management on the basis of value added requires information. It can be provided only by adequate analyzing data about value added, based on the defined value-added content and the value-added statement shown in the previous chapters.

The fundamental purpose of analyzing the value added is to direct business toward socially responsible and sustainable development of the organization. Main users of this information are management, employees and other internal or external stakeholders.

Analyzing the value added does not require substantial new methods and tools, but must take into account new data and content of categories.

Under "the analysis tool" is understood individual element of analysis technique or method. Such tools can be classified into the following sets:

1. Indicators as *pointers* (sizes, changes, differences) as absolute values (e.g. amounts)
2. Indicators as *ratios* (relationships between individual categories):
   a. Coefficients (showing mutual comparisons of categories)
   b. Indices (showing dynamics, change over time)
   c. Structures or degree of participation (showing the composition of the whole by individual parts)
3. Graphic tools (e.g. tables, graphs, figures, diagrams, flow charts)
4. Mathematical and statistical tools (e.g. financial mathematics, higher mathematics and probability calculus, statistical methods).

Indicators as pointers have following basic forms:

1. .Actual item
2. . Business flows (changes of actual items):
   Casual flows
   Execution flows
3. Deviations from the planned or comparable category.

One of the basic methods of analyzing business efficiency and risk is to analyze operating, financial and total leverage. This will be done in next sections, of course from surplus value added view. After that other indicators will be discussed.

6.6 Operating Leverage for Surplus Value Added

The Equation of surplus value added was written in Sect. 8.2:

$$SVA = LC - CLC + EBT - OCC \tag{6.1}$$

Surplus value added therefore consists of labor costs (LC), and reduced by consumption costs of labor (CLC) and $EBIT$ that is reduced by opportunity costs of capital owners (OCC). $EBIT$ is therefore reshaped to *net earnings before interest and taxes* ($NEBIT$). From now on, the Eq. 6.1 will be simplified with net categories net cost of labor (NLC) and net earnings before interest and taxes (NEBIT). It is than written as:

$$SVA = NLC + NEBIT \tag{6.2}$$

Introducing variable (VC) and fixed costs (FC) to Eq. 6.2 and comparing them to total revenues (TR), a new equation is:

$$\frac{SVA}{TR} = \frac{S - VC - FC_{corr} + NLC}{TR}. \tag{6.3}$$

In the Eq. 6.3, fixed costs (FC_{corr}) are corrected by addition of consumption costs of labor (CLC) and opportunity costs of capital owners (OCC). It can be:

$$\frac{SVA}{TR} = 1\frac{VC}{TR} - \frac{FC_{corr}}{TR} + \frac{NLC}{TR}. \tag{6.4}$$

Equation 6.4 is rewritten as:

$$\frac{SVA}{TR} = \frac{NLC}{TR} + \frac{TR - VC}{TR} - \frac{FC_{corr}}{TR}. \tag{6.5}$$

The second fraction on the right side is *a contribution margin ratio*. The Eq. 6.5 shows that the share of surplus value added (SVA) in total revenues depends on: the share of net labor costs, contribution margin ratio (CMR) and the share of fixed costs, that impacts the break-even point of SVA (BEP_{sva}).

Traditional calculation for the degree of operating leverage (DOL) is:

$$DOL = \frac{TR - VC}{TR - VC - FC} = \frac{TR - VC}{EBIT} \tag{6.6}$$

Similarly, we can define the degree of operating leverage (DOL_{corr}) for the surplus value added:

$$DOL_{corr} = \frac{TR - VC}{TR - VC - FC_{corr}} = \frac{TR - VC}{NEBIT} \tag{6.7}$$

Table 6.5 A comparison of two different degrees of operating leverage

No.	*Categories*	*Initial state*	*Increase 10% TS*	*Decrease 10% TS*	*Index 3/2*	*Index 4/2*
	1	*2*	*3*	*4*	*5*	*6*
1	Total revenues (TR)	40,000	44,000	36,000	110	90
2	Variable costs (VC)	20,000	22,000	18,000	110	90
3	Contribution margin (CM) 1 – 2)	20,000	22,000	18,000	110	90
4	Contribution margin ratio (CMR) (3/1)	0,50	0,50	0,50	100	100
5	Fixed costs (FC)	10,000	10,000	10,000	100	100
6	Labor costs (LC)	4,000	4,000	4,000	100	100
7	EBIT = (1 –2 – 5)	10,000	12,000	8,000	120	80
8	Degree of operational leverage (DOL) (3/7)	2				
9	Level of break-ever seilcs (5/4)	20,000	20,000	20,000	100	100
10	Margin of safety (1 – 9)	20,000	20,000	20,000	100	100
11	Margin of safety ratio (10/1)	0.50	0.50	0.5U	100	100
12	Consumption costs of labor (CLC)	1,500	1,500	1,500	100	100
13	Opportunity costs of capital (OCC)	1,000	1,000	1,000	100	100
14	FC_{corr} (5 – 12 + 13)	8,500	8,500	8,500	100	100
15	LC_{corr} (6 – 12)	2,500	2,500	2,500	100	100
16	*NEBIT* (7 – 9 – 10)	11,500	13,500	9,500	117	83
17	Operational leverage degree of SVA DOL_{sva} (3/16)	1.74				
18	FC_{corr}/FC(14/5)	0.85	0.95	0.95	100	100
19	NEBIT/EBIT	US	1.13	1.19	98	103
20	DOL/DOL_{sva}	1.15				

(continued)

Table 6.5 (continued)

No.	*Categories*	*Initial state*	*Increase 10% TS*	*Decrease 10% TS*	*Index 3/2*	*Index 4/2*
	1	*2*	*3*	*4*	*5*	*6*
21	Level of break-even sales for *SVA* (14/4)	17,000	17,000	17,000	100	100
22	Margin of safety for *SVA* (1 − 21)	23,000	27,000	19,000	117	83
23	Margin of safety ratio for *SVA* (22/1)	0.575	0.61	0.53	107	92

Source Own research

Table 6.5 shows that the degree of operating leverage calculated by traditional method is two (2). Therefore, increased or decreased total revenues for 10% affects *EBIT* by 20%.

Original fixed costs are corrected by subtraction of labor costs (*LC*) and addition of opportunity costs of capital (*OCC*). Hence, they are lowered by 500 €. It caused an increase of *EBIT* that became ***net earnings before interest and taxes*** (*NEBIT*) in the amount of 11,500 €.

The degree of operating leverage of *SVA* is 1.74. It means that increased or decreased total revenues for 10% affects change of *NEBIT* by 17,4%.

Therefore, the operational risk is lower in the case of surplus value added. At the same time, the amounts of increase and decrease of *EBIT* and *NEBIT* are equal.

NEBIT is 15% higher that *EBIT*. This is the reason why the degree of traditional operating leverage (*DOL*) is by the same percentage higher than the degree of operating leverage in the case of surplus value added (DOL_{sva}).

Traditionally calculated margin of safety is therefore lower than margin of safety for surplus value added. Therefore, also margin of safety ratio is higher for *SVA*.

Table 6.5 allows some conclusions:

1. The amounts of increase and decrease of *EBIT* and *NEBIT* are equal.

2. Increasing the surplus of added value allows the adaptation of its structure in accordance with the distribution policy among stakeholders.
3. The decrease in surplus value added (due to the decrease in total revenues) is relatively smaller than the decrease in *EBIT*, which in principle enables a partial transfer of risk to all stakeholders of the company, especially to employees.
4. The assessment of the break-even point for surplus value added and the corresponding safety intervals provides additional information, thus enabling a wider range of structured business decisions.
5. Operating leverage enables the determination of the volume of business, which already brings value added.
6. Operating leverage somewhat simplifies the sensitivity analysis of the business system.

In summary, it can be seen that *NEBIT* becomes an important category instead of *EBIT*. The difference is shown at calculation of break-even point and margin of safety and its ratio.

The difference in margin of safety in terms of value added is greater for labor costs, which reduce fixed costs when calculating the break-even point. This shows that labor costs can be a kind of reserve in reducing the volume of business, but it depends on the negotiating position of the union and on previous agreements on possible risk-taking.

Depending on the outcome of the negotiations, the level of leverage for value added can be calculated differently. With its help, the percentage increase in value added can be calculated and planned, which is the ultimate goal of calculating business leverage for value added.

6.7 Financial Leverage for Surplus Value Added

In the model, operating leverage is the assumption of unchanged interest costs when changing the volume of revenues. This is not entirely realistic, since a larger volume of business requires also greater funding volume.

This fact has two implications for the traditional model of financial leverage:

1. The financial debt is generally cheaper than equity, because it does not carry the same risk (equity is more expensive for a risk premium).
2. Interest is a deductible item from the tax base, resulting in an additional reduction in the debt price, due to the "tax shield."

In the surplus value-added model, the assumptions of financial leverage are changed:

1. Investors normally expect higher return comparing to creditors but only a part of this return presents fixed costs of financing, in line with the contract. This assumption has been already considered in the model of operating leverage, where the opportunity costs of capital increased fixed costs as shown in the Table 6.5 The other part of the expected return is incorporated in the surplus value added and therefore depends on the volume of *SVA*. It means that this part of return is really riskier and depends also on company's distribution policy regarding surplus value added.
2. The deductibility of the interest from the tax base has a total arbitrary character, because it is regulated by the tax legislation. This is just an expression of the tendency to reduce the credit risk of banks. The better position of creditors is entirely due to the contractual relationship, which is purely administrative in nature and has no basis in business or economic logic. There is no study that would economically justify such an arrangement. Most authors, especially in Western professional literature, do not usually deal with this, but take such an arrangement as a given fact despite it means an important and unnecessary motive for higher indebtedness of organizations.

   Despite of such regulation, creditors cannot totally avoid the credit risk. This is evidenced by the need for additional reservations and collaterals and debt write-offs. Especially when writing off debts, the dominance of business logic is shown. It turns out that this is not a contractual provision but a partnership, where the risk must be shared among the stakeholders. This thesis is also confirmed in Sharia law, where there is no talk about interest.

   Similar patterns are in the system of project financing—however, it is usually only a smaller part of banks' offerings.

The possible change of creditors into partners, of course, requires participation in management, for which most banks today are not qualified. Such a change seems idealistic today, but the very model of surplus added value is also idealistic (for now).

On the above discussion, consistent with this idealistic view, there is no need to address financial leverage in the surplus value-added model, because it simply does not exist anymore. It could be discussed only in a transitional period until the changes in tax legislation, but it will not be dealt in this book.[6]

6.8 Economics of the Organization, Based on the Surplus Value Added

The findings in the previous chapter and the definition of surplus value-added point to significantly changed the starting points of the theory of the organization's economics. These are mainly:

1. Fundamental organization's goal is surplus value added according to Fig. 7.3 in the Sect. 7.3. Profit is no more the main goal on the level of an organization.
2. Changing the main goal leads to changes of vision, mission, values and strategy of an organization. These changes will be directed to sustainable development considering the interests of stakeholders and economic, social and ecological bottom line. Shareholders' value as a criterion of decision-making is no more appropriate.
3. Several management and analytical models are no more suitable to support the strategy. Among them are, especially models of: Economic Value Added (*EVA*), Weighted Average Cost of Capital (*WACC*), Capital Asset Pricing Model (*CAPM*), financial leverage model.
4. Several management models need to be changed, adapted and redirected, for example, Balance Score Card (*BSC*), 6 Sigma, *PEST* analysis, management by objectives.
5. Models of total quality management need to be changed and adopted. Especially, models of measuring business excellence (e.g.

[6] Such a model of financial leverage was discussed in Bergant (2017, pp. 76–91).

Malcolm Baldridge National Award, EFQM Award) should be adopted accordingly.

6. Several methodologies of business analysis need to be changed, adopted or further developed (e.g. Cost–Benefit analysis, DuPont analysis, benchmarking, analysis of early warning signs, performance analysis, operating leverage analysis and analysis of ratios).

Above-mentioned changes show fundamental differences from traditional economics of an organization. Changes are listed very briefly but it is obvious that they require further development of the theory of economics and its practical implementation. Both of them depend on further development of education at all levels of business schools.

An important task of each organization will be to develop a comprehensive and efficient information system for external and internal reporting and planning, based on the surplus value added. A special area that will need huge changes is computer-based decision-making system, together with business intelligence tools.

To achieve better information system, several changes in accounting standards will be needed as a base for the improvement of accounting information system in order to get additional accounting statements and information, especially from the surplus value-added statement. This is the right way to improve integrating reporting of organizations in line with their social responsibility.

6.9 Some Starting Points for Analyzing the Surplus Value Added

Analysis of value added is, of course, only a partial analysis of an organization's sustainable development, as it requires more complex approaches (e.g. Schaltegger et al. 2006, pp. 102 and 689).

Riahi-Belkaoui (2010, p. 64) believes that value-added analysis can be used in addition to conventional analysis to obtain better assessments of a company's financial position, performance and leadership.

Some authors (e.g. Sarkar and Nandi 2011, p. 94) consider value-added indicators to be an important tool for measuring business performance because "traditional indicators are not relevant for analyzing a company's value added."

The role of surplus value-added analysis can be viewed from the perspective of different purposes, for example, for:

- presentation of the achievements of the organization
- increasing knowledge about sustainable development
- alternative views on understanding of business
- promoting behavior and performance in many respects.

According to the content, the analysis of surplus value added (*SVA*) can be divided for example into:

- analysis of accounting surplus value added
- analysis of extended surplus value added
- analysis of surplus value added
- analyzing the surplus value added in relation to the invested intellectual capital.

The development of surplus value-added indicators in all the above areas of analysis is possible in particular by comparing:

- by periods (past, present, future) to get flows and trends of *SVA*
- value added structures
- items of the selected income statement
- the relevant balance sheet items
- economic, social and societal point of view
- computationally related indicators
- causal relationship between indicators
- organizations within different industries.

This shows a number of possible approaches to analyzing the surplus value added that could be considered even in an independent monograph, which is beyond the scope of this work.

6.10 Accounting Ratios About Surplus Value Added

In the theory, there are already known several indicators about value added, however, the value added is calculated in traditional way (as labor costs plus *EBIT*). These ratios should be adapted in the following for analyzing surplus value added and limited to the level of the organization. Of course, additional information is possible and necessary also at lower levels of analysis (e.g. organizational units, projects, products).

Many authors (e.g. Yogesha and Mahadevappa 2014, p. 24; Mandal. and Goswami 2008; Riahu-Belkaoui 2010, p. 61, Shodhganga 2017) discuss indicators about value added as a traditional accounting category. In the following, ratios that are adapted to surplus value added (*SVA*) and also some additional indicators will be briefly presented.

1. *About the operations management efficiency*
   SVA / Total assets, (SVA – Fin. Costs)/ Equity, SVA / Material costs, SVA / Total revenues, SVA / Fixed assets, SVA / Machine hours, SVA / Capital employed.
   An interesting productivity ratio offer Haller and Stolowy (1999, p. 10). Here is adapted to *SVA*:

$$\left(\frac{\text{Surplus value added}}{\text{Capital employed}} \times \frac{\text{Surplus value added}}{\text{Number of employees}}\right)^{1/2}.$$

   The square root of the product of both indicators should therefore indicate the total productivity of capital and labor.
   From a theoretical point of view, the indicator can be criticized for many things, but its change in different periods of the same organization (with appropriate explanations of the movement of the numerator and both denominators) can provide additional information on productivity.[7]

   Important ratio of labor productivity is:
   SVA / All payments to employees,
   where payments to employees consist of minimum wages, basic salaries and participation in *SVA* in line with Sect. 8.3.
2. *Rate of surplus value added* (*RSVA*):

$$RSVA = \frac{\text{Surplus value added } (SVA)}{\text{Consumption of labor } (CLC) + \text{Opportunity cost of capital } (OCC)}$$

   RSVA shows the efficiency of labor and capital fixed costs.

[7] An in-depth and mathematically supported discussion of productivity in relation to value added can be found in the *OECD* Manual (2001) and Hulten (2009).

3. *About the structure of SVA*:

$$Creditors/SVA, Taxes/SVA, Employees/SVA, Dividends/\ SVA, \\ Management\ awards/SVA, Retained\ SVA/Total\ SVA$$

4. *About operating leverage*:

$$SVA/Net\ costs\ of\ labor = 1 + NetEBIT/Net\ costs\ of\ labor, \\ NetEBIT/EBIT$$

5. *Other possible ratios*:

$$(SVA/Equity)/ROE, (SVA/Total\ assets)/ROA,\ SVA/Profit \\ (Retained\ SVA + Depreciation)/\text{Long} - \text{term liabilities}, SVA/Net\ cash\ flow.$$

Deeper explanation of the expressive power of these ratios exceeds the scope of this work. In general, the indicators of surplus value added are primarily a starting point for additional information with which the company indicates its social responsibility. They can be further enriched with non-accounting information.

Questions for Discussion

6-1 What can we learn from the history of value-added statement?
6-2 What are the reasons for a significant expectation gap between the praxis of publication of value-added statements and the actual use of this information?
6-3 Do you find some shortcomings in empirical research of value-added statements?
6-4 What are main possible users of value-added statement?
6-5 What are main objectives of value-added statement?
6-6 What is the content and main expressive power of value-added statement?
6-7 What types of value added statement can be developed?
6-8 What are the advantages and disadvantages of surplus value-added statement?
6-9 What kind of analysis tools do you know?
6-10 What are the characteristics of operating leverage for surplus value added?

6-11 Is there a need to address financial leverage in the surplus value-added model?

6-12 Discuss the impact of surplus value-added model on conventional business economic models.

6-13 What accounting ratios about surplus value added would you prefer?

References

Arangies, G., Mlambo, C., Hamman, W. D., Steyn-Bruwer, B. W. (2008). The Value Added Statement: An Appeal for Standardization. (Retrieved: April, 2020). *Management Dynamics*, Vol. 17, No. 1/2008, pp. 31–43. https://mpra.ub.uni-muenchen.de/25970/1/MPRA_paper_25970.pdf.

Aruwa, A. S. Suleiman (2008). The Worth of Disclosures in the Value-added statements and Pattern of Value Added Distribution. *Journal of Finance and Accounting Research*, No 1/2009. (Retrieved: April, 2020). http://www.academia.edu/222418/THE_WORTH_OF_DISCLOSURES_IN_THE_VALUE_ADDED_STATEMENT_AND_PATTERN_OF_VALUE_ADDED_DISTRIBUTION.

ASSC-Accounting Standard Steering Committee (1975). *The Corporate Report*. (Retrieved: January, 2016). http://www.ion.icaew.com/clientfiles/6f45ef7e-1eff-41ff-909e-24eeb6e9ed15/the%20corporate%20report2.pdf.

Baba, Hideaki, Ishida, Yu, Aoki, Takahiro (2015). Social Accounting for Nonprofit Organizations: Visualizing the Invisible Value of Social Impacts. *Kansai University Review of Business and Commerce*, No. 16/2015, pp. 1–22). (Retrieved: June, 2020). http://baba-hi72.up.seesaa.net/image/KandaiReview2015_baba_etal.pdf.

Barloworld Limited (2017). Integrated Report 2017. (Retrieved: March, 2020). http://www.barloworld-reports.co.za/integrated-reports/ir-2017/value-added-statement-and-highlights.php.

Bergant, Živko (2017). Appropriate Consideration of Value-Added Law as a Precondition of Social Responsibility. 12th International Conference About Social Responsibility in Maribor. (Retrieved: December, 2019). http://www.irdo.si/irdo2017/referati/plenarna-bergant.pdf.

Blue Label Telecoms (2018). Annual Report 2018. (Retrieved: March, 2020). https://www.bluelabeltelecoms.co.za/online_reports/ar2018/value-added-statement.php.

Brennan, M. Niamh (2008). Corporate Governance, Accountability and Mechanisms of Accountability: Overview. *Accounting, Auditing & Accountability Journal*, Vol. 21, No. 7, pp. 885–906.

Centenary Bank (2018). Annual Report 2018. (Retrieved: April, 2020). https://www.centenarybank.co.ug/uploads/page/Annual_report_2019.pdf.

Coper D. J., Sherer M. J. (1984). The Value of Corporate Accounting Reports: Arguments for a Political Economy of Accounting. *Accounting, Organizations and Society*, No 3–4/1984, pp. 207–232.

Donleavy, D. Gabriel (2015). Usefulness Unfulfilled: A Performance Review of Value-Added Statements. *International Journal of Critical Accounting* No. 4/2015, pp. 315–334.

EU (2008). *Commission Regulation No 1126/2008*: Adopting Certain International Standards in Accordance with Regulation (EC) No 1606/2002 of the European Parliament and of the Council. *Uradni list Evropske unije*, 29.11.2008. Appendix: International accounting standards (*IAS*). (Retrieved: March, 2020). http://eur-lex.europa.eu/legal-content/SL/TXT/PDF/?uri=CELEX:32008R1126&from=EN.

First National Bank Ghana Limited (2018). Financial Report 2018. (Retrieved: April, 2020). https://www.firstnationalbank.com.gh/downloads/Ghana/financial-reports/Annual_Report_and_Financial_Statements_31December2018.pdf.

Friedman, Milton (1970). The Social Responsibility of Business Is to Increase Its Profits. *New York Times*, September 13, p. 33.

Grupo Carrefour Brasil (2020). Financial Statements 2019. (Retrieved: April, 2020). https://www.grupocarrefourbrasil.com.br/wp-content/uploads/sites/174/2019/09/Grupo-Carrefour-Brasil-Financial-Statements-31.12.2018_final.pdf.

Haller, Axel, Stolowy, Hervé (1999). *Value Added in Financial Accounting:* A Comparative Study of Germany and France. (Retrieved: January, 2016). https://www.researchgate.net/publication/29865542_Value_Added_in_Financial_Accounting_A_Comparative_Study_of_Germany_and_France.

Hulten, R. Charles (2009). Growth Accounting. *Working Paper* No. 15341. (Retrieved: May, 2020). http://www.nber.org/papers/w15341.

Ianniello, Giuseppe (2010). *The Voluntary Disclosure of the Value-Added Statement in Annual Reports of Italian Listed Companies.* (Retrieved: March, 2016). http://www.agriculturejournals.cz/publicFiles/25300.pdf.

ICA-The Institute of Chartered Accountants of India (2014). *Developments in Financial Reporting.* Chapter 10. Unit 1: Value-Added Statement. (Retrieved: January, 2016). http://www.icaiknowledgegateway.org/littledms/folder1/Chapter-10-developments-in-financial-reporting.pdf.

IFRS—International Accounting Standards Board (2018). *Conceptual Framework for Financial Reporting.* (Retrieved: June, 2020). https://www.ifrs.org/-/media/project/conceptual-framework/fact-sheet-project-summary-and-feedback-statement/conceptual-framework-project-summary.pdf.

Islam, Fakhrul (2019). The Voluntary Disclosure of Value-Added Statement in Financial Reporting-A Study on Listed Companies of Bangladesh. (Retrieved: April, 2020). https://www.researchgate.net/publication/330497717_The_voluntary_Disclosure_of_Value_Added_Statement_in_Financial_Reporting-A_Study_on_listed_Companies_of_Bangladesh.

Kaur, Prabhjot (2020). Value-Added Statement (VAS). (Retrieved: April, 2020). http://www.yourarticlelibrary.com/accounting/financial-reporting/value-added-statement-vas/57379.

Khoshkho Omid Imani, Fahim, Seyed Reza Seyed Nezhad, Mokhtari, Masoud (2013). The Impact of Net Value Added on Predicting the Earnings and Operating Cash Flow: An Empirical Study Base on Tehran Stock Exchange. *Management Science Letters* No 3/2013, pp. 2923–2932. (Retrieved: April, 2020). https://pdfs.semanticscholar.org/c5ed/237265d3caaf1061a96d082e57a9cc4050aa.pdf?_ga=2.147408817.784419649.1587388447-1321762634.1587388447.

Machado, A.V. Márcio, Macedo, M. A. da Silva, Machado, R. Márcia (2016). Analysis of the Relevance of Information Content of the Value-Added Statement in the Brazilian Capital Markets. (Retrieved: October, 2016). http://papers.ssrn.com/sol3/papers.cfm?abstract_id=2601211.

Mandal Niranjan, Goswami, Suvarun (2008). Value-Added Statement (VAS) – A Critical Analysis. *Great Lakes Herald*, No. 2 (2008). (Retrieved: May, 2015). http://www.greatlakes.edu.in/pdf/Herald/Vol2/Value%20Added%20Statement%20-%20A%20Critical%20Analysis.pdf.

McLeay, Stuart (1983). Value Added: A Comparative Study. *Accounting, Organizations and Society*, Vol. 8, No. 1/1983, pp. 31–56. (Retrieved: April, 2020). https://www.researchgate.net/profile/Stuart_McLeay/publication/221953528_Value_Added_A_Comparative_Study/links/00b495264ab1aea7aa000000.pdf.

Migros Group (2018). Annual Report 2018. (Retrieved: March, 2020). https://report.migros.ch/2017/en/overview-of-migros/environment-commitment/value-added-statement/.

Miller, B. W., Paul, Bahnson, R. Paul (2002). *Quality Financial Reporting*. New York: McGraw-Hill.

Mook, L. Ingrid (2007). *The Expanded Value-Added Statement*. Doctoral dissertation, University of Toronto. (Retrieved: January, 2016). http://home.oise.utoronto.ca/~lschugurensky/Mook_Thesis.pdf.

Morley, F. Michael (1979). The Value-Added Statement in Britain. *The Accounting Review* No. 3/1979, pp. 618–629.

Netcare Limited (2017). Annual Integrated Report 2017. (Retrieved: March, 2020). https://www.netcare.co.za/InvestorReport/netcare_annual-2017/downloads/Netcare_IAR_2017_Value-added_statement.pdf.

OANDO Plc (2018). Oando Energy and Trading. Annual Reports 2018. https://www.oandoplc.com/wp-content/uploads/2019/04/Financial StatementFull.pdf.

OECD Manual (2001). Measuring Productivity. (Pridobljeno: May, 2020). https://www.oecd.org/std/productivity-stats/2352458.pdf.

Oshika, Tomoki, Saka, Chika (2015). Created Value as Sustainability KPI for Integrated Reporting. (Retrieved: January, 2016). http://www.insead.edu/facultyresearch/areas/accounting/events/documents/OshikaandSaka-2015.pdf.

Perera, L. Aldama, Zicari, Adrián (2012) Value-Added Reporting as a Tool for Sustainability: A Latin American Experience. *Corporate Governance*, Vol. 12, No. 4/2012, pp. 485–498. (Retrieved: January, 2016). http://live.v1.udesa.edu.ar/files/MBA/Papers/Value_added_reporting_Zicari_2012.pdf.

Perrot, Pascal (2006). Définition et mesure de la »valeur ajoutée sociale« dans les associations. RECMA – *Revue internationale de l'economie sociale*, No. 301/2006, pp. 42–60. (Retrieved: April, 2020). http://www.recma.org/sites/default/files/301-042060.pdf.

Petty, William (1690). *Political Arithmetic*. (Retrieved: January, 2016). https://www.marxists.org/reference/subject/economics/petty/index.htm.

Pong, Chris, Mitchell, Falconer (2014). Accounting for a Disappearance: A Contribution to the History of the Value-Added Statement in the UK. *Accounting Historians Journal*, No 2/2014. (Retrieved: January, 2016). http://www.accountingin.com/accounting-historians-journal/volume-32-number-2/accounting-for-a-disappearance-a-contribution-to-the-history-of-the-value-added-statement-in-the-uk/.

Prasad, Suresh (2015). *Preparation of Gross/Net Value-Added Statement for Companies*. (Retrieved: April, 2020). https://www.scribd.com/document/370437728/Preparation-of-Gross-Net-Value-Added-Statement-for-Companies.

Riahi-Belkaoui, Ahmed (2010). *Wealth and Value Added: Reporting, Analysis, Prediction, and Taxation*, April, 2020. Pridobljeno.

Reichmann, Thomas, Lange, Christoph (1981). The Value-Added Statement as Part of Corporate Social Reporting. *Management International Review* No 4/1981, p. 17–22.

Sarkar, R. Chitta, Nandi, C. Kartik (2011). Corporate Social Performance Through Value Added Reporting – A Case Study of Hindustan Petroleum Corporation Ltd. *International Journal of Research in Commerce and Management*, št. 6/2011, pp. 89–95. (Retrieved: January, 2017). http://ijrcm.org.in/article_info.php?article_id=914.

Schaltegger, Stefan, Bennet, Martin, Burrit, Roger (2006). *Sustainability Accounting and Reporting*. Dordrecht: Springer.

Shodhganga (2017). *Analysis of Value Added Ratios.* (Retrieved: May, 2020). https://shodhganga.inflibnet.ac.in/bitstream/10603/144387/17/17_Chapter-5.pdf.

Singh, Pooja (2013). *A Critical Analysis of Value Added Reporting Practices in Selected Indian Companies.* Doctoral dissertation, Faculty of Commerce, Dayalbagh, AGRA. (Retrieved: January, 2016) http://shodh.inflibnet.ac.in:8080/jspui/bitstream/123456789/2045/1/synopsis.pdf.

Singtel (2019). Annual Report 2019. (Retrieved: 2020). https://cdn.aws.singtel.com/annualreport/2019/files/Group_Value_Added_Statements.pdf.

Suojanen, W. W. (1954). Accounting Theory and the Large Corporation. *The Accounting Review*, Julij, 1954, pp. 618–629.

Stanton, B. F., Jinkins, E. John, Ahearn, C. Mary, Hanson, D. Gregory (1992). Perspective on Farm Size and Structure Provided by Value-Added Measures. *The Journal of Agricultural Economics Research*, Vol. 44, No. 2/1992, pp. 36–44. (Retrieved: April, 2020). http://ageconsearch.umn.edu/bitstream/138012/2/5Stanton_44_2.pdf.

Unilever Nigeria Plc (2018). Annual Report. (Retrieved: March, 2020). https://www.unilever-ewa.com/Images/unilever-audited-financial-statements-ye-31-december—2018_tcm1283-535769_1_en.pdf.

Van Staden, Chris (2000). *The Value-Added Statement: Bastion of Social Reporting or Dinosaur of Financial Reporting?* (Retrieved: January, 2016). http://poseidon01.ssrn.com/delivery.php?ID=364085089029103082121125101025126110062049053076063030120001106113095066076064105069032124000100104011004099125064081002024107015062036037082105104113015000025066080052110082122017094127000064113028095078086069016099103089073101064088079094016085&EXT=pdf.

Van Staden, J. Chris (2001). *Aspects of the Motivation for Voluntary Disclosures: Evidence from the Publication of Value-added statements in an Emerging Economy.* (Retrieved: January, 2016). http://www.massey.ac.nz/massey/fms/Colleges/College%20of%20Business/School%20of%20Accountancy/Documents/Discussion%20Papers/206.pdf.

Van Staden Chris, Haller Axel, Landis Cristina (2013). Value Added Information as Part of Sustainability Reporting – Initial International Insights. (Retrieved: January, 2016). http://www.apira2013.org/proceedings/pdfs/K248.pdf.

Volkswagen Group (2017). Annual Report 2017. (Retrieved: March, 2020) https://annualreport2017.volkswagenag.

Yogesha, B. S., Mahadevappa, B. (2014). Analysis of Value Added Ratios of Indian Oil Corporation. *Journal of Humanities and Social Science*, Vol. 19, No. 11, pp. 18–25). (Retrieved: December, 2016). http://iosrjournals.org/iosr-jhss/papers/Vol19-issue11/Version-5/E01911151825.pdf.

CHAPTER 7

Management and the Value Added

7.1 Introduction

There are many definitions of management in the literature. Briefly, most authors agree that management is a process aimed at achieving the goals of the organization set by governing bodies.

Management must be integrated into a complete business process. Similarly, as has been used a systemic approach in Sect. 2.2 in the study of accounting, such an approach can also be used for positioning of management within the entire business system. Therefore, partial systems can be used as shown in Fig. 7.1.

Figure 7.1 shows the operational, informational and managerial partial system with their basic functions.

Operational partial system encompasses *operating* parts of six basic business functions: producing, purchasing, marketing (selling), human resource management, investment and technical function.

Informational partial system encompasses four basic information functions: past data processing, future data processing, analyzing of data, controlling of data processing.

As accounting is usually the largest part of an information system, Fig. 2.1 in Sect. 2.2 is now better understandable, showing parts of all four information functions as components of accounting.

Ž. Bergant, *Accountancy and Social Responsibility*,
Palgrave Studies in Impact Finance,
https://doi.org/10.1007/978-3-030-77928-3_7

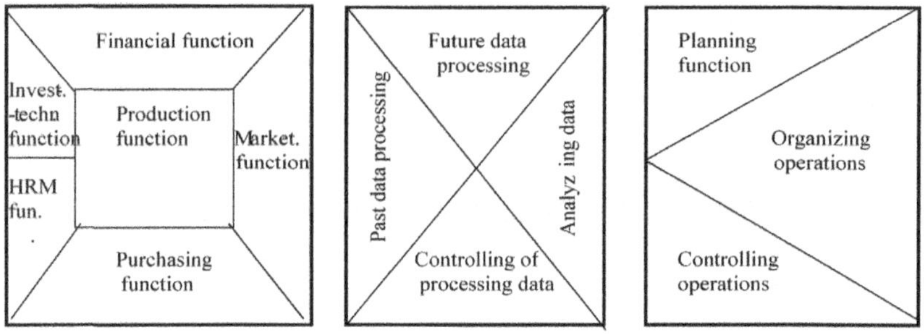

Fig. 7.1 Partial systems with basic business functions (*Source* Own research)

Managerial partial system encompasses three basic managerial functions: planning, organizing the operations and controlling the operations.

At the same time, the extension of the basic business functions (purchasing, production, revenues, financial, personnel investment-technical) must be taken into account also across all partial systems of the organization. Namely, each of these functions has its own information partial system and also management partial system, which are parts of the organization's entire information and management system.

Planning as one of the basic managerial functions could be strategic, tactical or operational. It should be differentiated from forecasting that is one of information functions (future data processing). Forecasting and planning together form parts of total planning process of organization's operations.

It is also necessary to understand the difference between the managerial control function and the control function in the information system. While management control involves the oversight of the entire business of an organization, control as an information function is limited to oversight what is happening within the information system. The accounting manager is responsible for the latter.

The main characteristic of partial systems is their interconnectedness. Changes in managerial partial system require changes in operational and informational partial systems. Changes in operational partial system require changes in informational partial system. Changes in informational partial system mean changes in total business system from information point of view.

7.2 A Comprehensive Model of Management

Management can be studied and defined from many aspects, such as in terms of partial systems (e.g. Fig. 7.2), time dimension, level of business, business functions, human aspects and the like.

Therefore, a more comprehensive view of management is important as a starting point for its more detailed consideration. In doing so, we proceed from the following:

1. Management encompasses three basic functions: planning, organizing business process and controlling the operations.
2. Operations have two dimensions: the level of organization and the level of employees.
3. Managerial process takes place with coordination and decision-making on all areas of organization's business.

Considering the above, management can be defined as a coordination and decision-making in the areas of business and human resources management. It is shown in the Table 7.1.

Table 7.1 shows the areas of management coordination and decision-making that apply to all three levels of management: top management, middle management and lower management.

Table 7.1 shows also two main dimensions of management: management of organization and management of people (leadership).

In addition to these two dimensions, it is essential to consider the third important dimension of management, that is, *ethics*. Without this dimension, the organization has no long-term viability. Unethical behavior has been empirically proven to diminish the value of the organization. Ethics is not just about how to satisfy stakeholders, but simply about what is right and fair, what constitutes excellence and success (Gill 2006). Ethics in accountancy will be discussed later. As mentioned earlier, the ethical aspect is an integral part of the value-added law, which only confirms the above claims.

There is, however, another dimension that pervades all management, and just as ethics is not shown in Table 7.1. This is ***risk management***. It can be defined as the fourth dimension of management. It must be taken into account in the organization's operations. Not least because the entire business organization in accordance with the law of value added is intended for risk management, thus creating the value added.

Table 7.1 Areas of managerial coordination and decision-making

Leadership (individual level\Management of Organization	*Communication*	*Motivation and development of employees*	*Behavior and leadership style*
Planning operations:			
Strategic			
Tactical			
Operational			
Preparing operations (organizing):			
Organizing planning			
Implementing			
Normative regulation			
Recruitment			
Operating			
Controlling			
Organizational processes			
Controlling operations			
Controlling			
Inspecting			
Auditing			

Source Own research

7.3 A Management Model for a Sustainable Development

The profession largely recognizes the importance of social responsibility, but it has not yet found a definitive evidence to support such claim. Empirically, such a proof is impossible, since we are talking about a distant future, and the study of the direction of the movements in the past is insufficiently convincing, especially for those people who have short-term interests.

Therefore, another path is needed. The starting point of the model is the assumption that sustainable development is a fundamental purpose (as a moving target) of an organization because it is consistent with the concept of its social responsibility.

Therefore, business decisions must be geared toward proper economic, social and environmental performance. This requires information from all three domains. Many authors talk about the *triple bottom line* (Elkington et al. 1998). This implies a focus on total net value added, as defined in Sect. 4.6. This is also supported by an empirical study justifying value added as one of the key indicators of sustainable development (Oshika and Saka 2015, 14). Donleavy also notes the positive impact of value added on the company's market value (Donleavy 2015, 325 and Zeng 2013).

Based on the above starting points, the model in Fig. 7.2 is proposed. A precondition for sustainable development as a long-term goal is that organization behaves accordingly to social responsibility in three areas: economic, social and ecological. That is shown in Fig. 7.2.

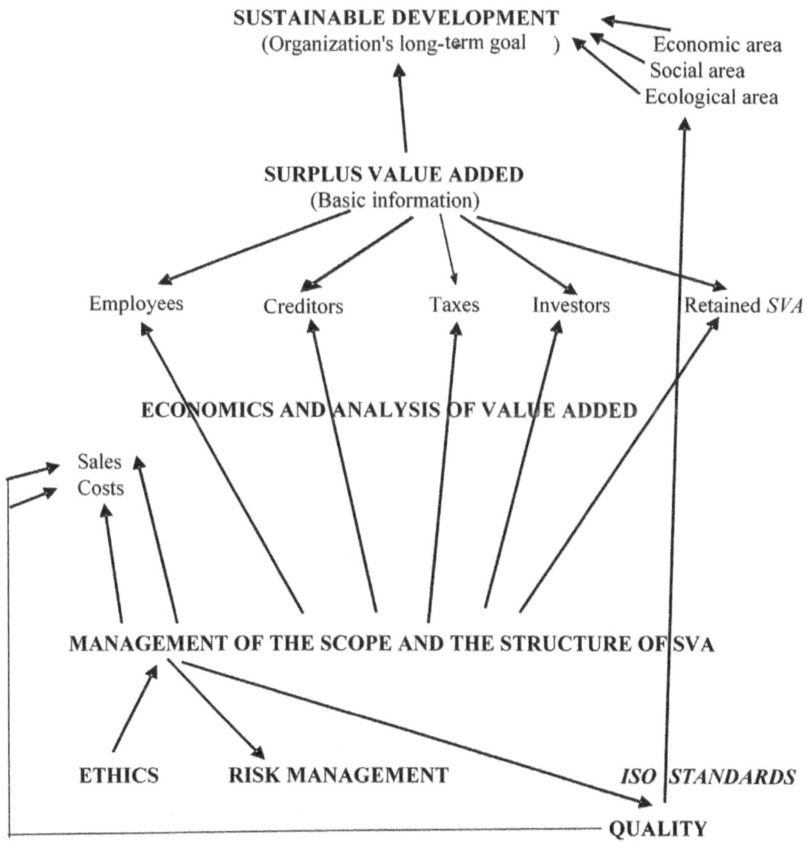

Fig. 7.2 Management model on the basis of the value added (*Source* Own research)

Figure 7.2 shows the value added as basic information about organization's performance to achieve sustainable development. Here should be immediately emphasized that the value added in Fig. 7.2 is in its widest definition, i.e. also with non-accounting expressed achievements or returns (e.g. expanded value added). The structure of value added, however, is shown only from an accounting point of view.

Figure 7.2 defines two basic orientations (focuses) of business management:

1. The *volume* of surplus value added (creating *SVA*) through maximizing revenues and optimizing costs.
2. The *structure* of surplus value added (distributing *SVA*) through adequate economic policy of value added that encompasses planning, investing, remunerating, borrowing, tax optimizing and dividend policy.

The appropriateness of decisions in three areas of social responsibility (economic, social and ecological) can be measured by principles and recommendations of *ISO* standards on quality of business in these areas (BSI 2020), which is also indicated in Fig. 7.2.

The quality management is focused on the current operations through quality of revenues and by costs management that is a matter of *ISO* standards as well.

One of basic dimensions of management is risk management, which is also shown in Fig. 7.2.

Last but not least, organization's management must consider ethics' principles in creating and distribution of surplus value added. That is also shown in Fig. 7.2.

The emphasis on value added is important because the management profession still mainly clings to traditional shareholder's value as the goal of business. However, shareholder's value approach means a short-sighted view that is not suitable to achieve long-term goals (Byars and Stanberry 2018, p. 13).

Allegation of sustainable development as the ultimate goal, in principle, does not necessarily conflict with the traditional corporate objective to increase shareholder's value. It depends primarily on a time horizon in which all interests are to be satisfied. However, this requires a profound change in organizational culture, values, decision-making and behavior of the organization. This means that the organization must recognize and take into account the full range of critical economic, social and environmental costs, associated with its operations (Elkington et al. 1998, p. 154).

Elkington's view is therefore relatively optimistic, despite the fact that such changes obviously require a long period of time. Changes in organizations cannot happen without changes in the political, economic and sociological system, that is, in the whole of society, which Elkington also emphasizes (Elkington, ibid.).

Proper compliance with the value-added law requires a radical change in the perception of relationships in the organization, risk-taking on the part of stakeholders in society and in their participation in value added.

It can be expected that value-added management methods and techniques will constantly change and complement each other, but in accordance with the principles illustrated in Fig. 7.2.

However, Fig. 7.2 does not mean that value added can be defined as direct information about the performance of an association, although performance by its basic definition means achieving the goals. Sustainable development, as a fundamental objective, is so complex that achieving the desired added value as a benchmark, despite its importance, would be too much simplified. Nevertheless, the surplus value added remains an important goal in deciding the business of a company. The organization cannot be successful in long-term if it does not contribute to the welfare of the stakeholders and society as a whole.

7.4 Cybernetic Model of Management and Value Added

In making its decisions, the management, in accordance with the principle of feedback, establishes a link between the current situation and the future behavior of the business system. This closes the management circle with feedback. Therefore, a consistent value-added management leads to the model in Fig. 7.3.

Figure 7.3 shows in particular the following:

1. The main red thread of management runs vertically through all three functions: planning, organizing and controlling. Within all three functions, both dimensions of management should be

emphasized: the aspect of organization's operations and the aspect of leadership.
2. Two basic areas of organizational management are outlined: creating and guiding value added to stakeholders.
3. Both areas are also subject to business planning.
4. From a development perspective, it is important to decide on the retained added value that is final effect of guiding value added.
5. Retained value added is mainly intended for increasing capital, financing investments and the development.
6. Through development, innovation with creativity, strategic, internal and external risk management, organization's management shapes the economic policy.
7. Strategic risks are connected by business decisions of management.
8. Internal risks are subject of entropy and internal frauds.
9. External risks are subject of external impacts and frauds.
10. Economic policy is focused on creating value added.
11. Organization's management manages risk through an appropriate organization of operations.
12. All areas of operations are monitored by the controlling function.

It should be remembered that principles of ethics and quality of operations permeate all the links shown in Fig. 7.3.

Due to the focus on value added, the differences in the management between for-profit and non-profit organizations[1] are also significantly reduced.

7.5 Human Resource Management and Value Added

Chapters 5 and 6 emphasize the general importance of human labor. Therefore, the importance of human resource management (*HRM*) that includes also knowledge management in an organization is also understandable. This is confirmed by both practice and theory with numerous works of authors and university curricula. The need for greater regulation and protection of workers has been recognized as well (e.g. Del Castillo 2020).

[1] More about these differences in Epstein and McFarlan (2011).

In the following, *HRM* will be discussed only in terms of value added. The main starting points are:

1. Employees in business[2] bear relatively the greatest risk. Their normal life depends on employment. The populist claim that the owner of the capital injection is most at risk, is merely in the function of justifying his profit appropriation, which is, allowed by the current legal order without proper logic.
2. Employees are bearers of the intellectual capital (they revive it through their work), which the company must maintain and increase. They create value added, since without work the company would not be able to operate and the invested capital would remain without profit.
3. Employees are important holders of long-term interests in the organization, and also of social responsibility as a condition for sustainable development.
4. Employees are legitimate contributors to an organization's monitoring and controlling system. Namely, the short-term and narrow interests of the owners of the capital, the management and "their" supervisory boards are often dangerous from a long-term point of view. Therefore, the role of workers and their representatives within the trade union is also very important from a supervisory perspective.

The next starting point is the claim that the huge differences between the market and book values of organizations can be explained partly[3] by the use of "invisible assets" (Milost 2012, p. 128). These assets encompass intangible assets, intellectual capital[4] and human capacities (Milost, *ibid.*).

Intangible assets are subject to accounting standards, but due to a conservative approach, they allow only a small portion of those assets to be recorded.

[2] The term "employees" encompasses all kinds of their work in an organization, including precarious work. More about precarity in Garben (2019).

[3] It is difficult to attribute the entire difference between the market value and the book value of an individual company to intellectual property, partly because of the unrealistic presentation of intangible assets, partly because of the changing market value of a share (Brennan 2001).

[4] More about history of intellectual capital in: Dumay et al. (2020).

Much broader is the idea of intellectual capital that is given a special attention also in the literature. It represents the collective knowledge and the root of an organization (Meihami et al. 2014, p. 45). It is not "pure intellect" but also a degree of "intellectual action" and an ideological process (Meihami, ibid.). Most authors agree that intellectual capital increases the value of organization's equity (e.g. Marr et al. 2004; Joia 2000; Roos et al. 2001; Riahi-Belkaoui 2003, Chen et al. 2004; Mostafaei 2015).

Probably among the first to adopt the idea of intellectual capital was the Swedish corporation Skandia that has developed also a visualization of capital forms in Fig. 7.4.

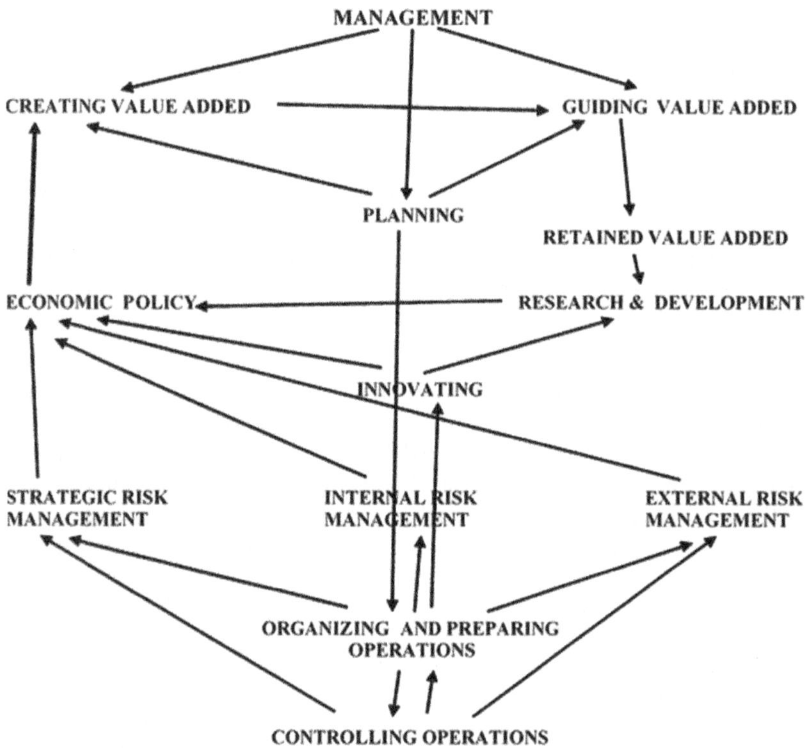

Fig. 7.3 Management on the value-added basis (*Source* Own research)

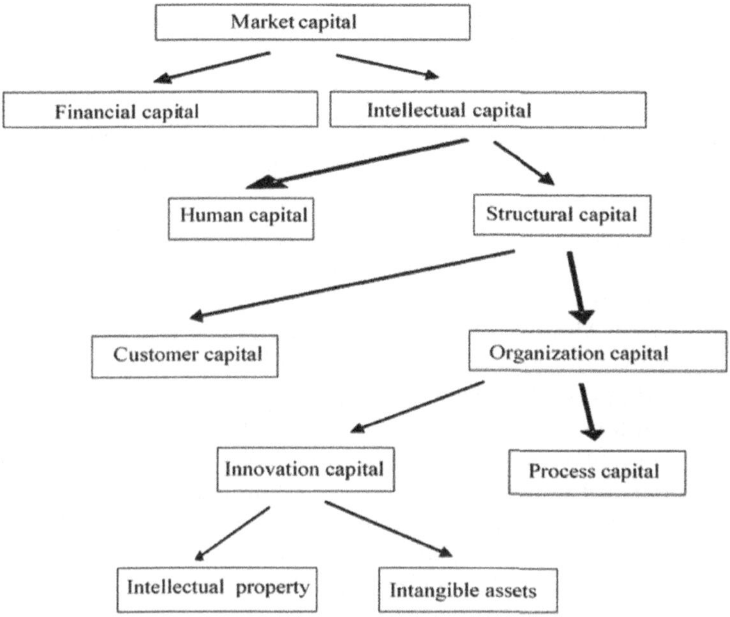

Fig. 7.4 Elements of Intellectual Capital (widely known as "Skandia" model) (*Source* [Mouritsen et al. 2001, p. 405])

Figure 7.4 simplifies the difference between financial capital and the market value of the organization that is shown as intellectual capital. Other impacts on organization's market value are ignored.

Nevertheless, Fig. 7.4 is good enough to illustrate that the intellectual capital is a complex and heterogeneous phenomenon. Similar sketches use later also other authors, however, with smaller differences in the structure of the intellectual capital (e.g. Joia 2000, p. 70, Roos et al. 2001; p. 7, Marr et al. 2004, p. 554).

The empirical results show that organizations' intellectual capital has a positive impact on creating the value added (Riahi-Belkaoui 2003, p. 230) and on economic performance (e.g. Mostafei 2015, p. 2907, Carrington 2013, p. 292).

Structural capital is defined as the knowledge that stays within the organization at the end of working day.

Empirically are proven links between different types of intellectual property (especially human capabilities and other elements) (e.g. Cabrita and Vaz 2006). On this premise, some authors estimate the elasticity of intellectual capital by the relationship between the change of intellectual property and the market value of organizations (e.g. Joia 2000, p. 83).

Numerous models of measuring the intellectual capital with relatively detailed criteria and the content of proposed intellectual capital statements have been developed on the above bases (e.g. Liebowitz 2000; Joia 2000; Chen et al. 2004; Marr et al. 2004; Miltiadis et al. 2008; Mostafei 2015; Kianto et al. 2020).

The Danish Ministry of Science, Technology and Innovation has even issued a manual for producing an intellectual capital statement with very detailed indicators (Knowledge 2003).

Some authors (e.g. Andriessen 2004, p. 9) critically consider these experiments and point to some insurmountable differences between the book and market value of the society. He claims that using the concept of book value implicates taking an internal perspective; however, using the concept of market value implicates taking an external perspective on the organization. It is therefore impossible to make book value equal market value (Andriessen, ibid.).

In any case, the positive side of assessing the intellectual capital is that it draws attention to the soft components of an individual business system, which, despite the difficulties in measuring them, must not be forgotten. Therefore, the "need for practitioners and researchers to agree on standard guidelines for management reporting on intellectual capital" is understandable (Rahim et al. 2011, p. 58).

Employees are considered to be the owners of ***human capital***. Human capital is the primary factor for developing structural capital. Therefore, the growth of structural capital depends on human capital (Mostafaei 2015, p. 2900).

It is quite true that structural capital exists objectively and independently of human capital (Mostafei, ibid.), but it is also true, that structural capital has no business effects without current work of employees. Even more, "any form of capital is only productive if related to another" (Mouritsen et al. 2001, p. 413). Therefore, employees have to be motivated not to wait for directions so they are seen to be self-directing (Mouritsen et al., ibid.). When motivating employees, management must take into account that the risks of employees are relatively hidden (Taleb 2012, p. 84), so the level of their feeling of threat may be low. This can lead to less flexibility and therefore to even more risk exposure (Taleb 2012, p. 85).

Human capital is obviously a central term in the frame of intellectual capital. It has received a significant amount of attention (Guthrie 2001, p. 33). Human capital is the foundation of intellectual capital as a primary element to perform its functions. "It refers to such factors as employees' knowledge, skills, capabilities and attitudes in relation to fostering performances which customers are willing to pay for and the company's profit comes from" (Chen et al. 2004, p. 201). Human head is the carrier of knowledge and skill (Chen et al., ibid.).

The importance of human capital is particularly high in terms of value added and, consequently, in terms of human resource management. The traditional approach, namely treats human resource management as a cost and not as an investment, which creates difficulties in the human capital development (Guthrie 2001, p. 33).

The key to understanding the unique impact of a firm's workforce on its capital structure decisions is to understand how labor is different than capital. People can do things that capital cannot. Their creativity produces valuable tangible and intangible assets in the form of new ideas, processes and know-how (Matsa 2018, p. 1). "Hiring employees, however, exposes a firm to labor frictions. Unlike capital, people cannot be owned and can act strategically" (Matsa 2018, p. 2).

"Human capital (and intangible assets that it creates) is becoming an increasingly critical asset for contemporary firms. (Matsa 2018, p. 34). Employees are not automata operating valuable physical assets, but are valuable assets themselves, operating commodity-like physical assets. (Zingales 2000).

Accountants are increasingly convinced that human capital should also be properly addressed in accounting statements (e.g. Kaye 2012; Stanko et al. 2014; Okeke 2016; Koster 2017).

The International Integrated Reporting Council (*IIRC*) in London also follows these trends (Arvidson 2019, p. 57).

Human resources accounting is a direct part of the social accounting and aims to provide information on the evaluation of one of the most important components of the organization, namely human capital (Ionel et al. 2020, p. 925).

Special emphasis on employee management is given also by the standard *EN ISO* 9000 2015 (points 5–7).

Based on the above, it can be concluded that the accounting of human capital is still in development, but it will be the subject of intensive research in the future. This claim is entirely in line with the direction of accounting in sustainable development from the perspective of social responsibility.

State-of-the-art research has developed well beyond simply showing that labor affects also finance (Matsa 2018, p. 33). It is additional reason to discuss organization's financial policy in the next two sections.

7.6 Investment Policy

Guiding added value from sustainable perspective affects the organization's financing in two areas:

1. Decisions regarding long-term investments, in particular capital investments or capital expenditures. There are two aspects regarding these types of investments. The first aspect contains the investment decisions of the organization, however, the second aspect contains the decisions of the outside investors and stakeholders.
2. Establishing and maintaining an adequate structure for financing the operations and capital adequacy of the organization.

Ad 1)

A number of expert bases are available to make organization's investment decisions. Among them, the net present value (*NPV*) is widely recognized as the most useful one, or as a method with the least disadvantages (e.g. Brigham et al. 1999, p. 205). It is confirmed also in recent literature concerning corporate social responsibility (e.g. Idowu and Louche 2011, p. 219). Net present value is the present value of the cash flows at the required rate of return of the project compared to the initial investment, so it is based on the discounted cash flow approach. Therefore, it allows finding the difference between the present inflows and the initial investment outlay. Nevertheless, *NPV* has huge disadvantages that stems from the numerator and from the denominator (discount rate) as well. They are already broadly discussed in professional literature and this topic is beyond of the scope of this work.

The *NPV* method could be additionally useful when calculating a new indicator, the ***net present value of surplus value added*** (*NPVSVA*), where *SVA* is used as a numerator. In Sect. 6.6, surplus value added was defined as a sum of net cost of labor (*NLC*)[5] and net earnings before interest and taxes (*NEBIT*).[6] For the discount rate (i) in the denominator, the negotiated percentage of fixed cost of capital is used as shown in Eq. 7.1.

$$NPVSVA = \frac{SVA}{i} \tag{7.1}$$

The indicator *NPVSVA* in general shows a discounted future surplus value added. It can be calculated as follows:

$$NPVSVA(i, n) = \sum_{i=0}^{n} SVA_i/(1+i)^t \tag{7.2}$$

where

t is the time of the data.

i is the discount rate.

SVA_t is surplus value added, at time t.

The result of the Eq. 7.2 is, as a rule, higher than the result according the classical calculation of NPV. The difference, in its own way, shows the interval between both possibilities, profit and value-added approach. Value added approach encompasses higher risk for investor of additional capital but, at the same time, it follows the interests of stakeholders, not only shareholders. This approach therefore shows the efficiency of planned investments from social responsibility point of view.

Considering both indicators means to expand information about the effects of the investment that in principle allows better investment decisions.

Similar approach is recommended also at assessing the value of an organization, where often is used the method of net present value of cash flows.

It may be concluded that the principle of social responsibility should be followed also in investment policy. Traditional methods should be replaced by sustainable finance theory. It requires changing the investment culture and behavior of all market participants. Sustainability as an orientation requires three necessary conditions (Lagouarde-Segot and Paranque 2018, p. 8):

[5] Defined in Sect. 5.4.

[6] Defined in Sect. 6.6.

1. The rate at which renewable natural types of capital sources are used must be equal to the rate at which they are renewed.
2. The rate at which waste is produced must not exceed the rate at which the environment can assimilate it.
3. The rate at which non-renewable natural sources are exploited must not exceed the rate at which they are replaced by renewable resources.

In this way, the welfare of the next generations is prioritized. "The sustainability principle shifts the investment objective from the accumulation of money to the accumulation of value" (Lagouarde-Segot and Paranque 2018, p. 9). It means deep qualitative changes in the practice of finance (Lagouarde-Segot, ibid.).

Modern trends in socially responsible investing by external investors (institutional investors, different investment funds, mutual funds, exchange trading funds, different investors in communities, public funds etc.) show important increasing comparing conventional investments. Sustainable Investment Standards are being developed (Sustainability & Impact Investor Forum 2020).

Ad 2)

Organization's financial structure is at the heart of the corporate finance theory because of its connectedness with solvency that is a vital condition for doing operations. Therefore, this area is also usually governed by insolvency legislation.

The main question is, how to combine the principle of profitability with the principle of ability to pay? Above all, how to comply with both principles in the design of information for decision-making?

The structure of the financing of the organization in modern finance is addressed through a variety of theories, among them are the theory of the costs of financial distress (***trade-off theory***), pecking order theory, signalling theory and market timing theory.[7] None of them has so far received unequivocal confirmation in the empirical researches, however, a number of critical comments. At the heart of the debate is still the trade-off theory. Trade-off theory assumes that as debt grows, the value of an organization's equity increases (Stulz 1996, p. 9). In doing so, the risk

[7] More on those theories in: Samuels et al. (1995), Arnold (1998), Bessler et al. (2011) and Brigham et al. (1999).

posed by rising costs of financial distress is increasing. Further borrowing above the point of optimal financing structure, financial distress costs increase and begin to decrease the value of the equity of the organization.

Positive sides of the trade-off theory can be seen particularly in:

1. Principled explanation of the organization's behavior regarding its fundamental objective.
2. Interpretation of the impact of borrowing on the value of the organization.
3. Theoretical proof of the existence of an optimal financing structure.
4. Ability to unravel the recent developments related to the borrowing organization.
5. Promotion new research in the field of optimization of financing structure and generation of new theories.

Good financial theory should be primarily the basis for the formulation of appropriate information for business decision-making. Trade-off theory does not satisfy this criterion because it is not able to create a user-friendly model for decision-making in organizations. On the one hand, it shows the positive impact of borrowing ("tax shield effect"), on the other hand, it warns against excessive borrowing and provides a "penalty" in the form of high costs of financial distress. It therefore primarily interprets past events and remains less useful for decision-making. Experiments to design information for decisions on the optimal financial structure on such a basis usually remain at the level of bachelor's, master's, even doctoral thesis. A general form for the optimal financing structure determination does not exist.

The root cause of this theoretical "impotence" is in a numerous important shortcomings of the recent financial trade-off theory:

1. For each organization, the estimation of the costs of financial distress is extremely risky because these costs of a company are very difficult to calculate. The most difficult is it to estimate indirect costs which are generally higher than the direct costs of financial distress (Arnold 1998, p. 797).
2. The summing up different types of probability distributions, about occurrence of costs and revenues when estimating the costs of financial distress, are professionally unacceptable. This is reflected in the

fact that the companies, which very likely get very small gains, are exposed to very high (although unlikely) risks whose likelihood cannot be reliably estimated.[8]

3. There is the question, on whose behalf? The complexity of the calculations (in particular the large number of assumptions and subjective assessments in the calculations) is the cause of relatively unreliable results (e.g. the recommended intervals for borrowing from 20 to 40% of total liabilities).
4. The theory is based on a "cost–benefit" approach, which is a basic principle of economics. Such a view on the financial policy of the company could be in direct conflict with business ethics. Namely, decision-making, information and implementation in the field of solvency is to be assessed through an ethical point of view as well. Long-term sustainable development of the company and individual performance depend not only on the legality and narrow professionalism of action but also on the ethical and moral decision-making activities.
5. The assumption of long-term growth of the value of a common equity should also imply satisfied interests of other stakeholders, not only the interests of shareholders. The organization that operates immorally to internal and external stakeholders cannot be successful in the long-term. Such an assumption is theoretically necessary for compliance and integrity of the model, but does not provide proper basis for the creation of information for decision-making. The common practice confirms such a statement.
6. Entrepreneurial risk in relation to solvency significantly changes depending on the maturity structure of the debt, despite the unchanged ratio between foreign and own sources of financing. The risk increases if the share of short-term debt in all the company's debts increases and vice versa. The idea of the costs of financial distress does not take this fact into account. This significantly reduces the expressive power of information based only on the relationship between foreign and own liabilities (financial leverage factor). Management can not sufficiently well decide about the company's solvency on such a basis.

[8] More about the empirical problems of small probability in Taleb (2009, p. 748) and Taleb et al. (2009, p. 78).

The principles of managing current assets ("current asset management") and the principles of short-term financing try to reduce the disadvantage of trade-off theory regarding maturity. Both types of principles are covered in the literature with theory of working capital management. The authors derive from the basic principles of finance, which require consistency in maturity of liabilities with maturities of available sources of financing.

In the literature, this principle is known as the "maturity matching principle" or "maturity matching approach" (e.g. Walsh 1996, p. 148; Brigham et al. 1999, p. 635) or the "matching policy" (Rao 1987, p. 528). The simplification of this principle from an accounting perspective means a rule that permanent working capital (permanent current assets) should be financed on the long-term basis.

Deviations from this principle imply aggressive policy ("aggressive approach"), which means that also part of the permanent current assets is financed on the short-term basis. Aggressive policy takes a greater risk of insolvency, but has lower financing costs due to cheaper short-term loans. Deviation in the other direction is conservative policy ("conservative approach"), which means that also a part of periodical current assets is financed on long-term basis. Conservative policy takes a lower risk of insolvency, but higher financing costs due to more expensive long-term liabilities (loans and equity).

The recent theory of corporate finance therefore (in view of the selection of those policies) proposes trade-off approach between costs and benefits, in order to determine the best level of short-term financing (e.g. Smart et al. 2004, p. 798). Estimated costs of financial distress, however, remain an unsolved problem also in these cases.

There is the lack of a definition of permanent working capital in various authors' texts. Brigham understands it as current assets at the lower end of the cycle (Brigham et al. 1999, p. 635). Smart et al. (2004, p. 777) speak only of a constant part of current assets. Arnold adds also cash to the minimum inventories and receivables (Arnold 1998, p. 549). Samuels defines permanent working capital indirectly through seasonal, fluctuating current assets (Samuels et al. 1995, p. 721). Cohen (1990, p. 146) and Kilig (2006, p. 366) understand that inventories and trade receivables present a long-term working capital.

Numerous and vague definitions of the permanent working capital are the cause of huge difficulties in designing useful information for decision-making about the solvency of the organization. This weakness can be reduced with an approach, which is typical for the idea of capital adequacy, but should apply to non-financial organizations. It will be proposed in next section.

7.7 Model of a Comprehensive Financial Policy

Backgrounds of the model are as follows:

1. Management in its decisions should not take into account the organization's insolvency as an option. Such an alternative is unethical assumption of the potential benefits of the company's insolvency.
2. The short-term spontaneous liabilities (*SL*) in a given volume of business (Brigham et al. 1999, pp. 335 and 669) are relatively easy identifiable from payment deadlines in a particular industry known or contractually agreed. The organization should respect them as an ethical norm (my word is my bond). A possible extension of payment deadlines represents a hidden liquidity reserve for a case of force majeure.
3. If the organization wants to timely meet its business obligations, it is necessary to take into account the maturity of debts, which means that it is not enough just to monitor the leverage factor (the vertical structure of financing).
4. For the starting point, it is logically recommended that the long-term engaged current assets should be financed by long-term sources. Deviations must be carefully considered. This means that information for decision-making is based primarily on estimates of the ***actual*** and of the ***required*** (needed) working capital of the company.
5. The organization's insolvency should not be considered as an ethical option. It can be treated only as a theoretical possibility.

Figure 7.5 on the basis of the above assumptions presents a comprehensive financial policy, which is based on the capital adequacy of the company as a starting point.

The main characteristics of the elements in Fig. 7.5 are.

1. The upper part of the image on the abscissa and the ordinate axis show the net working capital which is actual (NWC_{act}) and net

working capital which is needed (NWC_{need}). The balance in capital adequacy is shown with a straight line with the inclination of 45^0. The points on this line show equality between actual net working capital and net working capital, which is needed ($K = NWC_{act}/NWC_{need} = 1$) at different volume of operations (sales revenue).

2. It is understood that the line ($K = 1$) represents a theoretical starting point, because it is merely incidental for a company to be on this line. Deviations are therefore normal; the most important is to create information on their movements in relation to the line. The ratio K may be greater or less than one, as shown in two dotted lines with a larger or smaller inclination.
3. The Point A_0 shows the optimal stock level (*Inv*) plus spontaneous trade receivables I,[9] (i.e. permanent current assets) minus permanent (spontaneous) current liabilities according the volume of business. The result is a rough estimation of net working capital, which is needed.
4. Point B_0 shows the volume of the actual net working capital, which is equal to the net working capital needed, that is shown by the point O_0 on the line that represents $K = 1$.
5. The point A_1 shows the increased need for net working capital if the volume of business increases from the point O_0 to the point O_1.
6. The point C shows a situation in which the actual net working capital is less than adequate, but the deficit still can be replaced by revolving short-term loans. Therefore, the point C represents the limit of short-term borrowing company or interval of financial *instability* (lability) in relation to the point B_0.
7. The point D shows a situation in which the actual net working capital is higher than adequate. The company has surplus of net working capital, which means the ability to long-term investing that could be financed with short-term loans. This is the interval of financial *stability* in relation to the point B_0.
8. The point B_1 with the distance to the point D shows a deficit of net working capital for the case, when the actual net working capital would not increase, albeit required because of an increase in the volume of business to the point O_1.

[9] Spontaneous receivables depend only on changes in the volume of business.

Based on the identified elements in Fig. 7.5, the following areas can be summarized in particular for analysis and business decisions that affect the optimal financing, and hence the solvency of companies:

1. It should be stated, what amount of net working capital is needed at a given volume of business. This means to find the point A_0 on the ordinate axis.
2. Furthermore, it is necessary to determine where the organization is on the abscissa axis, and how much actual net working capital it has in relation to the needed net working capital. It means, we have to analyze the capital adequacy of the company.
3. In accordance with the above point, after estimating the deficit of the net working capital, the ability of the company about revolving short-term loans in the future and risks in this regard must be analyzed. In this way, we can estimate the distance between the points C and B_0.
4. Any increase in the deficit (moving to the left from the point C) means an over-indebtedness of the company. It means too much short-term loans that should be renewed (revolved), which represent high risk. The costs of revolving short-term financing are too high (because of higher risk) and exceed the benefit in comparison with long-term financing. The solvency risk is unacceptable and unethical and it requires appropriate actions according to the sound financial policy and bankruptcy legislation as well.
5. Any movement from the point B_0 to the left (within the interval CB_0) still represents acceptable solvency risk, due to the possibility of revolving short-term loans. Among other things, it is necessary to consider the direction of movement of the net working capital deficit in the past and in the business plan for the future.
6. Any movement from the point B_0 to the right (within the interval B_0D) represents surplus of net working capital. At the same time, it shows the ability of investing and the ability to increase the volume of business, which would increase the need for net working capital in the amount of such surplus. At the same time, such a deviation means higher financial costs, which represent the cost of the investment capability of the company.
7. Any movement from the point D to the right means high (excessive) solvency and represents the surplus of net working capital, which is operationally unnecessary. It causes unnecessary costs

of funding the excessive solvency and/or excessive investment capabilities.

8. Company has optimal structure of net working capital (it means a quality of net working capital) in the point B_0. At this point, the ratio between long-term debt and equity is assumed adequate, considering the solvency risk. A higher proportion of long-term debt to total long-term liabilities means less ability to long-term borrowing (with the assumption of unchanged effectiveness of assets). By contrast, a smaller proportion of long-term debt leads to higher capital costs, which represent the costs of too high quality of net working capital. At the same time these are costs of the organization's ability to long-term borrowing.
9. When moving from point C to the right (it means increasing the actual net working capital), financing costs are constantly increasing. Management must analyze the indicated intervals to get information for decision-making.
10. The distance CB_0 is named ***the interval of financial instability***, because the organization has deficit of net working capital and does not have enough reserves to maintain solvency. Instability increases with movement toward point C. Increased attention is required in this interval, particularly monitoring and control of solvency and constant monitoring of the movement of point C as well.
11. The distance B_0D is named the ***interval of financial stability***, because the company has a reserve to the extent of surplus net working capital. Therefore, in this interval (and of course, also in the interval from the point D to the right) it is useful to decide about development projects and increasing business volume (or reducing long-term sources).
12. In the point A_0, an entity may decide on an alternative policy in managing current assets such as: relaxed, moderate and restricted (Brigham et al. 1999, p. 594). Restricted policy causes the reduction of the net working capital needed, while increasing costs because of too low inventories. Relaxed policy causes the increase of the need for net working capital, while increasing the costs of higher inventories (***Inv***) and also costs of higher trade receivables. In Fig. 7.5, this is shown with an interval from excessive permanent current assets to too low inventories, where lie the costs of non-optimal volume of current assets, which are engaged on long-term basis.

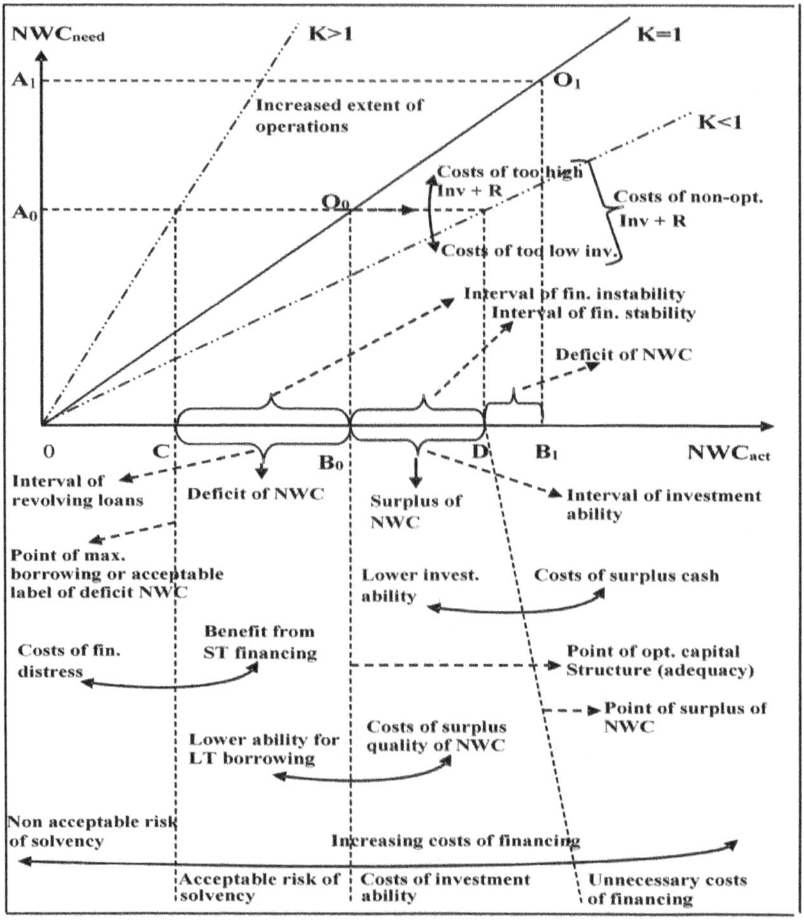

Fig. 7.5 Model of a comprehensive financial policy (*Source* Own research)

Management should be aware that all points on the abscissa and on the ordinate axis change their positions due to changes in the business and the business environment. It is of course recommendable to estimate the frame of these points in the organization's business plan.

It can be recognized that the limit (the point *C* in Fig. 7.4) is similarly soft as a border of too high financial distress costs. However, there is an important difference, especially in:

1. More acceptable criterion of how to define the point *C* (ethical or unethical approach).[10]
2. More reliable methodology of how to find this limit. It namely requires a deeper analysis of operations and organization's financial condition.
3. More reliable risk estimation due to carefully analyzing organization's ability to renew (revolve) short-term loans.

The trade-off theory determines the point *C* with respect to the assessment of costs and benefits. In Fig. 7.4, this point is determined with the clear goal that the company should not be insolvent at any time. Although this objective cannot be achieved in all circumstances, it is important that in such cases it can be confirmed or determined whether the management behaved professionally in accordance with the financial and sound management principles.

Determining the cost of financial distress requires a variety of information that is not always available. In contrast, the model in Fig. 7.4 uses predominantly accounting information, which is complemented by available environmental information.

We have already established that any estimate of the cost of financial distress does not provide reliable information for deciding the solvency of an individual company. The insolvency risk assessment, with the relevant information in accordance with the model in Fig. 7.4, is much more reliable to achieve the solvency objective of the company.

The exposed model covers all the main areas of financial policy decisions relating to the provision of solvency and connects them with the impact of such policies on the costs and profitability of equity.

The model takes into account the fundamental starting point about ethical decision-making, as it does not permit the costs of financial distress as an alternative in decision-making. Insolvency risk management is required to cope not only on the basis of professional principles but also on the basis of ethical principles.

Organization's insolvency as a result of failure of management in terms of due professional accountability (at a reasonable corporate risk) is unethical fact. It is therefore surprising that the concern for the ability to

[10] Here we follow the principle of fairness as more important (Rawls 1917, p. 347) than the principle of rationality (Rawls, 2011, p. 244). It means that debts should be paid (Kilpi 1998, p. 17).

pay is not elevated to the level of general principles in practice. Namely, addressing the solvency in the literature on the one hand is often limited to "liquidity ratios," on the other hand it is often insufficiently covered in some topics as: short-term financial management, cash management, management of working capital, capital structure, financial planning, budgeting and other areas of corporate finance.

The similar shortcomings recognized Dyck and Mulej: "Traditional concept of creditworthiness was too limited to financial aspects only and can no longer meet today's criteria" (Dyck et al. 1998, p. 348).

Last but not least, the above model is in full compliance with the fundamental principles of corporate social responsibility as it requires constant monitoring and planning of its solvency. Such contributions of accountancy and financial policy reduce the risk of insolvency and the associated potential damage to the organization and society as a whole.

Questions for Discussion

7-1 What are basic business functions?
7-2 Which partial systems encompass all business functions?
7-3 What is the difference between the managerial control function and the control function in the information system?
7-4 Discuss the four dimensions of management in an organization.
7-5 What is triple bottom line?
7-6 Discuss the main purpose of an organization from long-term point of view.
7-7 What is the basic information about achieving sustainable development of organization?
7-8 What is the role of *ISO* standards in the sustainable development framework?
7-9 Discuss the shareholder approach considering sustainable development.
7-10 Explain the management on the basis of value added.
7-11 Who bears relatively the greatest risk in business?
7-12 Who bears the intellectual capital?
7-13 How structured is structural capital?
7-14 Discuss the relationship between labor and capital.
7-15 Discuss the expressive power of net present value of surplus value added.

7-16 What is the main principle of trade-off financial theory?
7-17 What are the costs of financial distress?
7-18 What are advantages and disadvantages of trade-off theory
7-19 Explain the role of ethics in the solvency management.

References

Andriessen, Daniel (2004). IC Valuation and Measurement: Classifying the State of the Art. *Journal of Intellectual capital*, Vol. 5, No. 2, pp. 230–242.

Arnold, Glen (1998). *Corporate Financial Management*. London: Pitman Publishing.

Arvidson, Susanne (2019). *Challenges in Managing Sustainable Business*. Cham: Springer Nature.

Bessler, Wolfgang, Drobetz, Wolfgang, Grüninge, C. Matthias (2011). Information Asymmetry and Financing Decisions. *International Review of Finance* No 1/2011, pp. 123–154.

Brennan, M. Niamh (2001). Reporting Intellectual Capital in Annual reports: Evidence from Ireland. *I Accounting and Accountability Journal*, Vol. 14, No. 4, pp. 423–436.

Brigham, F. Eugene, Gapenski, C. Louis, Daves, R. Phillip (1999). *Intermediate Financial Management*. 6th Edition. Orlando: The Dryden Press.

BSI (2020). British Standard Institution. *ISO 26000 Guidance on Social Responsibility*. (Retrieved: April, 2020). https://www.bsigroup.com/en-GB/ISO-26000-Social-Responsibility/.

Byars, M. Stephen, Stanberry, Kurt (2018). *Business Ethics*. Houston, Openstax.

Cabrita Maria do Rosario, Vaz Jorge Landeiro (2006). Intellectual capital and value Creation: Evidence from the Portuguese Banking Industry. *The Electronic Journal of Knowledge Management* No. 1/2006, pp. 11–22. (Retrieved: January, 2017). http://www.ejkm.com/front/search/index.html.

Carrington, Donley (2013). An Empirical Study on the Impact of the Process of measuring *IC* on Performance. *The Electronic Journal of Knowledge Management*, Vol. 11, No. 4/2013, pp. 282–294. (Retrieved: February, 2017). https://www.google.si/?gws_rd=ssl#q=Carrington+Donley+An+Empirical+Study+pdf&*&spf=64.

Chen, Jin, Zhu, Zhaohui, Xie, Y. Hong (2004) Measuring Intellectual Capital: A New Model and Empirical Study. *Journal of Intellectual capital* No 1/2004, pp. 195–212. (Retrieved: January, 2017). http://citeseerx.ist.psu.edu/viewdoc/download?doi=10.1.1.195.4946&rep=rep1&type=pdf.

Cohen, Elie (1990). *Analyse Financière*. Paris: Economica.
Del Castillo, A. Ponce (2020). Labour in the Age of AI: Why Regulation Is Needed to Protect Workers. *Forsight Brief*, *No 8*. The European Trade Union Institute, Brussels. (Retrieved: May, 2020). https://www.etui.org/Publications2/Foresight-briefs/Labour-in-the-age-of-AI-why-regulation-is-needed-to-protect-workers.
Donleavy, D. Gabriel (2015). Usefulness Unfulfilled: A Performance Review of Value-Added Statements. *International Journal of Critical Accounting* No. 4/2015, pp. 315–334.
Dumay, John, Guthrie, James, Rooney, Jim (2020). Being Critical About Intellectual Capital Accounting in 2020: An Overview. *Critical perspectives on Accounting*, Vol. 70, July, 2020.
Dyck, G. Robert, Mulej, Matjaž, Knez-Riedl, Jožica, Jurše, Karin, Lutar-Skerbinjek, Andreja, Potočan, Vojko (1998). *Self-Transformation of the Forgotten Four-Fifths*. New York: Kendall/Hunt Publishing Company.
Elkington, John, Hailes, Julia, Makower, Joel (1998). *Triple Bottom Line*. Appendix 11. (Retrieved: April, 2020). http://archive.babymilkaction.org/pdfs/spinpdfs/appendices/triplebl.pdf.
Epstein, Marc, McFarlan, F. Warren (2011). Nonprofit vs. For-profit Boards. *Strategic Finance*, No. 3/2011, pp. 28–35.
Garben, Sacha (2019). Tackling Precarity in the Platform Economy-and Beyond. Social Europe. (Retrieved: May, 2020). https://www.socialeurope.eu/tackling-precarity-in-the-platform-economy-and-beyond.
Gill, W. David (2006). The Triple Bottom Line by Andrew Sawitz with Karl Weber. (Retrieved: April, 2020). https://static1.squarespace.com/static/57b0be1c579fb3136382b62d/t/57c8e87037c5815308cb0bb7/1472784496702/Savitz-A.-Triple-Bottom-Line.pdf.
Guthrie, James (2001). The Management, Measurement and the Reporting of Intellectual Capital. *Journal of Intellectual Capital*, Vol. 2, No. 1, pp. 27–41.
Idowu, O. Samuel, Louche, Céline, Edit. (2011). *Theory and Practice of Corporate Social Responsibility*. Heidelberg: Springer.
Ionel, C. Vatasoiu, Alina, Cornescu, Dumitru, I. Motoniu (2020). Human Resources Accounting – Accounting for the Most Valuable Asset of an Enterprise. (Retrieved: May, 2020). https://www.researchgate.net/publication/49615448_HUMAN_RESOURCES_ACCOUNTING_FOR_THE_MOST_VALUABLE_ASSET_OF_AN_ENTERPRISE/link/0f3196273829de2216413960/download.
Joia, L. Antonio (2000). Measuring Intangible Corporate Assets. *Journal of Intellectual Capital* No. 1/2000, pp. 68–84. (Retrieved: December, 2016). http://app.ebape.fgv.br/comum/arq/JIC.pdf.

Kaye, Leon (2012). Time to Start Valuing Human Capital as an Asset on the Balance Sheet. (Retrieved: May, 2020). https://www.theguardian.com/sustainable-business/valuing-human-capital-asset-balance-sheet.

Kianto, Aino, Ritala, Paavo, Vanhala, Mika, Hussinki, Henri (2020). Reflections on the Criteria Indian Sound Measurement of Intellectual Capital: A Knowledge-Based Perspective. Critical Perspectives on Accounting, Vol. 70, July, 2020.

Kilig, Levent (2006). *Compta Finance*. Paris: Groupe Eyrolle.

Kilpi, Jukka (1998). *The Ethics of Bankruptcy*. London: Routledge.

Knowledge (2003). *Intellectual Capital Statements – The New Guideline*. Copenhagen: Danish Ministry of Science, Technology and Innovation. (Retrieved: May, 2020). http://pure.au.dk/portal/files/32340329/guideline_uk.pdf.

Koster, E. G. Jan (2017). Human Capital as a Part of the Financial Balance Sheet. (Retrieved: May, 2020). https://www.eapm.org/human-capital-part-financial-balance-sheet/.

Lagouarde-Segot, Thomas, Paranque, bernard (2018). Finance and Sustainability: From Idea to Utopia. *International Review of Financial Analysis*, Vol. 55, January, pp. 80–92.

Liebowitz, Jay, Suen, Y. Ching (2000). Developing Knowledge Management Metrics for Measuring Intellectual Capital. *Journal of Intellectual Capital* No. 1/2000, pp. 54–67. (Retrieved: January, 2017). http://cos.ufrj.br/~jano/LinkedDocuments/_papers/aula05/Developing%20Knowledge%20Management%20Metrics%20for%20Measuring%20Intellectual%20Capital.pdf.

Marr, Bernard, Schiuma, Gianni, Neely, Andy (2004). Intellectual Capital – Defining Key Performance Indicators for Organizational Knowledge Assets. *Business Process Management Journal* No 5/2004, pp. 551–569. (Retrieved: January, 2017). https://pdfs.semanticscholar.org/be99/efdcf4dffc95763e175616928d63974e661a.pdf.

Matsa, A. David (2018). Capital Structure and a Firm's Workforce. *Annual Review of Financial Economics*, Vol. 10, No. 1, pp. 387–412.

Meihami, Bahram, Varmaghani, Zeinab, Meihami Hussein (2014). Role of Intellectual Capital on Firm Performance (Evidence from Iranian Companies). *International Letters of Social and Humanistic Sciences*, Vol. 12, pp. 43–50.

Milost, Franko (2012). Accounting for Invisible Business Assets of an Organization. Računovodsko obravnavanje nevidnih poslovnih prvin organizacije (In Slovene). *2nd Conference About Internal Reporting*, pp. 128–139. Ljubljana: ZES, ZRFRS, IPR.

Miltiadis, D. Lytras, Edvinsson, Leif, Ordóñez de Pablos, Patricia (2008). The Intellectual Capital Statements: Evolution and How to Get Started. (Retrieved: May, 2020). https://www.researchgate.net/publication/267301892_The_intellectual_capital_statements_Evolution_and_how_to_get_started.

Mostafei, Parasto (2015). An Empirical Investigation of Relationship Between Intellectual Capital and Different Dimensions of Company's Performance. *Science International* No. 3/2015, pp. 2899–2909. (Retrieved: January, 2017). http://www.sci-int.com/pdf/115352362899-2909%205+++.pdf.

Mouritsen, J., Larsen, H. T., Bukh, P. N. (2001). Valuing the Future: Intellectual Capital Supplements at Skandia. *Accounting, Auditing & Accountability Journal*, Vol. 14, No. 4, pp. 399–422. (Retrieved: December, 2020). https://www.researchgate.net/profile/Per-Bukh/publication/235295483_Valuing_the_future_Intellectual_capital_supplements_at_Skandia/links/02e7e52dff67e9c034000000/Valuing-the-future-Intellectual-capital-supplements-at-Skandia.pdf?origin=publication_detail.

Okeke, C. John (2016). Human Capital Accounting: A Literature Review. (Retrieved: May, 2020). https://www.researchgate.net/publication/288872492_Human_capital_accounting_A_literature_review.

Rahim, Azlina, Atan, Ruhaya, Kamaluddin, Amrizah (2011). Intellectual Capital Reporting in Malaysian Technology Industry. *Asian Journal of Accounting and Governance*, No. 2/2011 Intellectual Capital Reporting in Malaysian Technology Industry Intellectual Capital Reporting in Malaysian Technology Industry, pp. 51–59.

Rao, K. S. Ramesh (1987). *Financial Management*. London: MacMillan Publishing Company.

Rawls, John (1917). *A Theory of Justice*. Cambridge MA, Harvard University Press.

Riahi-Belkaoui, Ahmed (2003). Intellectual Capital and Firm Performance of U.S. Multinational Firms: A Study of the Resource-Based and Stakeholder Views. *Journal of Intellectual Capital* No 4/2003, pp. 215–226. (Retrieved: April, 2020). https://papers.ssrn.com/sol3/papers.cfm?abstract_id=365580&rec=1&srcabs=1152892&alg=1&pos=6.

Roos, Göran, Bainbridge, Alan, Jacobsen, Kristine (2001). Intellectual Capital Analyses As a Strategic Tool. *Strategy and Leadership Journal* No 4/2001, pp. 21–26. (Retrieved: January, 2017). https://pdfs.semanticscholar.org/2201/b9ec8834062d6cef991b76448262856e2e05.pdf.

Samuels, M. J., Wilkes, F. M., Brayshaw, R. E. (1995). *Management of Company Finance*. London: Chapman & Hall.

Smart, B. S., Megginson, W. L., Gitman, L. J. (2004). *Corporate Finance*. Mason, OH: Thomson, South-Western.

Stanko B. Brian, Zeller, L. Thomas, Melena F. Matthew (2014). Human Asset Accounting and Measurement: Moving Forward. *Lornal of Business & Economic Research*, Vol. 12, No. 2, pp. 93–104.

Stulz, René (1996). Rethinking Risk Management. *Journal of Applied Corporate Finance*, Vol. 9. No. 3, pp. 8–24.

Sustainability & Impact Investor Forum (2020). *Driving Value with Value*. (Retrieved: May, 2020). https://informaconnect.com/sustainability-and-impact-investor-forum/?vip_code=FKN2742GOOGLE&gclid=EAIaIQobChMIw_TU7_Oe6QIVhOJ3Ch0grABIEAAYASAAEgLI2_D_BwE.

Taleb, N. Nassim (2012). *Antifragile*. London: Penguin Books.

Taleb, N. Nicholas (2009). Errors, Robustness, and the Fourth Quadrant. *International Journal of Forecasting*, Vol. 25, pp. 744–759.

Taleb, N., Goldstein, G. D., Spitznagel, W. M. (2009). The Six Mistakes Executives Make in Risk Management. *Harvard Business Review*, October 2009, pp. 78–81.

Walsh, C. (1996). *Key Management Ratios*. London: Pitman Publishing.

Zeng, Tao (2013). Corporate Social Responsibility, Tax Aggressiveness, and Firm Market Value. (Retrieved: May, 2016). https://doi.org/10.1111/1911-3838.12090/epdf.

Zingales, L. (2000). In Search of New Foundations. *Journal of Finance*, Vol. 55, No. 4, pp. 1623–1653.

CHAPTER 8

Accountancy, Ethics and Sustainable Development

8.1 Introduction

My biggest problem with modernity may lie in the growing separation of the ethical and the legal (Taleb 2010, 62).

The manager, who likes to claim working in accordance with the law, arouses distrust in his observance of ethical criteria. Even more, "such behaving is not only false but highly dangerous" (Boatright 2000, p. 16), because not everything that is immoral is illegal.

Based on many years of experience as a management consultant I get similar feelings when seeing attempts to make a distinction between professional, business and personal ethics in professional literature. These dilemmas are somehow artificial and scholastic. From practical point of view, the same are discussions about different positions in ethics theory: absolutism, objectivism, subjective universalism, conventionalism, subjectivism, amorality and skepticism (Pojman and Fieser 2011, p. 17). Various theories of ethics can be seen also in diagrammatic forms (e.g. Gaffikin 2007, 5). These approaches are of course understandable and useful, especially from historical study aspects.

The need for posing and solving of ethical issues is obvious, because of the concern about the behavior of big business and growing neoliberalism and globalism. This need became a crucial factor for further development of society in line with social responsibility of individual persons

Ž. Bergant, *Accountancy and Social Responsibility*,
Palgrave Studies in Impact Finance,
https://doi.org/10.1007/978-3-030-77928-3_8

and organizations. This is especially important because the information age and the Internet increase the potential for unethical actions and behavior. This importance is shown also by ISO 26,000 (point 4.4), where recommendations are given for organizations to promote ethical behavior.

Business is a part of social system, and economic elements of major decisions cannot be isolated from their social consequences (Prindl and Prodhan 1994, 22). At the same time, "a society that leaves nothing to an individual's own sense of what is right and moral would no longer be a free society" (Prindl and Prodhan, ibid.). "Business has to take account of its responsibilities towards the society in coming to its decisions, but society has to accept its responsibilities for setting the standards against which those decisions are made" (Prindl and Prodhan 1994, 42).

The long-term sustainable development of the organization and the success of the individual therefore depend not only on the legality and narrow professionalism of operations, but also on the ethical decision-making and moral operation.

According to Blakburn (2001), there are seven threats to ethics, that are however actual even today: increasing secularization, a lack of belief in any universal principles of ethics, egoism and selfishness, belief in social Darwinism, determinism, unreasonable demands and false consciousness that fooled one into actions for the wrong reasons. In principle, these reasons are avoidable if the value-added law is fully recognized and properly considered (see Chapter 5).

Proudhon has said already in 1868 that "accounting should be regarded as a means of solving the most important of social problems of economy and justice" (Proudhon 1868). He should be understood as giving the importance of information role of accountancy that must consider its ethical aspects. These aspects matter because the ethical decisions that accountants make have an impact on other people and their behavior (McPhail and Walters 2009, p. 56).

"There seems to be lack of public and political engagement within the ethics of accounting. At a time when societal expectations are increasing and business is becoming more complex, the traditional resources that may have provided the grounds for addressing these problems in the past have diminished and there is growing concern that we lack the ethical capacity within the accounting profession to engage seriously with these challenges" (McPhail and Walters 2009, p. 8).

However, the above quotations, which substantiate the need for ethics in accounting, do not stress enough the feedback effect of accounting on the values in the society. Acccounting system namely does not follow only given rules. It also affects the rules and values in society. There is a huge difference between the accounting system that supports shareholders' interests and the system that supports stakeholders' goals. Some authors even make a difference between business and professional ethics on this basis (e.g. Balthazard 2015, p. 1).

A shift of mind is required from currently still too much widely accepted business goal, as to maximize shareholder's value (Idowu and Louche 2011). Below, the ethical aspects of accountancy will be considered from stakeholders' point of view. Namely, this is the only way to ensure the discussion in line with social responsibility and sustainable development of an organization.

8.2 Ethical Aspects of Accounting Information

Accounting information system must follow the most important goal of an organization. "Profits are to be generated but not at any cost to society and preferable in a way that supports society" (Brooks and Dunn 2018, p. 23). Although an increasing number of authors emphasize social responsibility and sustainable development of companies, the economic and accounting professions are not yet united in emphasizing value added as basic accounting information on sustainable development. This is evidenced in particular by the shy treatment of the statement of value added in accounting standards.

This poses important ethical dilemmas for the accounting profession. The solutions depend on the effectiveness of the influence of economic and social sciences on political will, especially in the formulation of accounting standards.

In these efforts, the responsibility of the accounting profession is not negligible. This also points to the ethical aspect of accounting professionals, which requires their active participation. It is the first and probably also the most difficult task of accountancy as a science today.

The second and not less difficult task is to achieve changes in tax legislation regarding the elimination of interest as a deductible item from the tax base in organizations. It was discussed in Sect. 6.7.

Both above-mentioned tasks are a precondition to construct an efficient information system in organizations for internal and external reporting to support decisions in line with social responsibility and sustainable development.

It should also be noted that the importance of ethical and social responsibility corresponds to the difficulties of making the necessary changes.

Next important ethical aspect deals with the quality of information. Firstly, mistakes and false explanations (see Sect. 3.5.2) should be eliminated to the greatest extent possible. These efforts are connected with the need for continuous learning and also with considering the achievements of other researchers and practitioners. In doing so, the importance of the participation of experts and the reduction of the limitation of their citation to individual areas as stated by Perera and Zicari (2012, p. 487) should be emphasized.

Secondly, the efficiency and the effectiveness of reporting (see Sect. 3.5.4) are important issues of ethics, because they are a precondition to achieve the trust and the reduction of uncertainty of information users.

Accountants are often economically dependent on their employers and under the pressure from the public and other stakeholders. That is why their independence is all the more important for ethical decisions and moral conduct. The independence of the individual is affected in particular by the following factors:

- Professionalism;
- psychological factors (to assess objectivity and ability regardless of the consequences);
- economic factors (economic independence);
- external influences (awareness of social responsibility, regulations and control).

8.3 Ethical Aspects of Management in Accountancy

It is obvious from Table 7 in Sect. 7.2 that ethical dilemmas in an organization can emerge on both dimensions of management: management of organization (planning, organizing and controlling) and leadership of employees (communicating, motivating and leading style). The ethics of management in accounting can be illustrated in Table 8.1.

Table 8.1 Model of ethics in the management of accountancy

Type of ethical relationship		*Ethical relationship in terms of partial systems*		
		Managing	*Informing*	*Operating*
Stakeholders' relationships	Owners			
	Management			
	Employees			
	Employees in outsourcing			
	Other stakeholders			
Relationships in the organization	Organization as a whole			
	Business functions			
	Business areas			
	Centers of responsibility			
External relationships	Accounting statements			
	Accounting reports			
	Occasional information			

Source Own research

The model in Table 8.1 is based on three pillars that represent relationships to stakeholders, relationships in the organization and external relationships. Each pillar represents different interests, principles and professional assessments, and within them there are also different possibilities to influence decision-making, information and implementation in the company's operations.

Under the first pillar, professional ethics in accounting contacts partially overlaps with owners' ethics, managers' ethics, personal employees' ethics and other stakeholders' ethics[1] in the organization.

In the context of employees precarious workers are included and also those who are not necessarily employees of the organization

[1] More about other stakeholders in Brooks and Dunn (2018, p. 248).

(outsourcing). There are also several ethics risks if stakeholders' expectations are not met (e.g. Brooks and Dunn 2018, p. 20).

Under the second pillar, professional ethics in accounting is reflected in the relationships at the level of business of the entire organization, at the levels of business functions, business areas and at the levels of individual centers of responsibility. These levels are interconnected (matrix organization), but they represent independent areas of interest in the organization.

Under the third pillar, professional ethics in accounting is reflected in the area of responsibility for financial statements, in the area of financial reports and, of course, in the area of occasional information.

All these relationships must be considered from all three partial systems (managerial, informational and operational) point of view. That is shown in Table 8.1 as well.

Table 8.1 has eleven different relationships and together with three aspects (partial systems) represents thirty-three areas where ethical dilemmas can emerge. Each of these areas requires its own consideration from enforcing and implementing ethics in accounting point of view. At the same time, Table 8.1 represents a comprehensive starting point for normative regulation in an organization.

8.4 Personal Ethics as a Base of Ethical Behavior of the Organization

The model in Table 8.1 in previous section does not apply only to the head of accounting, but also to all employees working in accounting tasks (not only in the accounting department). Therefore, the discussion is not only about "professional ethics of an accountant" but about "professional ethics in accountancy." The latter proves to be a more appropriate term.

There are numerous factors that influence the way individual person experiences ethical dilemmas. These factors are, for example (adapted from: McPhail and Walters 2009, p. 37):

1. *Individual attributes* (moral maturity, age, gender, nationality, profession, health).
2. *Contextual attributes* (local, regional, national, international, national culture, organizational culture, group and role, linguistic framing, place).

3. *Issue attributes* (nature of causes and consequences, social consensus, possibility of effect, temporal immediacy, proximity, concentration of effect).

Of course, an individual can act in a variety of roles (business or professional). Thus, it is possible to talk about personal ethics from a professional or business point of view. It follows from this statement that professional and business ethics are only two aspects of personal ethics. This means that there are not several *types* of ethics, but there is always only one: *personal ethics*. Therefore, business and professional ethics represent two partial systems (and not subsystems) of personal ethics.

In all cases of business ethics, the fundamental carrier of behavior and decisions is individuals. They are associated and interdependent and each of them contributes to overall ethics in an organization. Some of them have higher or lower impact. In this way, business ethics becomes a *resultant* or *synergy* (and not the sum) of personal ethics of all employees, an important part of organization's culture and a precondition of corporate social responsibility.

Business ethics is often defined as ethical behavior of organizations (e.g. Artur 2018, p. 1). Some authors understand business ethics as "an appliance, systematic study field, regarding the determination of moral principles and behavior codes, which regulate human relationship among organizations and govern the business people and/or managers' decisions" (e.g. Tomescu et al. 2015, p. 176).

Such and similar definitions and talking about how an organization "conducts its business," someone could wrongly understand as a personification of the organization and forgets that within are people, which make decisions in line with their *collective* ethics. This ethics is nothing more and nothing less than a resultant (synergy) of personal ethics. Employees and especially the management should not *hide themselves* behind the name of organization. So-called behavior and ethics of organization is, therefore, as a rule, personal behavior and ethics of organizations' top management. One is often not sufficiently aware of this fact.

In creating the resultant of personal ethics from business or professional point of view, some conflicts of interests may emerge. Above findings have important consequences regarding the resolution of these conflicts. The important question here is, which principles should prevail.

As the business and professional aspects are only partial systems, the principles of personal ethics and its values must be a fundamental priority. The predominance of short-term business interests always has negative consequences in the long run. Namely, advocates of the principles of personal ethics may be outvoted or neglected, but it results in deteriorating relationships and reducing work efficiency. In such a case, there is a high probability of deteriorating the image of the organization in its environment.

The predominance of the principles of personal ethics is therefore of a primary nature. Here, however, the premise of the fundamental criterion of ethical conduct is important. These must not be narrow and short-term interests, but a fundamental impact on the well-being of society, which means a broader view. It can be explained by the difference between self-interest and greed (Anderson 2000, p. 172; Brooks and Dunn 2018, p. 150).

Of course, in different societies, a common understanding of the particular contribution to their well-being could be different. Therefore, there could be different also a perception of moral behavior. Nevertheless, it does not neglect a fundamental criterion of ethical conduct (social well-being).

All said above is valid also for professional ethics of accountancy that depends on personal ethics of employees, working in accounting tasks. Innumerable codes of conduct are only means that individuals can use to improve or help to maintain the desired level of their behavior. But there can be also conflicts between different codes of conduct (Brooks and Dunn 2018, p. 415). These codes cannot set a general rule, what is good and what is bad in all situations to which an individual is facing, nevertheless how codes of conduct are broadly interpreted.

Adopting different ethical standards (e.g. ethical relativism) means a lack of consistency and integrity that likely damages one's reputation (Byars and Stanberry 2018, p. 21). A possibility of an universal ethical standard offers the criterion of social responsibility that will be discussed in the following chapters.

The ethical aspect is closely linked to the notion of accountability, which implies a broader perspective in relation to responsibility. Accountability in its broadest sense simply refers to the giving and demanding of reasons of conduct (Roberts and Scapens 1985, p. 447). Accountability» is a state of mind; an outward expression of inner responsibility felt by the

Table 8.2 The meaning of accountability

Activity aspect *Moral aspect external (to others moral pulls)* *Internal (to oneself) moral pushes*	*Legal aspect*	*Organizational aspect*	*Professional aspect*	*Political aspect*
	Liability Obligation	Answerability Obedience	Responsibility Fidelity	Responsiveness Amenability

Source Adopted from: Dubnick (2002, p. 20)

employee, which is driven by intrinsic rather than extrinsic motivators« (Head 2009, p. 1). This broader meaning can be illustrated in Table 8.2.

Table 8.2 offers a wide range of understandings of accountability from a variety of perspectives, thus also giving the individuals the opportunity to properly check and improve their behavior. In all cases, accountability is a two-way street: You want to know that you can count on people, and they want to know that they can count on you (Bustin 2014, p. xiii). It's good to keep in mind that talking about responsibility is easy, but it's harder to stick to it. This is what Bustin calls "the great paradox" (Bustin 2014, p. 52).

Some authors have found limits to the concept of accountability (e.g. Joannides 2012, p. 245), but it still remains more or less as an academic provocation (Riddle et al. 2018, p. 74). As stated above, all possible dilemmas can be and should be solved at the level of personal ethics and conscience that is the base of social responsibility as well.

8.5 Accounting Process Development

The fundamental factor of accounting development is undoubtedly the need for information. The information needs can be divided into the need for greater efficiency of accounting process and the need for new and more detailed information.

Information technology and its development also play an important role in this environment through allowing more effective processing of increased number of data and processing new, more complex information. At the same time, information technology generates possibility of emerging new information needs as well.

Therefore, accounting development is aimed to current and strategic development. It is shown in Fig. 8.1.

Information needs in Fig. 8.1 are classified according to their origin into:

- the need to improve the quality of information arising from the need for greater efficiency and effectiveness of the information system;
- the need for new information arising from the growth of business volume and the need for better risk management in business;
- the need for new information generated and enhanced by the IT development.

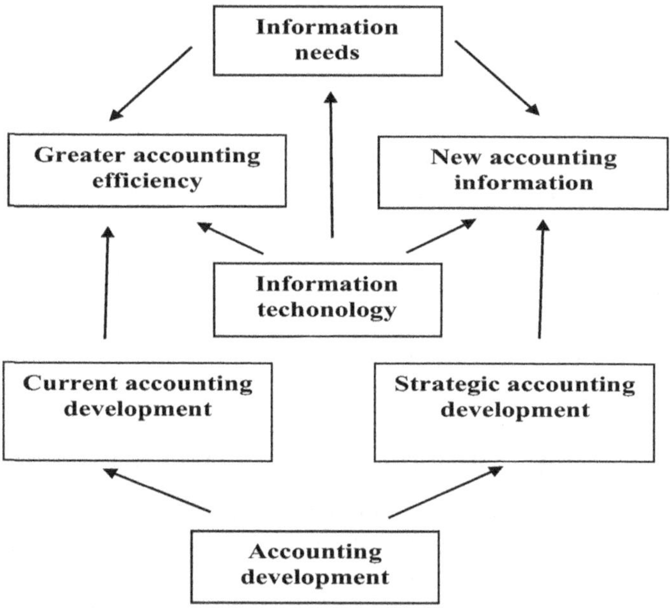

Fig. 8.1 Factors of accounting process development (*Source* Own research)

The need for accounting information is developing rapidly because of economic development but also due to the orientation of organizations toward more socially responsible operation and sustainable development.

In terms of improving the efficiency of the accounting information system, it can be discussed current (tactical) organizational development, but when new information in mind, it can be discussed strategic organizational development.

It should be emphasized that increasing the efficiency of the accounting information system is possible only by increasing the knowledge of accountancy that will be discussed later.

8.6 Accounting Department Development

From the organizational perspective, the changes of accounting department are interesting. These changes have some characteristics that could

Table 8.3 The development of accounting department organizational form

	Phase	*Organizational form*
1	Basic	The accountant in an organization performs also treasury tasks
2	Discovery	Treasury tasks are discovered but accounting and financial operations are still governed by the same person
3	Refinement	Special treasury department is established. Accounting department orientates to internal users, accountant becomes a controller
4	Centralization	Cost and management accounting is developing, an accounting services for a corporation and its subsidiaries are being developed
5	Enlightenment	The principle of rationalization of accounting is prevailing. IT support is developed. Accounting department is partially decentralized
6	Maturity	Accounting department becomes legal entity (accounting service) and offers services also in the free market, also as outsourcing. In this phase, a treasury function in its evolutionary cycle developed to "in-house bank"
7	New Era	Accounting service developed different kind of services and entered new fields of work. Diversified entities are also established (e.g. auditing, forensic services, evaluation services, consulting services, liquidation and receivership, actuarial and insurance work, taxation, investment advice)
8	Stabilization	Probably a new entity for accounting services is established for basic organization or corporation

Source Adapted and developed from the basic idea of Frampton (1987, p. 4)

be monitored. Table 8.3 shows eight principal phases in the development of accounting department.

Each phase of the development of the accounting department in Table 8.3 is in principle adapted to the current needs of the organization. As these are changing, so must change also the accounting department. In practice, all forms of accounting department can be found in different organizations.

Table 8.3 shows that development can initially take place from organizational forms with close connection with the treasury (financial) function to completely independent forms (internal and external accounting services) that are able to provide a competitive offer of accounting services.

Of course, this does not mean that a smaller organization may have lower quality accounting in terms of decision support or that for a small organization its financial function is less important.

In all these processes, it is necessary to ensure that the new volume of business does not increase the risk of the company beyond acceptable frameworks.

Based on Table 8.3, it is possible to better understand and to indirectly conclude something about the development of accounting knowledge or its conceptual framework.[2] This important task will be discussed in the next section.

8.7 The Development of Accounting Theory

The need for accounting theory was perceived relatively early (e.g. McCredie 1957; Hopwood 1987, p. 210). Its development is addressed by the authors (e.g. Godfrey et al. 2019) through typical periods: "pragmatic accounting" (1800–1955), "normative accounting" (1956–1970) and "positive accounting" (1970–2000).

In the following years, accounting theory has taken different approaches. "In particular, the professionals sought normative theories to unify accounting practice and make it more homogeneous, whereas academic researchers have sought to better understand the role and impact of different forms of accounting information" (Godfrey et al. 2019, p. 13). These two approaches are compatible in general,

[2] More about the history of accounting knowledge in Hines (1989, pp. 72–92).

because positive theory can help provide an understanding of the role of accounting while normative theories can improve the practice of accounting. But still, many normative theorists do not accept the value of positive accounting research (e.g. Tinker and Puxty 1995, p. 7; Godfrey et al. 2019, p. 29).

Despite several arguments for positive accounting theory (e.g. Godfrey et al. 2019, 435), both theories remain an open topic for further discussions that still take place (e.g. Al-Adeem 2010, 125).

The need for a single, consistent conceptual framework has soon gained quite widespread acceptance (e.g. Kempner 1968, p. 1; Hopwood 1987, p. 232; Miller 1998, p. 619; Jones 2015, p. 2). Nevertheless, there were, and they can be found also today, severe critics and appeals for further improvement regarding the proposed approaches (e.g. Hines 1989, 1992; p. 87; Montagna 1991, p. 98; Unegbu 2014, p. 13; Oldroyd et al. 2015).

Belkaoui established that an accounting theory is possible if it constitutes a frame of reference and includes three elements: encoding the phenomena to symbolic representation, manipulation according to rules and translation to real-world phenomena (Riahi-Belkaoui 2012, p. 109). A systematic approach to the formulation of an accounting theory includes several possibilities: practical, deductive, inductive, ethical, sociological, economic and eclectic (Riahi-Belkaoui 2012, p. 110).

Belkaoui thinks that a formulation of the objectives of financial statements is needed for formulating a conceptual framework for financial accounting and reporting. In doing so, he emphasizes three groups of interests (firms, users and accounting profession) and possible conflicts among them (Riahi-Belkaoui 2012, p. 164). On this basis, he suggests particular, general and qualitative objectives of financial statements (Riahi-Belkaoui 2012, p. 166).

In short, the fundamental objective of accounting information is divided into two possibilities: the usefulness for potential investors and creditors of enterprises and the usefulness for resource providers of nonbusiness organizations (Riahi-Belkaoui 2012, pp. 182, 185). It follows that there is no single objective for all organizations, except very large definition like "usefulness for users of accounting information."

In the last five years, it is not possible to find some additional important contributions to the development of accounting theory. Even more, there are some important books named "Accounting Theory," but almost all of them mention the theory only in an introduction and avoid its definition or deeper discussion. Classical example is Scott's monograph *Financial Accounting Theory* (Scott and O'Brien 2019). Scott and O'Brien see the fundamental problem of financial accounting theory "how to design and implement the concepts and standards that best combine two competing roles for accounting information: informing investors and improving contacting efficiency by motivating and evaluating manager performance" (Scott and O'Brien 2019, p. 25). It means that there are two different groups of interests even in enterprises. They of course require some different information. Such statement shows that the recent accounting theory is really in a blind alley.

It is difficult to avoid a feeling that critical remarks on the current development of accounting theory are so radical that they are no longer attractive to the academic sphere, which can no longer keep up with new trends and demands of society's development. It seems to be still valid today the statement, that "many accounting academics are ignorant of the literature written by accounting scholars from the 1920s through the 1960s" (Granof and Zeff 2008, p. A3). Suojanen, for example, is certainly among the forgotten authors. This is probably a consequence of enforcing the doctrine of neoliberalism. Riahi-Belkaoui in his monograph (2012) no longer mentions value added and the statement of value added, the importance of which he emphasized in 2003 (Riahi-Belkaoui 2003, p. 217) and still even in 2010 (Riahi-Belkaoui 2010, p. 18).

Among the first more radical authors is probably Al-Adem, who emphasizes the findings of his research, in particular, the following (Al-Adeem 2010, p. 125):

1. The diminishing level of published papers to advance accounting theory.
2. The decrease of accounting theory topics, while the use of the empirical archival method, the influence of economic and finance disciplines and financial accounting topics increased.
3. Focus on a scientific approach to academic accounting research has restricted the development of accounting theory.
4. The increase of empirical research became the dominant base for judging claims for knowledge causes other research to be ignored. They are unlikely to have a place in important accounting reviews. Faculty members in business fields, including accounting, are discouraged from working on such articles.

5. Questions about the normative topics that contribute to building general accounting theory are ignored.
6. It appears that accounting academics use empiricism in a narrow way. A discipline overly exposed to empiricism may subject itself to the need to borrow theories from other disciplines. The tendency toward doing such empirical studies is connected with utilizing theories (methodologies, models) from economics and finance.[3] In this way, these theories become the theoretical foundations for accounting theory.
7. Restricting the theoretical foundation in accounting academia has placed accounting in a "subservient" position to economics. The excessive citing from economic and finance sources makes the contents of accounting knowledge published in accounting journals to a large extent not differently from those in economic and finance journals. The number of empirical studies that can be classified as financial accounting papers increased, the number of papers about accounting theory decreased.
8. The heavy importation of theories and models from the economics and finance disciplines has created a dominant school of accounting research that is dependent on economics and finance-based theories and methodologies. Some examples about predicting economic or financial events (e.g. Altman model, bond-rating models, *CAPM* model) are still to be found also in 2012 (e.g. Riahi-Belkaoui 2012, pp. 363–433).
9. Positive accounting research has rejected normative theorizing in accounting, claiming that the proposed normative accounting theories serve as excuses for policy-makers.
10. The mainstream accounting researchers lack knowledge in other fields outside of economics and finance that prevents accounting research from benefiting from other branches of knowledge.
11. The schism between accounting academics and accounting practitioners broadened. What is considered empirical accounting

[3] A good example of this phenomenon is the recent use of securities market model, agency theory and stock valuation in dealing with accounting theory (Scott, O'Brien, 2019, p. 393). Even more, the critics of different accounting approaches (or theories) research their usefulness using economic and financial models and concepts (e.g. Godfrey et al., 2019, pp. 394–396).

research lies outside the domain of accounting practice and such results can be understood mostly by "elite" researchers.

All above findings are supported by cited author's research and relevant citations of professional literature. "General accounting theory remains neglected. As the limitations of financial empirical research in general and positive theorizing in particular are now acknowledged, it is time to reestablish research an activity supporting normative theorization" (Al-Adeem 2010, 144). "Building general theory for accounting that is capable of guiding practice and that is founded on a normative foundation becomes a necessity" (Al-Adeem 2010, 143).

On the above considerations, it is not surprising, that some authors describe accounting as a language of capitalism (Roberts and Scapens 1985, p. 448). Next radical author is probably Richard (2014), who stated that evolution of accounting goes in a dangerous direction. This process has permitted an unbridled acceleration of profit recognition, which contributed significantly to financial crises manifestation:

> With the appearance of *IFRS* capitalist accounting, modern capitalism looks as if it has reached its 'supreme stage' of recklessness. This situation is potentially unsustainable for three principal reasons. Firstly, the trend toward eliminating systematic depreciation and recognizing potential profits in financial accounting are the best way to induce the destruction of financial capital. Secondly, the limitations associated with the traditional accounting concept of capital (in the sense of a resource to be conserved), notably the exclusion of human and natural capital from this systematic conservation of capital, will likely render the continued conservation of financial capital impossible in the future. Thirdly, the monopolization of power over firms by shareholders, who dominate employees, will become progressively more unbearable, especially in the context of a growing illegitimacy of these shareholders. Keynes (1936, p. 376) proposed a gradual and mild "euthanasia of rentiers" to solve the economic problems of capitalism. It appears now that the solution is necessarily a more radical one in form of a new environmental accounting system based on a drastic redefinition of profit and power, in the frame of a new democratic governance of firms. (Richard 2014, p. 9)

Jones concluded that "accounting reports do not impartially mirror economic events: they reproduce and legitimize dominant power relations in society" (Jones 2015, p. 464). He asked himself: What about the future of financial accounting theory? (Jones 2015, p. 156). With emphasizing the importance of this question, he leaves it open, without a clear answer.

Based on the above, the following two relatively old citations are still relevant:

> For some of the accounting paradigms, some accounting academics may gain access to power and privilege, not because of the usefulness of their research, but because of the monopoly on some form of cultural capital (e.g., capital market research, positive accounting research). (Riahi-Belkaoui 1998, p. 10).
>
> When theory and practice do not coincide, there is something wrong with the theory. (Kinney 1986, p. 339).

Open questions in the accounting theory and its radical critics indicate the need for a different approach to build more consistent and useful theory. Such a possible approach will be discussed in the next chapter.

Questions for Discussion

8-1 How do you distinguish personal and business ethics?
8-2 What are today's main ethical dilemmas in accounting?
8-3 Name three pillars that represent an important dimension of ethics in corporate management.
8-4 Which is the second dimension of ethics in corporate management?
8-5 What factors influence ethical dilemmas of an individual person?
8-6 What means the ethics of an organization? Discuss a synergy of personal ethics of the employees.
8-7 Discuss a possibility of universal ethical standard.
8-8 What is the meaning of accountability?
8-9 What are main factors of accounting process development?
8-10 Discuss the development of accounting department.
8-11 Discuss the critics of current accounting theory.
8-12 Is there a need for a consistent accounting theory?

References

Al-Adeem, K. Rasheed (2010). *Accounting Theory: A Neglected Topic in Academic Accounting Research.* Doctoral dissertation. Cleveland: Case Western Reserve University.

Anderson, Elisabeth (2000). Beyond Homo Economicus: New Developments in Theories of Social Norms. *Philosophy & public Affairs*, Vol. 29, No. 2, pp. 170–200.

Artur, Victoria (2018). Business Ethics. (Retrieved: May, 2020). https://www.researchgate.net/publication/328789262_Business_Ethics.

Balthazard, Claude (2015). *Are Professional and Business Ethics the Same Thing?* (Retrieved: May, 2020). https://www.hrpa.ca/Documents/Designations/Job-Ready-Program/Are-professional-ethics-and-business-ethics-the-same-thing.pdf.

Blakburn, Simon (2001). *Ethics: A Very Short Introduction.* Oxford university Press.

Boatright, J. John (2000). *Ethics and the Conduct of Business.* Hoboken, NJ: Prentice-Hall Inc.

Brooks, J. Leonard, Dunn, Paul (2018). *Business and Professional Ethics for Directors, Executives & Accountants.* 8th Edition. Bosron: Cangage Learning.

Bustin, Greg (2014). *You Can Count On Me.* Mc Graw-Hill Education.

Byars, M. Stephen, Stanberry, Kurt (2018). *Business Ethics.* Houston, Openstax.

Dubnick, J. Melvin (2002). Seeking Salvation for Accountability. (Retrieved: July, 2020). http://mjdubnick.dubnick.net/papersrw/2002/salv2002.pdf.

Frampton, Paul (1987). Measuring and Evaluating the Benefits of an In-House Bank. *5th International Cash Management Conference.* London, 1987.

Gaffikin, Michael (2007). Accounting Theory and Practice: The Ethical Dimension. (Retrieved: May, 2020). https://www.researchgate.net/publication/30386402_Accounting_Theory_and_Practice_the_Ethical_Dimension.

Godfrey, Jayne, Hodgson, Allan, Tarca, Ann, Hamilton, Jane, Holmes, Scott (2019). *Accounting Theory.* 7th Edition. Milton: Willey.

Head, H. Joel (2009): Building an Accountable Workplace. (Retrieved: June, 2020). https://www.envisionexcellence.net/elements/uploads/files/Building-Workplace-Accountability-Whitepaper.pdf.

Hines, D. Ruth (1989). Financial Accounting Knowledge, Conceptual Framework Projects and the Social Construction of the Accounting Profession. *Accounting & Auditing Journal*, Vol. 2, No. 2.

Hines, D. Ruth (1992). *Accounting: In Communicating a World, We Create a World.*

Hopwood, G. Anthony (1987). The Archaeology of Accounting Systems. *Accounting, Organizations and Society*, Vol. 12, No. 3, pp. 207–234.

Idowu, O. Samuel, Louche, Céline, Edit. (2011). *Theory and Practice of Corporate Social Responsibility.* Heidelberg: Springer.

Joannides, Vassili (2012). *Critical Perspectives on Accounting*, Vol. 23, No. 3, pp. 244–257.

Jones, Stewart (2015). *The Routledge Companion to Financial Accounting Theory*. New York: Routledge.

Kempner, J. Jack (1968). The Basic Concepts of Accounting. *Montana Law Review*, Vol. 30, No.1, pp. 1–17.

Keynes, J. Maynard (1936). *The General Theory of Employment, Interest and Money*. London: Macmillan.

Kinney, W. R. (1986). Empirical Accounting Research Design for Ph.D. Students. *The Accounting Review*, Vol. 61. No. 2, pp. 338–350.

McCredie, Helen (1957). The Theory and Practice of Accounting. *The Accounting Review*, Vol. 32, No. 2, pp. 216–223.

McPhail, Ken, Walters, Diane (2009). *Accounting and Business Ethics*. London: Routledge.

Oldroyd, David, Tyson, N. Thomas, Fleischman, K. Richard (2015). American Ideology, Socialism and Financial Accounting Theory: A Counter View. *Critical Perspectives on Accounting*, Vol. 27, March 2015, pp. 209–218.

Perera, L. Aldama, Zicari, Adrián (2012) Value-Added Reporting as a Tool for Sustainability: A Latin American Experience. *Corporate Governance*, Vol. 12, No. 4/2012, pp. 485–498. (Retrieved: January, 2016). http://live.v1.udesa.edu.ar/files/MBA/Papers/Value_added_reporting_Zicari_2012.pdf.

Pojman, P. Louis, Fieser, James (2011). *Ethical Theory*. Boston: Wadsworth.

Prindl, R. Andreas, Prodhan, Bimal (1994). *Ethical Conflicts in Finance*. Oxford: Blackwell Publishers.

Proudhon, Pierre-Joseph (1868). *Solution du problème social*. Paris: Librairie Internationale.

Riddle, Stewart, Honan, Eileen, Bright, David (2018). *Writing with Deleuze in the Academy: Creating Monsters*. Singapore: Springer Pte Ltd.

Roberts, John, Scapens, Robert (1985). Accounting Systems and Systems of Accountability – Understanding Accounting Practices in Their Organisational Contexts. *Accounting, Organizations and Society*, Vol. 10, No. 4. pp. 443–456.

Miller, Peter (1998). The Margins of Accounting. *European Accounting Review*, Vol. 7, No. 4, pp. 605–621.

Montagna, Paul (1991). Accounting Elites and Accounting Theory. *Accounting, Organizations and Society*, Vol. 16, No. 1, pp. 93–99.

Scott, R. William, O'Brien, C. Patricia (2019). *Financial Accounting Theory*. Toronto, ON: Pearson Canada Inc.

Granof, H. Michael, Zeff, A. Stephen (2008). Research on Accounting Should Learn from the Past. *The Chronicle of Higher Education*, Vol. 54, No. 28, p. A34.

Riahi-Belkaoui, Ahmed (1998). *The Coming Crisis in Accounting*. Westport, CT: Quorum Books.

Riahi-Belkaoui, Ahmed (2003). Intellectual Capital and Firm Performance of U.S. Multinational Firms: A Study of the Resource-Based and Stakeholder Views. *Journal of Intellectual Capital* No 4/2003, pp. 215–226. (Retrieved: April, 2020). https://papers.ssrn.com/sol3/papers.cfm?abstract_id=365580&rec=1&srcabs=1152892&alg=1&pos=6.

Riahi-Belkaoui, Ahmed (2010). *Wealth and Value Added: Reporting, Analysis, Prediction, and Taxation*, April, 2020. Pridobljeno. https://www.researchgate.net/publication/247621754_Usefulness_of_value_added_reporting_A_review_and_synthesis_of_the_literature.

Riahi-Belkaoui, Ahmed (2012). *Accounting Theory*. 5th Edition. Hampshire: Cengage Learning.

Richard, Jacques (2014). The Dangerous Dynamics of Modern Capitalism (from static to IFRS' Futuristic Accounting. *Critical perspectives on Accounting*, Elsevier, Vol. 30, pp. 9–34.

Taleb, N. Nicholas (2010). *The Bed of Procrustes: Philosophical and Practical Aphorisms*. New York: Random House.

Tinker, T., Puxty T. (1995). *Policing Accounting Knowledge: The Market for Excuses Affair*. New York: Markus Weiner Publishers.

Tomescu, M. Ada, Romania, Oradea, Bodog, S. Aurelia (2015). *Business management and Business Ethics – Two Paradigms and Their Relationship*. (Retrieved: May, 2020). https://www.researchgate.net/publication/285381076_Business_Management_and_Business_Ethics_-Two_Paradigms_and_Their_Relationship.

Unegbu, O. Angus (2014). Theories of Accounting: Evolution & Developments, Income-Determination and Diversities in Use. *Research Journal of Finance and Accounting*, Vol. 5, No. 19, 2014. (Retrieved: January, 2020). https://arxiv.org/abs/1411.4633.

CHAPTER 9

Accountancy and Social Responsibility Aspect

9.1 Starting Points to a New Approach

First fundamental starting point is the orientation toward accountancy and no only to accounting. Such an orientation is in line with the definitions of both notions in Sects. 2.1 and 2.2.

Second starting point should be the fact that accountancy is normally the most important part of information system in every business system. This means that it must be focused on the fundamental objective of the business system.

This point deserves a deeper discussion, whereas it concerns the key question of why an entity or business system (company, association, state, institute, etc.) is established. There are of course numerous specific visions and missions of these entities. Do they have the same denominator?

Any form of bringing people together is, in principle, intended to exploit synergies for more efficient achieving a common goal. Do all these goals have something in common?

In Sect. 5.1, the creation of organizational systems was explained through human need to ensure adequate safeness. To minimize the risk people have to work and the result is value added and part of it means also a reserve to manage risks. Because of their interdependence, people must cooperate and their associations should contribute to increase the

Ž. Bergant, *Accountancy and Social Responsibility*,
Palgrave Studies in Impact Finance,
https://doi.org/10.1007/978-3-030-77928-3_9

reserves for managing risk of all. These reserves come from created value added that increase the well-being of the society as a whole.[1]

Above considerations are encompassed in the first part of *general value-added law* that was explained in Sect. 7.1. Created value added should be considered more in depth. Firstly, it should be understood in its broader way. It means as a value that does not diminish social welfare, although it is completely spent. It means that it encompasses also soft human performances (e.g. sociological, emotional and cultural achievements). Secondly, from measuring point of view, it must be viewed as *surplus value added*, that is explained in Sect. 6.4. Therefore, only value-added creating increases the social welfare.

Based on the above, a *surplus value added could be defined as a common denominator for all objectives in all organizations.* It means that business information system should measure and monitor the states and trends of surplus value added as main information for reporting about effectiveness and performance of an organization.

Such a statement is not totally new. Already in 1954 Suojanen wrote: "If the income, generated in the enterprise, is to be analyzed on the basis of social considerations, then the traditional type of income statement is insufficient" (Suojanen 1954, p. 395). The value-added frame of reference for the enterprise "is much more realistic and relevant *accounting theory* (stressed by Ž. Bergant) of the enterprise than under the presently employed proprietorship and entity theories" (Suojanen 1954, p. 396).

An attempt of improvement presents a contracting theory of organization that sought to take into account the interests of all stakeholders (e.g. Scott and O'Brien 2019, p. 312). It remained halfway through, as it still assumes profit as basic information.

Profit is today still important, mainly in companies, but not in the same manner in institutions and other associations. On the contrary, value added is important also in these organizations.

Profit is still important only for financial capital owners and investors, because it increases the value of their investments. But, there does not exist a scientifically accepted argument to justify a legal norm that profit belongs to investors of financial capital.[2] Furthermore, such a norm is

[1] More about well-being and its measurement see in Stiglitz et al. (2018).

[2] One of the arguments often used is that shareholders bear residual risk (Boatright 2000, p. 179) but it is not *all* the risk in an organization, especially in publicly held corporations. The important part of risk bears stakeholders.

not the basic characteristic of capitalism as a socio-economic system.[3] This is only an arbitrary and administrative norm that leads to "unsustainable nature of corporate capitalism and its moral emptiness" (Kazmi et al. 2015, p. 7) and further inequality as "the defining issue of our time" (Barack Obama 2012). "Corporates that operate only for their own and their shareholders' gain are responsible for exhausting limited and fragile natural resources and for increasing pollution" (Kazmi et al., ibid.). They neglect interests of other stakeholders (especially workers). According to value-added law (Sect. 5.1), such norm leads to increasing dissatisfaction and also to the entropy of the society as a whole. From the above perspectives, we can treat profit as an "original sin" that has misdirected the main attention of information systems in organizations.

The importance of stakeholders' interests is increasingly recognized, not only in professional literature (e.g. Freeman et al. 2010), but also in several important declarations that claims profitability as an intolerable yardstick (e.g. Democratizingwork 2020), and researches (e.g. *KPMG* 2020, 26). Their common demand is for redefining the purpose of a corporation and appropriate participation in profit or value added.

Next fundamental starting point to accountancy theory is based on the definition of accountancy according to Fig. 2.2 in Sect. 2.2. It means that accountancy in an organization encompasses two basic concepts: accounting and management in accountancy. Both of them have their own principles and rules that together form a comprehensive accountancy information system, including information-communication technology.

Such a system is oriented to measure and monitor created and distributed surplus value added in an organization. In this way, accountancy information system creates information about the organization's contribution to the social well-being in particular past and/or planned period. Accounting information, of course, does not include all "soft parts" of value added considered in a broader view, but offer sufficient basis for decision-making according to organization's social responsibility. At the same time, further analysis and information development are possible.

The above considerations are illustrated in Fig. 9.1. Three main areas of accountancy information system are shown: accounting process, management in accountancy and assets that are used to support the

[3] There are several authors who mistakenly believe that the appropriation of profits by the owners of capital is a base characteristic of capitalism (e.g., Kazmi et al. 2015). It is true, however, that in practice it looks like this.

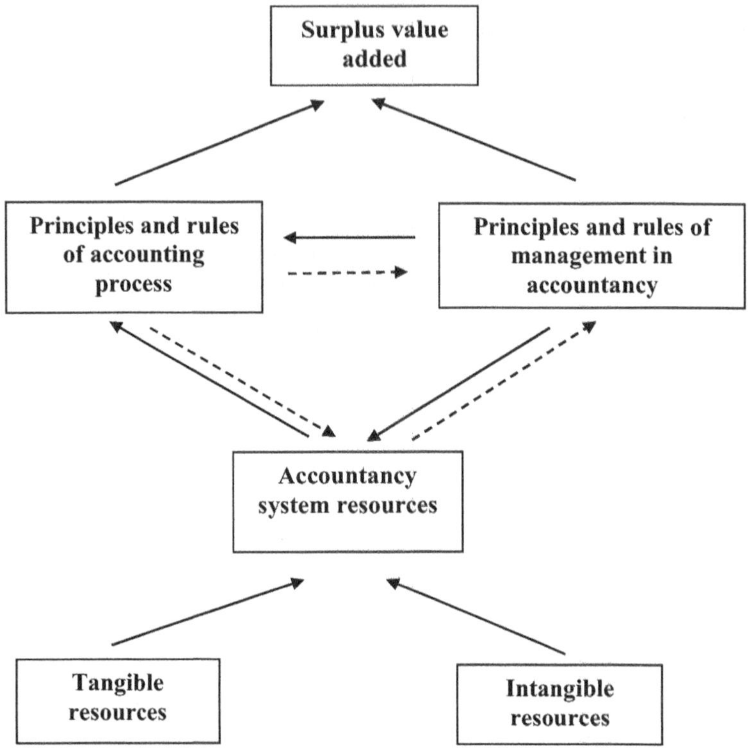

Fig. 9.1 Basic areas and focuses of accountancy theory (*Source* Own research [Bergant 2021, p. 3])

system. The system is oriented to provide information about the value added. It means that main information is about creating surplus value added and distributing it among stakeholders. This information allows to analyze the operating of an organization according its vision and mission. This does not mean that income statement would not be prepared. Profit still contains (in terms of a different view of business) some useful supplementary information as stated in Sect. 6.4.

The area of principles and rules of accounting process in Fig. 9.1 encompasses the main accounting concepts as (Kempner 1968): entity as a single of business organization, double entry system, going concern, historical cost and accrual concept. These concepts are related primarily to the balance sheet; therefore, the income statement is added (Kempner 1968, p. 13). Of course, the statement of surplus value added should be added as well. It means that this area is no more (or should not be) ruled totally by actual accounting standards that follow already obsolete principle of profit as a main category. The area of principles and rules of accounting process should generate the basic information about surplus value added.

The area of principles and rules of management in accountancy in Fig. 9.1 in principle encompasses all classical principles of management that are applicable in accountancy system. First of all, here are included management functions as planning, organizing and controlling. In this framework, ethical behavior, risk management and strategic focus in sustainable future are emphasized. All these activities are oriented toward effective management of accounting process to ensure in a timely manner true and fair information about surplus value added that is shown in Fig. 9.1.

The area of accountancy system resources in Fig. 9.1 encompasses tangible (e.g. fixed assets with hardware and communication equipment), intangible assets (e.g. software, data warehouse, licenses and patents). This area supports the efficiency of accounting process to achieve its goals. Figure 9.1 does not mean that the head of accountancy must also be the head of the computer center. However, he must play a decisive role in the development and use of information and communication technology that support accounting processes. Therefore, there is an urgent need for data science and analytic skills of accountants (Gould 2019).

All three areas above are closely interlinked. Accounting process needs computer support and maintenance, but also has a reciprocal effect on the development of computer equipment. Management takes care of the development and maintenance of information system resources, but also receives information about its additional capabilities and the possibility of developing new or higher quality information. Management directs and controls the operation of the accounting process, but also receives initiatives from it for more efficient operation or solving possible problems. This is shown by the dashed lines in Fig. 9.1, thus forming a comprehensive accountancy system. Therefore, accountancy theory must consider all three areas and also their connectedness.

Figure 9.1 allows the differentiation among responsibilities of individuals in accountancy. Such a differentiation helps in organizing efficient system in particular organization. At the same time, it suggests that several different experts may be involved in an accountancy system. In this way, it allows also the development of professionals on these topics.

9.2 Critical Discussion About Accountancy Theory Concept

The concept of accountancy theory in the previous section has some advantages and also some shortcomings. Among advantages can be found particularly:

1. The concept is based on the principles of the value-added law that are hardly to neglect. Namely, value-added law is valid as long as humankind exists. In this way, the theory gets a very solid basis for defining the goals of information system and the development of its principles and rules. On this starting point, some important lacks of traditional accounting theory may be resolved.
2. The surplus value-added basis in principle enables the satisfaction of stakeholders' interests, which significantly reduces problems in the relationships between people and organizations. It enables the interests of stakeholders to be satisfied, which significantly reduces dissatisfaction and entropy in society, especially by making it easier to manage inequalities between people.
3. Such a concept also changes our view of the world, which means that it has not only sociological but also its own philosophical and psychological dimensions that come from ethical dimension of the value-added law. In this way, it emphasizes the importance of human society as a whole.
4. The accountancy theory concept broadens the area of subject. This allows a comprehensive view that requires interdisciplinary approach. This confirms that accounting is not only a craft of book-keeping and reporting but also a demanding scientific field with a significant impact on the development and operation of society as a whole. This impact is based on the fact that organizations, individuals and society as a whole make their decisions and behave not only instinctively, but also to a significant extent on the basis of information.
5. The concept has an important impact on other disciplines. In the field of economics and finance, several already traditional models should be amended, supplemented or even omitted, for example: operating leverage, the role of margin, criteria of organization's performance and corporate governance, the role of capital market, evaluation of the value of shares and of the value of a firm equity,

risk management, capital asset pricing model (*CAPM*), weighted average cost of capital (*WACC*) financial leverage, economic value added (*EVA*), signaling theory, theories of optimal financial structure (see Sect. 7.7), etc.

6. The concept can no longer be blamed for importing models from economics and finance (e.g. Al-Adeem 2010, p. 127), but vice versa. It has a major impact on economic and financial thought, enabling new directions of research and development. Special attention may be paid to changes of certain criteria in further empirical researching of economic or financial subjects.
7. The concept may have an important impact on the selection of proper criteria of significance in further empirical researches. At the same time, it allows and enhances new possible directions of empirical and theoretical research.
8. The concept places social responsibility as an universal criterion of the adequacy of human behaving and acting.
9. Last but not least, the concept of accountancy theory allows direct links to practical questions and their discussions in the proper and constructive direction.

The main shortcoming of the above concept is its difficult realization in a short time. The difficulties are in general in three different fields: academic, legislation and practical sphere. Academic field has mainly subjective character, but it is no less difficult than others. It is very difficult to change the mental world, embodied in textbooks and school curricula. It is even harder to come to terms with the possibility that something was wrong. This requires time or even a change of generations. Therefore, mainly the young generation is the one that will accept and implement the changes.

The second shortcoming represents the difficulties to change an important part of legislation system that was widely accepted almost without great doubts and became self-understanding part of human life. Numerous regulations should be changed, for example on the field of corporate governance, taxation and a huge number of linked laws and other sort of regulations, including accounting standards. The changes will also affect auditing and auditing standards, in particular with regard to assessing the efficiency and effectiveness of operations. All changes require not only political will, but also adequate organization climate in societies of numerous countries in the world.

Once the problems in the above two areas have been solved, a lot of professional work remains, but it would mean easier problems compared to the ones listed. At the same time, it should be still borne in mind that "the transformation of accounting as a body of expertise takes place within and through an historically specific ensemble of relations, formed between a complex of actors and agencies" (Miller 1998, p. 618).

All changes could be done when recognizing that they are necessary and beneficial on long-term to provide sustainable future for next generations. Therefore, it is necessary to discuss the role of accountancy also from this point of view. By postponing this discussion and relevant research, accountancy will not develop in the right direction, which will continue to cause problems also in a society as a whole. The right direction for accountancy development is sustainable future that is discussed in the next section.

9.3 Sustainable Development and the Sustainable Future

"Sustainable Development Goals (*SDG*), adopted by all United Nations Member States in 2015, provides a shared blueprint for peace and prosperity for people and the planet, for now and for the future. At its heart are the 17 Sustainable Development Goals (*SDGs*), which are an urgent call for action to be taken by all countries—developed and developing—in a global partnership. They recognize that ending poverty and other deprivations must go hand-in-hand with strategies that improve health and education, reduce inequality, and spur economy" (Mulej 2020).

"In order to make the 2030 Agenda a reality, broad ownership of the *SDGs* must translate into a strong commitment by all stakeholders to implement the global goals. Division for sustainable development goals in *UN* aims to help facilitate this engagement" (Mulej, ibid.).

The distinction between the target state of organization's sustainability (which is a moving goal) and the process of sustainable development has to be raised in mind. The process is to be implemented to achieve its desired outcome (Schaltegger et al. 2006, p. 2).

There are several definitions of sustainable development and its meaning. Short but most comprehensive definition is the development, which fulfills the needs of the present generation without jeopardizing the possibilities of future generations to fulfill their needs. It has been already stated that a precondition for sustainable development is a proper behaving according to social responsibility in three areas: economic, social and ecological.

These areas (pillars of social responsibility) can be treated also as "special stakeholders" (Byars and Stanberry 2018, p. 93) or "sustainable development triangle" (Munasinghe 2007). It means that accountancy, as a basis of information system, has to consider their interests.

Today, there are four dimensions of sustainability recognized: ecosystem based, integrity, welfare and self-supply with the inclusion of public (Vovk Korže 2020).

Nevertheless, today it still has to be recognized that "the problems of sustainability of mankind and Earth are much more complex as it was understood during the end of twentieth century. The first part of the sustainable development – sustainability is much more important and has value for future of mankind. Second part *development* is misused term from industrial revolution and economics, and has nothing to do with Nature of Earth. Development could be a part of product, construction, man-made systems, repairs, machines, armaments, etc., and it is a part of human society of post-industrial era. The nature has no development what so ever and nature system is working on contents and interdependences, interactions and co-operation relations" (Mulej 2020).

Therefore, "the transition from sustainable *development* to sustainable *future* is needed for survival of mankind" (Mulej 2020). Such consideration leads to a short definition: "*sustainable future of mankind is a harmony of the humankind system/civilization with system of nature/biosphere of the Planet Earth*" (Mulej, ibid.).

In the following sections, the notion of sustainable development will be understood as *sustainable future*. The accountancy will be discussed also from this point of view.

9.4 Accountancy and the Sustainable Future

Accounting has long been used in a traditional way: for management and external users. Changes have taken the form of triple bottom line accounting and reporting. In recent time it is discussed as sustainability accounting and reporting (Schaltegger et al. 2006, p. 6).

Some authors have raised concerns about the conceptual standing of the triple bottom line and prefer three *P's*: people, planet, profit (e.g. Organicsoul 2020). Further discussion is above the scope of this work, because these concerns cannot diminish the importance of accountancy development. For example, there are also important contributions to environmental management accounting (e.g. Soonawalla 2006, pp. 380–407).

Godfrey et al. defined sustainability accounting and reporting as a subset of social accounting. Some authors even mean that sustainability accounting is not necessarily covered by traditional accounting function and not necessarily concerned with the financial success of the entity (Godfrey et al. 2019, p. 486). Such a statement could be questioned regarding recent developments in sustainability reporting.

An important recent contribution to accounting regarding sustainability future is guided by Global Reporting Initiative (*GRI*) that have already changed the word *development* to *future* (GRI 2015) and offered the integrated reporting system within the GRI standards (GRI 2016). For example, such a contribution is possible especially in developing useful tools for measuring the efficiency of investments in social and ecological area and in sustainability reporting (e.g. Communities Scotland 2006; Valvassori and Vaccari 2009). Detailed discussion of GRI standards is above the scope of this work.

A very interesting approach was presented by Širovnik, who linked all three sustainable aspects (economic, environmental and social) to the mathematical model and obtained a new category: sustainable net present value (Širovnik 2016, p. 44).

The above considerations point to the need for further development of accounting theory, which is otherwise constantly evolving. More about history of accounting theory can be found in Unegbu (2014). Today accounting theory achieved the status that is best represented by the international accounting standards. These standards are focused primarily to external reporting, which is mostly named as financial accounting. Internal reporting however is treated in numerous professional literatures through other accounting disciplines (e.g. cost accounting and management accounting) as good accounting practices.

Such approach to accounting theory has at least three important drawbacks. *Firstly*, it treats accounting only as a process (e.g. Hendriksen 1965) and basic accounting principles (e.g. Smyth 2018). Therefore, it neglects the management aspect (management partial system) that is an integral part of accountancy, which is shown in Fig. 2.2 in Sect. 2.2. *Secondly*, it neglects the importance of connectedness of accounting with actual economic system, which dictates criteria and main information of business success. *Thirdly*, it neglects also the impact of accounting theory on socio-economic and political development. This effect is otherwise recognized, but the authors usually do not connect accounting theory close enough to social responsibility aspects.

From sustainable future point of view, the accountancy should be regarded in line with Fig. 2.2 in Sect. 2.2, from *two aspects*: development of accounting process and development of managing in accounting.

Organization's orientation to sustainable future should be reflected in the *accounting process* in several areas and especially in: collecting appropriate data from economic, social and ecological aspects, designing information for long-term decision-making, external and internal reporting.

The main difficulties come from requiring appropriate data. In all of three areas named above, emerge problems that are not sufficiently solved, yet neither in theory and therefore nor in practice. The most important reason lies in the fact that all three areas are intrinsically linked. Sustainability spans engineering, biology, economics, psychology, politics and touching effectively all aspects of science in some way. Due to interactions between causes and effects, no discipline of science is capable of framing correct question in manner that can lead to complete answers (Nuttal and Young 2017, p. 12). Therefore, a different way should be found. It is possible to find several indicators to achieve a better basis to determine how different alternatives contribute to sustainability future (e.g. Nuttal and Young, ibid.).

It must be confessed that accounting principles severely limit the choice of data that can be presented in financial statements. Therefore, some authors speak of accounting, which through communication creates the world (e.g. Hines 1992) and influences a reality that does not exist independently of accounting (Hines 1988).

Changes in accounting standards are really changing the perception of the reality of doing business and thus also possible decisions about a sustainable future.

Management in accounting should reflect decisions in an orientation especially in: planning and organizing accounting process, human resource management (education and motivation), efficient controlling, ethical deciding, advanced information and communication technology, fraud preventing and supporting economic, social and ecological principles.

The main concept of understanding the accountancy as a theory in an organization as considered above is shown in Fig. 9.2 that shows a

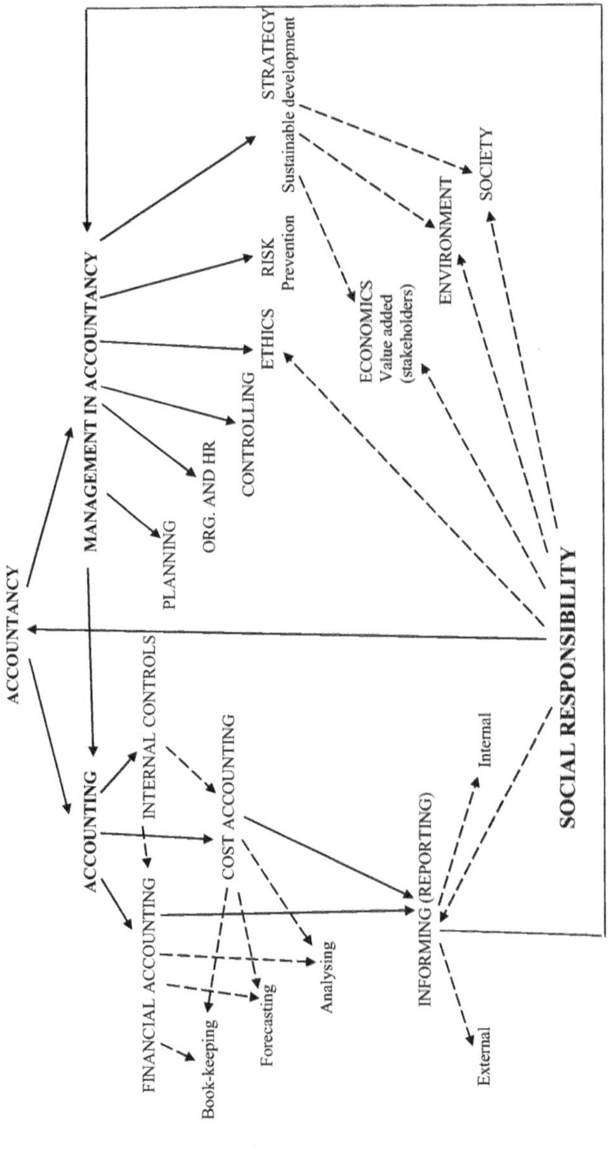

Fig. 9.2 The concept of accountancy theory (*Source* Own research)

comprehensive field of accountancy theory in relation to social responsibility.

In the framework of accounting, Fig. 9.2 shows reporting (internal and external) as the main connection that primarily means taking into account the interests of all stakeholders in an organization.

In the framework of management in accountancy the main connections are ethics (it was discussed in Chapter 8) and strategy that should be directed to sustainable future. It means that the main objective of accountancy to follow should be surplus value added, considering environmental and social issues.

From environmental point of view, accountants cannot ignore ***natural capital*** that is used to increase ***artificial capital***. By depleting natural capital, the environmental crisis develops. This requires further research and development of new accounting approaches (e.g. Hopwood 2009). At the same time, this fact concerns also accountancy ethics (McPhail and Walters 2009, p. 114).

Regarding the social contract theory, it is argued that corporate management seeks to comply with the expectations of society, thereby gaining organizational legitimacy (Jones 2015, p. 517) as a general perception of entity's behavior.

Figure 9.2 shows a relevant contribution of accountancy theory to organization's proper performance and thus to gain wanted image and legitimacy.

Social responsibility aspect of accountancy stems from social responsibility of organization that is important also within the social identity theory and philosophy (Gholami et al. 2012, p. 10111). Socially responsible accountancy includes operating and behaving in both parts of accountancy: accounting and management.

The line from social responsibility to accountancy in Fig. 9.2 shows the fundamental dependence of accountancy as a whole on the principles of social responsibility. These principles apply to both organizations and individuals. Therefore, some of these principles will be discussed in the next chapter.

Figure 9.2 can show also something more. On the first sight one could conclude that the creation and growth of surplus value added are continuous objectives that have no limit but this impression is not accurate. In every system, two opposite processes take place. These are processes of reinforcing (strengthening) and balancing (Hutchens 2001, p. 64). Everybody knows that too much medicine pills is a poison. Sometimes things have to be driven to the absurd to see or prove the wrong direction. In nature, there are numerous examples of strengthening and balancing. Even a man whose weight is constantly growing has increasing problems.

Several examples can be found also in an organization. One of the most important ones is a process of growth that has its limitations. It is common knowledge that a company cannot grow indefinitely. An increase in revenues and value added do not always mean success. It is very likely that growth increases also internal problems in an organization and its processes of entropy. These problems cause a decrease of operating efficiency and diminish organization's contribution to the society welfare.

A contribution to the social welfare is to be therefore a *limited factor* to ensure balanced growth of the organization. At the same time, it is a criterion of its social responsibility. This role of social responsibility is shown also in Fig. 9.2.

These findings are additional reasons to discuss social responsibility in next sections.

9.5 Social Responsibility Aspect

During the last forty years or so, the concept of social responsibility has been transformed from an irrelevant idea to one of widely accepted approaches to understanding business and all global developments.

Understanding and addressing the social responsibility (*SR*) is one of the conditions for shaping and establishing economic democracy toward achieving a sustainable development. The basic justification for the need for economic democracy is already rooted in the fundamental principles of social responsibility. Authors as well as international institutions in many ways define social responsibility. Among them is very important *ISO* standard with its seven principles: responsibility for the impact (accountability), transparency of data, ethical behavior, respect for interests of stakeholders, respect for the rule of law, respect for international norms of behavior and respect for human rights (*ISO* 26000). Here are some other short examples: responsibility for future generations, for workers and human creativity, for income inequality, for governance, for the elderly, for entrepreneurship, for health, for politics and for history.

Social responsibility can be considered as the responsibility of different entities and/or activities (states, communities, business, students, etc.); however, perhaps the biggest focus in the literature is on corporate social responsibility (*CSR*).[4] Such a view is supported by numerous authors (e.g. Wan-Jan 2006, p. 176; Khan et al. 2012; MPRA 2016) several professional editions, especially from Institute for Corporate Culture Affairs (*ICCA*) in its Handbook (ICCA 2006) and A–Z (ICCA 2010). Nevertheless, besides *CSR*, there are individual persons as an important area for considering social responsibility (e.g. Benabou and Tirole 2010; Joseph 2014; Davis et al. 2017). It will be discussed in Sect. 10.5.

Above citations of course, did not exhaust all definitions and aspects of social responsibility in the extensive literature. The existence of a large number of different definitions of social responsibility points to its many aspects and to its importance as well. Therefore, there are also some attempts of systematic approaches to different aspects and taxonomy of social responsibility (e.g. Bergant 2020).

A socially responsible company adjusts its relationship toward its owners, employees, business partners, narrower and broader business, social environment and nature in accordance with the principles of sustainable future. It requires a comprehensive treatment in terms of both internal users (management) and external users of information. Corporate social responsibility should be disconnected from short-term or individual successes, but needs to be understood from a long-term perspective with a forward-looking approach (Idowu and Lauche 2011, p. 265).

Recent understanding of social responsibility considers (Agwuezie 2019, p. 4):

- A new stakeholder approach as opposed to the traditional view of promoting the exclusive interests of stockholders;
- Managerial values and discretion as being key promoters of socially responsible actions and the notion of organizational moral responsibility analogously to that of individuals;
- New aspects in corporate legitimacy;
- Alternatives to the traditional view of corporate governance;
- The role of an interventionist government in enhancing corporate socially responsible behavior.

A paradigm shift is evident: from accountability to shareholders to accountability to stakeholders (Jamali 2008, p. 229; Brooks and Dunn

[4] More definitions of corporate social responsibility see also in Noufe (2016).

2018, p. 508). Yet, today this shift is still not done totally. It can be seen in professional literature[5] and in numerous organizations, but it is far from being seen in the society as a whole. Some obstacles will be discussed in the next section.

9.6 Critical Remarks on Recent Achievements

Despite important development in recent times, there could some weaknesses be found that function as obstacles to further growth, introduction and exercise of social responsibility paradigm.

Firstly, the greatest emphasis seems to be placed on corporate social responsibility. This is understandable, given the importance of this area of human activity and regarding a relatively long period[6] to recognize the impact of corporate social responsibility on profitability and market share of companies. However, there is less attention given to the individuals within the company (employees), thus overlooking their individual interests and needs (Kazmi et al. 2015, p. 755). As a result, there is a bit slower development of social responsibility in other areas of society, e.g. governmental bodies and administration, associations, communities and individual citizens.

Secondly, the most common recommendation of the authors of corporate responsibility is to improve the information in terms of completeness, transparency and accuracy that should reflect the accountability of companies. (e.g. Brooks and Dunn 2018, p. 21). The authors mostly find the rationale for CSR that is based on a moral argument, on a rational argument, or on an economic argument (D'Amato et al. 2009). Different authors and researchers still try to highlight these arguments (e.g. Tsoutsoura 2004, Khan and Majid 2013; Zakari 2017). Boatright claims that "the ***ultimate*** objective of the firm is not shareholders' wealth maximization but maximization of wealth for the whole society" (Boatright 2000, p. 186). "If the value of a firm is taken to be its value as an ongoing entity that is capable of creating wealth for society indefinitely into the future, then managers cannot consider the interests of individual shareholders or

[5] A comprehensive approach is given in Brooks and Dunn (2018, p. 514).

[6] Lee in the year 2008 states thirty years of researches that means about fifty years today (Lee 2008, p. 69).

current stock price, but must take into account the interests of all of the groups that make up the corporation" (Boatright 2000, 190).

"The literature shows that corporate leadership should have a holistic approach to engage with stakeholders and that the vital link between business and stakeholder management is leadership" (Chow 2007). Lord Drayson (Minister of State for Science and Innovation in UK) said "all successful companies must not only create wealth efficiently and sustainably, but increase their value added year on year" (Drayson 2009). Straub claims that socially responsible business can succeed only if it becomes a movement (Straub 2018).

As a rule, such and similar statements and/or recommendations have (and will have also in future) a relatively small effect, so they lack decisive arguments for a change in behavior and action. Adizes states that critics (e.g. World Economic Forum in Davos in 2020) of corporate policy that is directed to shareholders' value are not able to make changes that are needed. Therefore, "new eco-political theories of social responsibility will remain on paper because the power structure—the dynamics of the economic system—has not changed" (Adizes 2020). He even named coronavirus pandemic, as a missed opportunity to make strategic changes that humanity needs to survive (Adizes 2020).

Thirdly, accounting standards still require profit and loss statement (income statement) as basic information of company's performance. International accounting standards (*I*AS) reflect a political consensus that aims to provide the world's capital markets with a common language for financial reporting. International Financial Reporting Standards (*IFRSs*) form the basis of accounting in numerous countries.

Only *GRI* Standards, which in the context of economic disclosures (GRI 2016, Discloser 201-1) speak about ***created economic value***, represent a milder requirement. Created economic value is namely intended for distribution among employees, equity investors, payments to the state, community investment and retained value. However, *GRI* standards remain at the level of recommendations for ***additional*** disclosures to official accounting standards.

It should be noted that all the recommendations and theoretical findings are not enough for decisive changes in defining the basic criteria for business performance. This means that talking today about social responsibility remains still at the level of declarations and recommendations that do not have the decisive force to implement the changes. This will continue until it is generally accepted that profit is not and cannot be fundamental information about an organization's performance.

Fourthly, the recognition of value added as fundamental information of organization's performance is not enough. The value-added law has to be considered. It means that a proper system of distributing value added among all stakeholders, who bear a risk, should be established. Otherwise, the entropy of all organizational systems will grow uncontrollably.

Fifthly, it is not possible to implement the necessary changes without the support of individual countries, which must first implement changes in their operations and thus set an appropriate example. One of these changes is the recognition that the state is also an important stakeholder in companies, due to three aspects:

1. The state bears the risk in the operations of companies, as their poorer performance reduces the tax contribution to the state treasury.
2. At the same time, the state creates the conditions for the operation of companies and thus contributes to their better functioning and reduction of their own tax risk.
3. The state is the most important guardian of the social well-being of all citizens in its broadest sense.

Therefore, the state should not be indifferent toward companies that do not contribute to social well-being. These are companies that do not create surplus added value, as this lowers the overall level of social well-being.

The role of the stakeholder gives the state the right and duty to protect the level of social welfare. Therefore, it can and must intervene in the case of loss-making or negative surplus value added. The state must therefore have the right to demand appropriate explanations from the management and owners of such companies and the preparation of appropriate rehabilitation programs. This does not mean an implementation of a state capitalism, but the timely cessation of negative effects on the level of social welfare. Of course, the state should require the same measures from public companies and other organizations owned by it.

All this, of course, requires appropriate changes in legislation and a lot of political will. However, only in this way can important steps be taken toward the introduction of social responsibility and contribution to a sustainable future.

Sixthly, a contribution to the social welfare is not in general recognized as a growth-limiting factor, ensuring appropriate balance as it was stated in Sect. 9.4. The best description of this balance is the most comprehensive quality of life that depends on education, living conditions, daily activities, opportunities for participation in political process, natural and social environment and factors that affect the economic, social and personal security of people (Aorta Size, Mulej 2020, p. 3).

Seventhly, it must be acknowledged that changes begin with individuals who can and should also influence public policy. The role of science and education is therefore most important for raising their awareness, so the academic sphere cannot escape its responsibility.

Concerning the value-added law, social responsibility can be defined as ***the responsibility of individuals and organizational systems of all forms and levels in the creation and distribution of value added, that is, in increasing the welfare of the whole society.***

Additional role of social responsibility is a criterion for appropriate behavior of organizations or individuals. The role of individual persons is worthy additional discussion in the next section.

9.7 Different Behavior of People

Individuals directly or indirectly manage all organizational systems. Therefore, the key issue is the responsibility of the individual persons and their work in terms of social responsibility. There is no doubt that people are different in their thinking and actions. With these actions is increased or reduced the level of human well-being (social welfare). Therefore, people behave differently in a socially responsible way.

If we want to understand this diversity, we must first ask ourselves about the causes, because only on this basis we can systematically achieve the increase of people's awareness of their social responsibility. This is undoubtedly a complicated task. For the start, it would be useful to see some examples of different people's behavior.

9.7.1 The First Example

The organization (including its stakeholders) is the subsystem of the environment where it operates. Therefore, it assumes a part of the interests of this environment. In exchange, it demands to take over a part of the interests of the organization. The same applies inwardly: The society takes a part of the employees' interests and therefore requires the employees to take part of the interests of the community. Therefore, so-called personal, professional and business ethics are partially overlapping, which can be a source of different ethical dilemmas.

Such dilemmas are the most solvable from the social responsibility of individuals' point of view, which is particularly characteristic of personal ethics. Yet in everyday life we often do not behave according to this principle. Why?

9.7.2 *The Second Example*

It often happens that the behavior of our good acquaintance or even a friend, about whom we have a very good opinion as a person, is so changed that he or she disappoints us when he or she appears in another environment (e.g. on television, in a local community, in a political party, in a new, more responsible job). He or she is the same person, yet behaves and acts differently. Why?

9.7.3 *The Third Example*

Cipolla divided the behavior of individuals into four quadrants depending on whether they work for their own and/or for the common benefit (Cipolla 1988, pp. 49–61):

1. Intelligent people (acting for their own and for the common benefit),
2. Thieves (operating for their own benefit, although to the detriment of the community),
3. Constrained people (acting for the benefit of the community, but to their own detriment),
4. Stupid people (acting at their own detriment and also to the detriment of the community).

Although such a classification is relatively superficial and probably also a scientifically inadequate thesis, we can summarize in particular the following:

- Undoubtedly, different people behave differently in relation to the two judgments shown (own and common benefit);
- The individual can be with his or her particular action (of course, at different times, environments and situations) practically within all of four quadrants, defined by Cipolla.

Most persons would probably want to be in the first quadrant, but all of us are not there. Why?

9.7.4 *The Fourth Example*

Taleb quotes two brothers (Geoff and Vince Graham), who summed up the ludicrousness of political classification like this:

> I am at the Fed level, libertarian,
> at the state level, Republican,
> at the local level, Democrat,
> and at the family's and friends' level, a socialist.

If this saying doesn't convince you of the fatuousness of left vs. right labels, nothing will (Taleb 2018, 61).

However, this is reality in numerous countries. Why?

9.7.5 *The Fifth Example*

People are different and they see the same things differently. There is a connection with the need as a factor that is most influenced by personal viewing of the environment. But there is a need as the most influential factor in personal viewing of the environment. Every human behavior is conditioned by the force in itself.[7] People have obviously different needs and different internal factors. Why?

9.7.6 *The Sixth Example*

Rus wrote visionary some time ago: "The most comprehensive exit from these obstacles is the development of the new morale of all humanity, and the much greater participation of ordinary people in decisions at national

[7] More about it in Green (2018, p. 2).

and global level" (Rus 1976, p. 71). Why is he looking for an exit in the new morality?

We did not find comprehensive answers to the questions in the professional literature. Therefore, we will try to find them below. Namely, a man with analytical thinking is not satisfied with unconvincing answers to questions that begin with the word "Why."

The first answer to the questions asked is the diversity of individual interests. It is quite simple but the answer why we have different interests, is already more demanding. As an appropriate starting point for thinking, there are different needs of individuals, but we have to explain why their needs are different.

It is therefore useful to focus on the basic, fundamental human need, that is, one's existence. On this basis, we have already come up with the creation of a general value-added law (*VAL*), which was explored in Chapter 5.

Despite the clear message of the *VAL* that ethical action is a prerequisite for the existence of humanity, all of us do not act in this sense. Again: Why?

The response of user in a form of behavior in taking decisions can be and should be studied through several possible types or aspects. Greene has found eighteen laws of human nature that illustrate numerous possibilities of human behavior (Greene 2018). All of them are excellently analyzed. Nevertheless, one cannot find the answer to the question: Why there are so many different types of behavior?

It is possible to search for a response in one's sense of risk that shapes the interests of the individual person and forces or motivates him (or her) to act. This process is a relatively complex one. In next section, we will try to study it in a simplified manner.

9.8 Risk as a Red Thread of an Individual's Activity

The process from one's sense of risk to one's performance is shown in Fig. 10.1. Many risks endanger the existence of people, but it is impossible to objectively assess them in their entirety.

This is illustrated in Fig. 9.3 (Bergant 2019, p. 8) as an objective risk state. An individual person may have only a more or less approximate subjective sense of these risks, which is influenced by both received

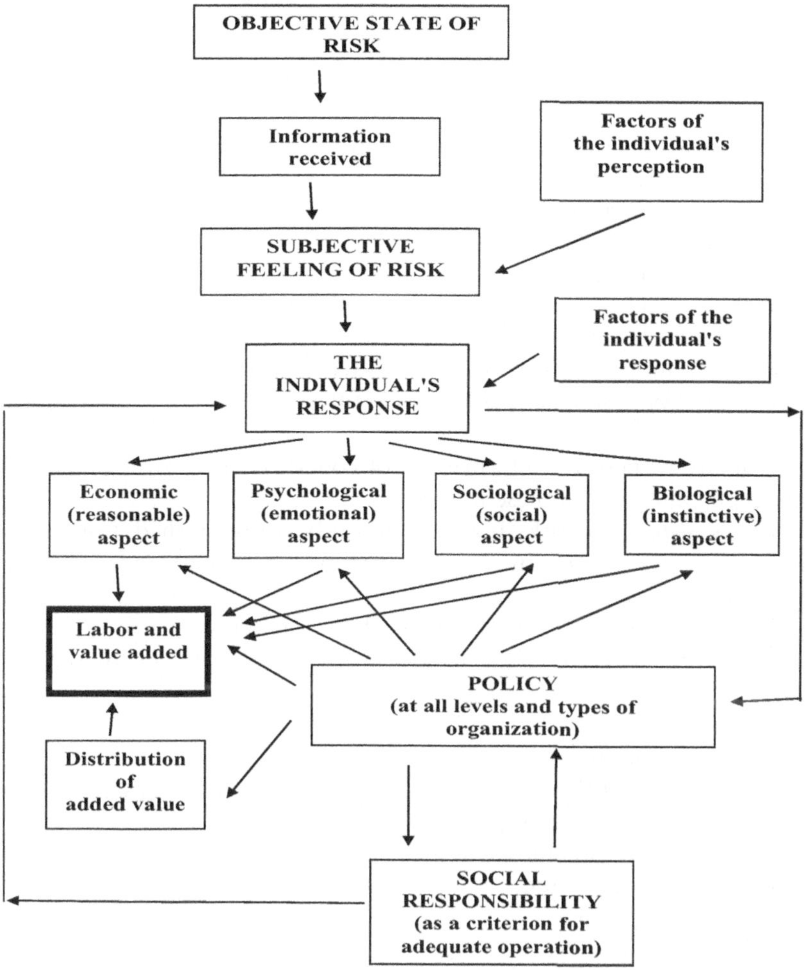

Fig. 9.3 Process from an individual's sense of risk to actions (*Source* Own research)

information and factors that influence his or her ability to perceive and understand this information.

Factors that influence ability to perceive and understand information are numerous. For illustration purposes among them are, in particular:

- genetic characteristics and intellect, or character;
- education and skills;
- values, culture, ethics and norms accepted and practiced;
- spirituality;
- knowledge of the environment and the relationship with the environment;
- material situation and standard of living;
- experiences;
- status and responsibility;
- forms and levels of association or organization (e.g. family, company, different bodies and communities);
- distribution of probability and its "tails" (Taleb 2009, pp. 54–67);
- degree of abstraction (sub-consciousness) and the time dimension.

The ability to perceive information, of course, changes over time, even under the influence of these factors.[8]

One's *sensing* of risk, however, must be distinguished from one's *response* to this feeling. In this way, it is much easier to understand the whole process.

The individual responds to his or her own sense of risk under the influence of many additional factors. To illustrate, we can list them in particular:

- interest and life goals;
- assessment of the costs and benefits in the broadest sense;
- sense of responsibility;
- a sense of exploitation and inequality;
- feeling of neglecting;
- desire for revenge;
- jealousy and envy;
- personality (character) characteristics, pride and ethical norms;
- the degree of flexibility;
- religious belief;
- characteristics of the degree of hierarchy and extent of permitted behavior (competences);

[8] Increasing knowledge, e.g., enhances the ability to perceive the risk, but it does not reduce the sense of risk and sensing in all cases; however, it can even increase it (e.g. Beck 1992).

- the struggle for power and the exploitation of the weaknesses of others;
- competitive advantages and disadvantages;
- age and ambition;
- current position;
- time dimension;
- selection of methods and knowledge of risk assessment;
- different risk assessments (importance, volume and probability);
- knowledge and experience of risk management;
- other characteristic and personality traits of the information user.

In this work, we will not deal more closely with particular factors. They are listed primarily for illustration and justification that, in the same circumstances, two different people usually feel differently, also at the same level of information, and therefore, they respond differently.

The form or content of the response expresses the interest or motive for the performance and behavior of an individual person. The response, of course, can be spontaneous, emotional or rational. It can also be considered from the four aspects shown in Fig. 9.3.

9.8.1 *Biological (Instinctive) Aspect*

This aspect is surely the most natural, original (spontaneous) and therefore also subconscious and accordingly very strong, as it strives for the preservation of the human species.

9.8.2 *Sociological Aspect*

This aspect takes into account that the individual's response to a sense of risk influences the formation of relationships with other people, as well as the anthropological dimension of his or her functioning.

9.8.3 *Psychological Aspect*

This aspect takes into account the emotions and other characteristic features of the individual person, which give an additional dimension to his or her response to the sense of risk. A particular example of this aspect is the response in the form of fear, which can have an extremely strong influence on the performance and behavior of an individual person.

9.8.4 Economic Aspect

This aspect involves the operation of a person, aimed at creating value added in its broadest sense, as a material source for its existence and risk management reserves. It is based on the value-added law with all its consequences and a reason-based risk management (definition, evaluation, avoidance, reduction, redistribution and acceptance). In this context, it will not be superfluous to emphasize the importance of an individual's sufficient accounting literacy, which is necessary in order to be able to make appropriate decisions from an economic and financial points of view.

Within the relationships among reason, emotion and instinct, extreme (even negative) responses are possible, but they must be managed reasonably. In this context, e.g. the environmental activity of preventing and detecting fraud is extremely important.

In Fig. 9.3 the arrows show the connection between the listed economic, psychological, sociological and biological aspects of the response (interest) with the central point (Labor and value added), which is boldly surrounded and shows the total effect of all factors on performance of the individual and thus on the creation of added value.

The policy at all levels and types of organizations and associations of individuals is embedded in all points of the process, which is shown by appropriate arrows. The fundamental responsibility of all types of policies is reflected in particular on the impact on:

- the behavior and activities of individuals;
- the field of labor and its consideration;
- asserting the category of added value as the basic information on sustainable development from an economic point of view;
- starting points and basic criteria for distribution of value added;
- promoting and enforcing the principle of social responsibility in all areas of people's operations.

This is shown in Fig. 9.3 with the corresponding arrows.

The social responsibility of an individual is a reflection of his personal maturity. It is at the same time an obligation to behave properly and the right to cooperate in society. Therefore, social responsibility is a fundamental criterion for the proper response of the individual person. It is shown in Fig. 9.3 with the arrow from Social Responsibility to Individual Response.

Therefore, it represents the responsibility of the individual person to act socially responsibly and to shape politics at all levels and types of organization. This is also shown in Fig. 9.3 with the arrow from Individual Response to Policy.

The feedback loop in Fig. 9.3 (the arrow pointing from Social Responsibility to Policy) emphasizes the social responsibility of policy-makers and policy operators.

Figure 9.3 shows the way a person operates in a risk-dependent manner and provides an opportunity to optimally resolve possible ethical dilemmas in all areas of activity of both the individual and all types of organizations.

Figure 9.3 therefore shows the risk as the red thread of all people's activity, since the risk is their common denominator. It can be a starting point in particular for:

- understanding of the diversity of people and their functioning, and on this basis for empathy to the other people and consequently for better communication;
- easier solving problems and unifying common goals;
- easier policy-making at all levels and types of organizations;
- adequate and objective treatment of the individual (without stereotypes and prejudices);
- easier agreement on basic values, as it confirms ethical action as an integral part of the value-added law;
- effective improvement of the functioning and proper modification of social systems;
- more appropriate evaluation of the performance of individuals and communities;
- effective basis for comprehensive measures to increase the well-being of society and social responsibility (in the economic, social and environmental spheres) and thus to ensure sustainable development.

Many feedback loops in the process from the risk to the performance of an individual show the cybernetic character of the model in Fig. 9.3, which also provides answers to the questions asked in Sect. 9.7. The common denominator of all individual responses is the risk that a person feels and also behaves on these bases. It is the ***fundamental reason*** for the differences in the functioning and behaving of people.

The model does not only provide answers to the question in the introduction, but offers also a basic judgment (criteria) of the adequacy of the behavior and functioning of the individual person. This criterion is the contribution to social well-being or added value in the broadest sense, regardless of the currently environment. This means that this criterion is always the most important one, despite the possible current partial or short-term interests of the individual person or organization.

Although all four aspects are present in an individual person, the structure of their intensity is always completely different. This is the main cause of the different behaving of people.

Figure 9.3 shows that people are and will be different regarding emotions and responses. "Rationality is a subjective phenomenon, since an individual from time to time can be both rational and irrational in reaching decisions" (Ogu 2013, p. 98). "Economic and social theory can advance only if it takes account of historical, cultural and institutional specifics" (Hodgson 2012, p. 104).

The model has also a strong philosophical dimension in terms of people's action and meaning of life. It does not explain only the diversity of people's behavior and actions, but it also gives an answer as to what kind they are supposed to be. The model provides an understanding of today's reality, which, under the influence of neoliberalism, puts us in the face of difficultly solvable problems, such as inequality of people, wars, migrations, dangerous threats to the environment, which pose ever greater risks for the existence of mankind. Moreover, the model redirects postmodern ethics from the delusion of the ideological and idealistic orientation to the Christian goodness of people.

It is not about a naive-optimistic elevation of morality or moralization, but about establishment of the importance of proper action for the sustainable future and existence of mankind. The basic ethical principle, which is already contained in the law of added value, is confirmed, and we quoted it at the beginning of this section. The model therefore gives a theoretical overall basis for the design of appropriate policies at all levels, which should contribute to improving the organization and functioning of social systems, and thus to raising social welfare. Of course, the role and responsibility of individuals in shaping these policies is the most important factor.

The model, under consideration of an innovative approach to making a difference between the individual's ***ability to perceive*** and his or her ***ability to respond*** to the risk, allows for further studies, such as:

- study of influential factors;
- study of the influences of factors and links between them;
- study of individual's responses from different perspectives;
- possibilities of use of the model in individual areas (e.g. studying the efficiency and effectiveness of the information process).

9.9 Individual's Accounting Statements

The outcome of individual's operations is included in the overall operating result of the company as a whole. Therefore, the individual also has his own statement of surplus value added. It has a general form as follows:

1. **EFFECTS**
    a. Revenues
    b. Non-monetized effects on:
        i. complacency;
        ii. family and friends;
        iii. organization or association;
        iv. other people;
        v. broader society.
2. **CONSUMPTION**
    a. Material costs of all goods;
    b. Negative synergies in operation;
    c. The effort to cope with entropy in the group.
3. **CREATED SURPLUS VALUE ADDED (1–2)**
4. **NEGATIVE VALUE ADDED (2–1)**.

Individual person has also personal balance sheet from the social responsibility point of view. It can be in general form as shown in Table 9.1.

Accordingly to Table 9.1, a consolidated balance sheet could be created at higher levels of human associations and of course, a consolidated

Table 9.1 Personal balance sheet

Assets	*Liabilities*
Tangible assets	Financial capital
Patents and licenses	Intellectual capital
Knowledge and skills	Non-material value added
Cash and cash equivalents	Value added of current period
Financial receivables	Financial debts
Other receivables	Other debts
Natural goods	Obligations toward the environment
Spiritual wealth	Obligations toward the society
Emotional intelligence	Obligations toward the family and friends
Total assets	Total liabilities

Source Own research

balance sheet of a total humankind. This may be less useful from a strictly analytical point of view, but it is an important starting point for holistic thinking and awareness that each good has its own source and/or obligation.

Personal accounting statements show that accounting thinking and accounting approach is welcomed also in personal thinking and skills. It helps to see the position of individual person from an additional point of view.

Now is the time to find the role of accountancy theory and practice, which will be done in the next chapter.

Questions for Discussion

9-1 Discuss main starting points to a new concept of accountancy theory.
9-2 Which are basic areas of accountancy theory?
9-3 Discuss advantages and disadvantages of the new concept of accountancy theory.

9-4 How do you see the difference between sustainable development and sustainable future?
9-5 Discuss the role of accounting standards within the process of accountancy development.
9-6 What are main drawbacks of recent accounting theory?
9-7 What is the role and structure of management in the accountancy?
9-8 Discuss the social responsibility of accountancy.
9-9 What is a limiting factor of the company's growth?
9-10 Discuss the stakeholder role of the state.
9-11 Discuss different definitions of social responsibility.
9-12 Discuss the possibility of shifting from accountability to shareholders, to accountability to stakeholders.
9-13 Why are today's discussions about social responsibility becoming similar to philanthropy?
9-14 What is the basic prerequisite for social responsibility not to be on the level of declarations anymore?
9-15 How would you substantiate the state as an important stakeholder in organizations?
9-16 How would you define social responsibility in connection to value-added law?
9-17 Discuss the universal criterion for appropriate behavior of organizations and people.
9-18 Why people behave and think differently?
9-19 Why is it important to distinguish one's ability to perceive and ability to respond to the risk?
9-20 What is the red thread of all people activities and behaving?
9-21 Do you find personal accounting statements useful?

References

Adizes, Ichak (2020). *Why We Are NOT Socially Responsible*. Adizes blogs. Adizes Institute: July 3, 2020. https://www.ichakadizes.com/post/why-we-are-not-socially-responsible.

Agwuezie, O. Remi (2019). *The Concept of Corporate Social Responsibility*. (Retrieved: July, 2020). https://www.academia.edu/38797711/THE_CONCEPT_OF_CORPORATE_SOCIAL_RESPONSIBILITY.

Al-Adeem, K. Rasheed (2010). *Accounting Theory: A Neglected Topic in Academic Accounting Research.* Doctoral dissertation. Cleveland: Case Western Reserve University.

Beck, Ulrich (1992). *Risk Society.* London: Sage.

Benabou, Roland, Tirole, Jean (2010). Individual and Corporate Social Responsibility. (Retrieved: July, 2020). https://www.researchgate.net/publication/48264162_Individual_and_Corporate_Social_Responsibility.

Bergant, Živko (2019). The Quality of Accounting Information and User's Social Responsibility: Social Aspect. *International Journal of Advances in Management and Economics.* (Retrieved: December, 2019). http://www.managementjournal.info/index.Php/IJAME/article/view/617/514.

Bergant, Živko (2020). Starting Points to Comprehensive Treatment of Social Responsibility. *International Journal of Advances in Management and Economics*, Vol. 9. No. 1, pp. 1–7.

Bergant, Živko (2021). Accountancy Information System for Sustainable Future. *International Journal of Latest Research in Humanities and Social Science (IJLRHSS)*, Vol. 4, No. 1, pp. 01–07.

Boatright, J. John (2000). *Ethics and the Conduct of Business.* Hoboken, NJ: Prentice-Hall Inc.

Brooks, J. Leonard, Dunn, Paul (2018). *Business and Professional Ethics for Directors, Executives & Accountants.* 8th Edition. Bosron: Cangage Learning.

Byars, M. Stephen, Stanberry, Kurt (2018). *Business Ethics.* Houston, Openstax.

Chow, Hoi Hee (2007) Aholistic approach to business management. *Singapore management Review*, Vol. 29, No. 1, pp. 73–84.

Cipolla, M. C. (1988). *Allegro ma non troppo.* Bologna: Societá editrice il Mulino.

Communities Scotland (2006). Making the Case: Social Added Value Guide. (Retrieved: May, 2020). http://www.forthsectordevelopment.org.uk/documents/Making%20the%20case%20-%20SAV%20guide.pdf.

D'Amato, Alessia, Henderson, Sybil, Florence, Sue (2009). *Corporate Social responsibility and Sustainable Business.* Greensboro: Center for Creative Leadership.

Davis, López S., et al. (2017). Introducing Personal Social Responsibility as a Key Element to Upgrade CSR. *Spanish Journal of Marketing – ESIC*, Vol. 21, No. 2, pp. 146–163.

Democratizingwork (2020). Work: Democratize, Decomodify, Remediate. (Retrieved: July, 2020). https://democratizingwork.org/.

Drayson, Paul (2009). The 2009 Value Added Scoreboard. The Top 800 and 750 European Companies by Value Added. BIS, Department for innovation & Skills, UK. http://webarchive.Nationalarchives.gov.uk/20100908131539/http://innovation.gov.uk/value_added/downloads/2009_ValueAdded_Analysis.pdf.

Freeman, R. Edward, Harrison, Jeffrey, Hicks, Andrew, Parmar, Bidhan, Simone de Cole (2010). *Stakeholder Theory: The State of the Art*. Cambridge: Cambridge University Press.

Gholami, Sajad, et al. (2012). Social Responsibility Accounting: From Theory to Practice. *Journal of Basis and Applied Scientific Research*, Vol. 2, No. 10.

Godfrey, Jayne, Hodgson, Allan, Tarca, Ann, Hamilton, Jane, Holmes, Scott (2019). *Accounting Theory*. 7th Edition. Milton: Willey.

Gould, Stathis (2019). *Building Data Science and Analytics Capabilities in Finance and Accounting*. (Retrieved: July, 2020). https://www.ifac.org/knowledge-gateway/preparing-future-ready-professionals/discussion/building-data-science-and-analytics-capabilities-finance-and-accounting (*IFAC* Knowledge Gateway).

Greene, Robert (2018). *The Laws of Human Nature*. New York: Penguin Random House LLC.

GRI (2015). Global Reporting Initiative. Informing Decisions, Driving Change: The Role of Data in a Sustainable Future. (Retrieved: June, 2020). https://www.globalreporting.org/resourcelibrary/Informing-decisions,-driving-change-The-role-of-data-in-a-sustainable-future.pdf.

GRI Standards (2016). Consolidated Set of *GRI* Sustainability Reporting Standards 2016. (Retrieved: May, 2020). http://www.ekvilib.org/wp-content/uploads/2018/03/GRI-standardi-2016.pdf.

GRI (2016, Discloser 201-1). *GRI* 201: Economic Performance. (Retrieved: July, 2020). http://www.ekvilib.org/wp-content/uploads/2018/03/GRI-standardi-2016.pdf#page=90&zoom=100,0,0.

Hendriksen, Eldon (1965). *Accounting Theory*. Homewood: Richard D. Irwin, Inc.

Hines, D. Ruth (1988). Financial Accounting: in Communicating Reality, We Construct Reality. *Accounting, Organization and Society*, Vol. 13, No. 3, pp. 251–261.

Hines, D. Ruth (1992). *Accounting: In Communicating a World, We Create a World.*. Doctoral dissertation. Lancaster University, 1992.

Hodgson, M. Geoffrey (2012). On the Limits of Rational Choice Theory. *Economic Thought* No. 1/2012, pp. 94–108.

Hopwood, G Anthony (2009). Accounting and the Environment. *Accounting, Organization and Society*, Vol. 34, No. 3–4, pp. 433–439.

Hutchens, David (2001). *The Tip of the Iceberg*. Waltham: Pegasus Communications, Inc.

ICCA (2006). *The ICCA Handbook on Corporate Social Responsibility*. Chichester: Wiley.

ICCA (2010). *The A to Z of Corporate Social Responsibility*. Chichester: Wiley.

Idowu, O. Samuel, Louche, Céline, Edit. (2011). *Theory and Practice of Corporate Social Responsibility*. Heidelberg: Springer.

Jamali, Dima (2008). A Stakeholder Approach to Corporate Social Responsibility: Afresh Perspective into Theory and Practice. *Journal of Business Ethics*, Springer, Vol. 82, No. 1, pp. 213–231. (Retrieved: July, 2020). https://www.academia.edu/15824941/A_Stakeholder_Approach_to_Corporate_Social_Responsibility_A_Fresh_Perspective_into_Theory_and_Practice.

Jones, Stewart (2015). *The Routledge Companion to Financial Accounting Theory*. New York: Routledge.

Joseph, Augustine (2014). The Need of Personal Responsibility and Integrity in Corporate Social Responsibility Theories. *International Journal of Recent Advances in Organizational Behavior and Decision Sciences*, Vol. 1, No. 1, pp. 45–67.

Kazmi, B. Ali, Leca, Bernard, Naccachew, Philippe (2015). Is Corporate Social Responsibility a New Spirit of Capitalism? *Organization*, Vol. 23, No. 5, pp. 742–762. (Retrieved: June, 2020). https://www.researchgate.net/publication/288021009_Is_corporate_social_responsibility_a_new_spirit_of_capitalism.

Kempner, J. Jack (1968). The Basic Concepts of Accounting. *Montana Law Review*, Vol. 30, No.1, pp. 1–17.

Khan, Majid, Majid, Abdul (2013). The Effect of Corporate Social Responsibility on Profitability and Market Share: A Case of Cement Industry of Pakistan. *Academic Journal of Management Sciences*, Vol. 2, No. 1, pp. 44–62.

Khan, T. Muhammad, et al. (2012). Corporate Social responsibility (CSR) – Definition, Concepts and Scope (A Review). *Universal Journal of Management and Social Sciences*, Vol. 2, No. 7, pp. 41–51.

KPMG. (2020). *The Social Contact in the 21st Century*. McKinsey Global Institute. (Retrieved: June, 2020). https://www.mckinsey.com/~/media/McKinsey/Industries/Social%20Sector/Our%20Insights/The%20social%20contract%20in%20the%2021st%20century/MGI-The-social-contract-in-the-21st-century-Executive-summary-final.pdf.

Lee, P. Min-Dong (2008). A Review of the Theories of Corporate Social Responsibility: Its Evolutionary Path and the Road Ahead. *International Journal of Management Reviews*, Vol. 10, No. 1, pp. 53–73.

McPhail, Ken, Walters, Diane (2009). *Accounting and Business Ethics*. London: Routledge.

Miller, Peter (1998). The Margins of Accounting. *European Accounting Review*, Vol. 7, No. 4, pp. 605–621.

MPRA (2016). Corporate Social Responsibility: A Review on Definitions, Core Characteristics and Theoretical Perspectives. *Mediterranean Journal of Social Science*, Vol. 6, No. 4, pp. 63–95.

Mulej, Matjaž (2020). *Sustainable Future Concept vs. Sustainable Development After 15 years (Remembering Timi Ečimović, 1941–2018)*. (Retrieved: June,

2020). 15th IRDO International Science and Business Conference. June, 2020, Maribor. http://www.irdo.si/irdo2020/referati.html.

Munasinghe, Mohan (2007). Sustainable Development Triangle. (Retrieved: May, 2020). https://editors.eol.org/eoearth/wiki/Sustainomics_and_sustainable_development.

Noufe, Daniel (2016). Corporate Social Responsibility and Financial Performance: A Literature Review. (Retrieved: July, 2020). https://www.academia.edu/32452298/Corporate_Social_Responsibility_and_profitability.

Nuttall, Douglas, Young, Lay (2017). Building the Framework for Absolute Sustainability. *OIDA International Journal of Sustainable Development, Canada*, Vol. 10, No. 11, pp. 11–32.

Obama, Barack (2012). Remarks by the President at the Associated Press Luncheon. (Retrieved: Julij, 2020). https://obamawhitehouse.archives.gov/the-press-office/2012/04/03/remarks-president-associated-press-luncheon.

Ogu, I. Michael (2013). Rational Choice Theory: Assumptions, Strengths, and Greatest Weaknesses in Application outside the Western Milieu Context. *Arabian Journal of Business and Management Review* (*Nigerian Chapter*), Vol. 1, No. 3, pp. 90–99.

Organicsoul (2020). Understanding the Triple Bottom Line, Its Shortcomings, and the Solution. (Retrieved: May, 2020). http://www.organicsoul.com/understanding-the-triple-bottom-line-its-shortcomings-and-the-solution/.

Rus, V. (1976). *Etika in Socializem* (In Slovene). Ljubljana: Mladinska knjiga.

Schaltegger, Stefan, Bennet, Martin, Burrit, Roger (2006). *Sustainability Accounting and Reporting*. Dordrecht: Springer.

Scott, R. William, O'Brien, C. Patricia (2019). *Financial Accounting Theory*. Toronto, ON: Pearson Canada Inc.

Širovnik, David (2016). Sinthesis of Sustainable Systems by Maximizing Sustainable Net Present Value. (In Slovene). *Sinteza sistemov z maksimiranjem trajnostne neto sedanje vrednosti*. Master's Thesis. Maribor. (Retrieved: April, 2020). https://dk.um.si/Dokument.php?id=105690.

Smyth, Danielle (2018). What Are the Basic Accounting Theories? (Retrieved: January. 2020). https://bizfluent.com/about-5121481-basic-accounting-theories.html.

Soonawalla, Kazbi (2006). *Contemporary Issues in Management Accounting*. Oxford: Oxford University Press.

Stiglitz, E. Joseph, Fitoussi, Jean-Paul, Durand, Martine (2018). *For Good Measure: Advancing Research on Well-being Metrics Beyond GDP*. Paris: *OECD* Publishing.

Suojanen, W. W. (1954). Accounting Theory and the Large Corporation. *The Accounting Review*, Julij, 1954, pp. 618–629.

Taleb, N. Nicholas (2009). Errors, Robustness, and the Fourth Quadrant. *International Journal of Forecasting*, Vol. 25, pp. 744–759.

Taleb, N. Nassim (2018). *Skin in the Game: Hidden Asymmetries in Daily Life*. New York: Random House.

Tsoutsoura, Margarita (2004). Corporate Social Responsibility and Financial Performance. (Retrieved: July, 2020). https://escholarship.org/uc/item/111799p2.

Unegbu, O. Angus (2014). Theories of Accounting: Evolution & Developments, Income-Determination and Diversities in Use. *Research Journal of Finance and Accounting*, Vol. 5, No. 19, 2014. (Retrieved: January, 2020). https://arxiv.org/abs/1411.4633.

Valvassori, Antonella, Vaccari, Vittorio (2009). Sustainability Report: Present Status and Future. (Retrieved: may, 2020). https://www.researchgate.net/publication/265676522_SUSTAINABILITY_REPORT_PRESENT_STATUS_AND_FUTURE

Vovk Korže, ana (2020). Understanding Sustainability Today. 15th IRDO International Science and Business Conference. June, 2020, Maribor. (Retrieved: June, 2020). http://www.irdo.si/irdo2020/referati.html.

Wan-Jan, W. Saitfuk (2006). Defining Corporate Social Responsibility. *Journal of Public Affairs*, Vol. 6, August–November, 2006.

Zakari, Murtala (2017). The Relationship Between Corporate Social Responsibility and Profitability: The Case of Dangote Cement Plc. *Journal of Finance and Accounting*, Vol. 5, No. 4, pp. 171–176.

CHAPTER 10

The Role and Position of Accountancy

The reflections so far in all previous chapters make it possible to find the position of accountancy in relation to social responsibility and to a sustainable future.

Firstly, it is necessary to change the notions about the *sustainable future* that was discussed in Sect. 9.4, to *sustainable society*. This notion better reflects an objective and its content that is not postponed to the not exactly defined future but is understandable and means a better starting point to measure its achievement. Besides, such a notion is mentioned according the basic human need (existence of an individual) that is fundamental starting point of value-added law. Namely, sustainable society can be defined as a sum of all people with their needs and includes all synergies based on their interdependence and cooperation. At the same time, it includes a precondition of sustainability that means also appropriate safeness of people.

In short, a sustainable society is not a "no-growth" society—it is rather a society that recognizes the limits of growth and looks for alternative means of improvement. Human development is not about having more, but about being more. It means a quality of life instead of the quantity of things (Mulej 2020). "What really counts in life money can't buy" (Hoffer 2020).

Ž. Bergant, *Accountancy and Social Responsibility*,
Palgrave Studies in Impact Finance,
https://doi.org/10.1007/978-3-030-77928-3_10

Šarotar Žižek and Mulej have exposed the foreseen path to the establishment of society welfare. This path is based on several characteristics that can be also main characteristics of sustainable society (Šarotar Žižek and Mulej 2020):

1. Preserving nature
2. Happy, personally and socially responsible, respected, content and satisfied people
3. State-of-the-art technology
4. Happy family
5. The participation of people
6. Long-term business success
7. Responsible owners
8. Socially responsible values, culture, ethics and norms
9. Thoughtful consumerism
10. Diversity management
11. Universal basic income
12. Solidarity
13. Free time and leisure
14. Systems/orders (e.g. political, legal, economic, social, health)
15. Democracy.

Above defined sustainable society can play an important role as a fundamental objective of people for their functioning and behavior.

Secondly, it is necessary to consider that every objective has three dimensions: its *setting* after appropriate discussion (governmental and/or managerial aspect), *criteria* of appropriate decisions and performance (analytical aspect) and *information* that allow monitoring the achievements (information aspect).

It can be illustrated for the purpose of sustainable society as shown in Fig. 10.1.

Sustainable society on the *top of the triangle* is a final consensus in the society about its fundamental objective. Its main characteristic is that it is horizontal goal that suits to big majority of society members. It is also a moving goal that follows changes in a society.

The adopted goal requires the definition of a *criterion* that notes the situation in relation to the goal and thus provides a basis for appropriate planning, decision-making and behavior of members of society. The

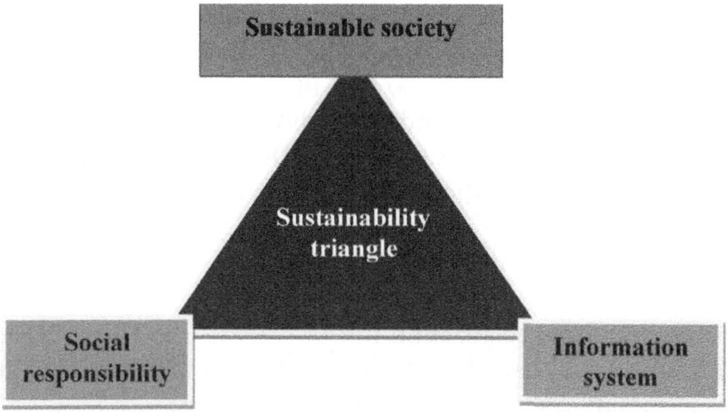

Fig. 10.1 Sustainability triangle (*Source* Own research [Bergant 2021, 4])

main criterion for achieving sustainability and effectiveness in society is social responsible behaving that according to its fundamental definition reflects in contributions of individuals and organizations of all forms and levels to the well-being of the whole society.[1] This second aspect shows that a criterion and a precondition for sustainable society are important characteristics of social responsibility.

Determining the criteria in more detail is a common task of the user and the analyst, but it must be based on the value added to be requisitely holistic. In the opposite case (e.g. profit based), an entropy in business system increases as a result value-added law.

The third corner of the triangle means the information system that is relevant for the design and implementation of the strategy to achieve the objective and which show and explains the deviations from the planned goals. Every information system is "a source of power" and has crucial role on all decisions, activities and the development of democratic society. It includes also nonfinancial information (e.g. Baumüller and Schaffhauser 2018).

The main important part of such information system is of course accountancy, which is dealt in detail in Sect. 9.4 and illustrated in Fig. 9.2. It can be seen that accountancy is, as a source and reflection of social responsibility, also a prerequisite for achieving sustainable

[1] More about well-being metrics in Stiglitz et al. (2018).

society by deriving and developing relevant information for decision-making process. It is also shown in Fig. 10.1. The role of the head of accountancy is therefore similar to that of a navigator on board of a ship on the high seas. Ratnatunga and Alam show that extensive management accounting backgrounds of CEOs and CFOs ensure the significant use of accounting information in the governance process (Ratnatunga and Alam 2011, p. 373).

Relevant information is mainly intended for:

1. management of organization for:
   - decision-makings at all levels of organization, business functions and responsibility centers to achieve business goals;
   - internal governance bodies (e.g. employees' ownership);
   - measuring organization's performance for the needs of motivation system;
   - measuring organization's social value (e.g. Eurodiaconia 2016);
   - fraud prevention and assets protection;
2. Other internal users (e.g. internal control bodies, employees and unions).
3. External users (e.g. ownership bodies, investors, creditors and business partners, state authorities).

Each of the three aspects presented in Fig. 10.1 represents a specific area of topics that are closely related to each other, but each area has its own logic and thus its own way of development. Each aspect has its own deeper theoretical and practical dimensions. Some of them were discussed in Chapters from 3–9. A harmony among these three aspects represents *an ideal of sustainable society*. Sustainability triangle illustrates a harmony of relationships among its angles; therefore, it is an equilateral triangle.

This ideal position presents an ultimate objective of human activities in long-term and should be continuously implemented and maintained. Activities that cause or increase a disharmony in the sustainability triangle can be assumed as not socially responsible. However, still today, a harmony inside sustainability triangle is not yet achieved. It cannot be achieved without deep changes in accounting system (Gray and Bebbington 2000; Gray and Milne 2002) and without understanding the content of sustainability triangle as well.

The sustainability triangle can be viewed as the underside (foundation) of the *sustainability pyramid* as well. The top of pyramid represents the main characteristic of social society: social well-being, as an ultimate goal that is supported through implementing and maintaining the sustainability triangle.[2] For individual person, the top of pyramid can be the feeling of happiness or satisfaction.

The interior of the sustainability pyramid is subject to constant changes and entropy processes. All human actions should be aimed at striving to use the synergies to establish and maintain harmony within the sustainability triangle. In this way, we would also improve the level of well-being of society.

Figure 10.1 shows also a position and most important role of accountancy in supporting activities to function according to social responsibility. In this way, its fundamental principles are considered in order to achieve goals of sustainable society.

Accountancy, on the one hand, derives from the basic needs of people (value-added law), and on the other hand, enables appropriate decision-making to meet these needs. This means that accountancy as a theory and practice is woven into the foundations of the philosophical, psychological, sociological and other social sciences. Hence is derived the great (social) responsibility of accountancy theory as a science and at the same time the (social) responsibility of accountancy professionals in practice.

This responsibility primarily lies in the academic field that must recognize its role in social development. Academics in accountancy are the ones who have to provide and formulate the information and explain it properly and present it convincingly. This poses a major challenge for further work on the development of accountancy and reporting, but it must be independent of the many current economic and financial models, which no longer have a place in Fig. 10.1. Recognizing this role of accountancy is the first important stage in its development toward a relevant, socially engaged science.

Questions for Discussion

10-1 How do you understand sustainable society?
10-2 What dimensions has every objective?
10-3 Discuss sustainability triangle.

[2] In Christian religion, the sustainability pyramid can be compared by the doctrine of the Holy Trinity (Father, Son and Holy Spirit) as three persons in one Godhead.

10-4 What is the main criterion for achieving sustainability in society?
10-5 Why profit based information increase an entropy in business system?
10-6 Explain the role of information system in the sustainable triangle.
10-7 What is the role and intention of accountancy in the information system?
10-8 Explain connections between three aspects and harmony inside of sustainability triangle.
10-9 How do you understand the sustainability pyramid?
10-10 What is going on inside the sustainability pyramid?
10.11 What represents the top of sustainability pyramid?
10.12 Describe the role of the accountancy theory regarding sustainability pyramid:

References

Baumüller, Josef, Schaffhauser-Linzatti, Michaela-Maria (2018). In Search of Materiality for Nonfinancial Information-Reporting Requirements of the Directive 2014/95/EU. (Retrieved: July, 2020). https://www.researchgate.net/publication/326997551_In_search_of_materiality_for_nonfinancial_information-reporting_requirements_of_the_Directive_201495EU.

Bergant, Živko (2021). Accountancy Information System for Sustainable Future.

Eurodiaconia (2016). *Measuring Social Value*. (Retrieved: July, 2020). https://cmsimpact.org/wp-content/uploads/2016/01/Eurodiaconia-Measuring-Social-Value.pdf.

Gray, Rob, Bebbington, Jan (2000). Environmental Accounting, Managerialism and Sustainability: Is the Planet Safe in the Hands of Business and Accounting? (Retrieved: October, 2020). https://www.st-andrews.ac.uk/media/csear/discussion-papers/CSEAR_dps-sustain-envaccman.pdf.

Gray, Rob, Milne, J. Markus (2002). Sustainability Reporting: Who's Kidding Whom? (Retrieved: October, 2020). https://cgi.st-andrews.ac.uk/media/csear/discussion-papers/CSEAR_dps-sustain-whoskidding.pdf.

Hoffer, Frank (2020). *Beyond "Green Growth"*. Social Europe. (Retrieved: July, 2020). https://www.socialeurope.eu/beyond-green-growth.

Mulej, Matjaž (2020). *Sustainable Future Concept vs. Sustainable Development After 15 years (Remembering Timi Ečimović, 1941–2018)*. (Retrieved: June, 2020). 15th IRDO International Science and Business Conference. June, 2020, Maribor. http://www.irdo.si/irdo2020/referati.html.

Ratnatunga, Janek, Alam, Manzurul (2011). Strategic Governance and Management Accounting: Evidence from a Case Study. *ABACUS, Journal of Accounting, Finance and Business Studies*, Vol. 47, No. 3, pp. 343–382.

Šarotar Žižek, Simona, Mulej, Matjaž (2020). Society & Welfare. (Retrieved: July, 2020). http://www.irdo.si/irdo2020/referati/a2-1-sarotarzizek&mulej.pdf.

Stiglitz, E. Joseph, Fitoussi, Jean-Paul, Durand, Martine (2018). *For Good Measure: Advancing Research on Well-being Metrics Beyond GDP.* Paris: *OECD* Publishing.

CHAPTER 11

Summaries of Findings and Main Points

Taking into account the relatively complex discussion in the whole work, a summary of the major findings may be useful for the reader to get a brief overview of the content. It will be done following the red thread of the whole work.

* * *

To highlight a relationship between accounting and social responsibility and also the relationship between accounting and accountancy in an organization should be defined. Accountancy has a broader notion and presents an accounting information system that includes accounting as its subset and management in accountancy according to Fig. 2.2. Using the partial system approach, it is possible to differentiate organization's management and accountancy management through the difference of their tasks and responsibilities. At the same time, it is possible to make a difference between accounting department as an organization's unit and the accountancy function that is interwoven through the whole organization.

* * *

Ž. Bergant, *Accountancy and Social Responsibility*,
Palgrave Studies in Impact Finance,
https://doi.org/10.1007/978-3-030-77928-3_11

The main process of accounting (from data to an information) is discussed separately from other particular accounting processes. The information is a result of cooperation between the designer and the user of information that means a significant impact of users on the quality of information system. The accounting information functions (book-keeping, forecasting, analyzing and controlling) are studied from partial systems' (managerial, informational and operational) point of view.

* * *

A difference between creating accounting information and accounting reporting is emphasized. The last one is discussed through four aspects (managerial, informational, operational and quality). Some important delusions in current financial analysis in theory and practice are shown. Quality of reporting is divided into its efficiency and effectiveness. The quality of decision-making depends not only on the quality of information but also on the user's response. Appropriate user's response shows the quality of reporting.

* * *

A sense of threat to existence is the origin of basic human needs. It is transformed into the right to work. For incapacitated people it is transformed to their *right to solidarity*. Human work in a broader sense creates the value added that means an increase of welfare of people and presents also a source of reserves for risk management. Value added reflects the social utility of a system and is a prerequisite for its long-term survival. Therefore, it is main information from long-term view. Value added should be understood in its broader sense as its contribution to the well-being of society. From the above considerations, the general value-added law is formulated. It has its own creative and distributive dimensions that work regardless of the socio-economic system or human history and in all types of organizations. Value-added law requires the distribution of value added between all stakeholders that bear risk according to their work contribution. In opposite, the inequality is devastating and the entropy of the system increases.

* * *

Basic labor costs as a compensation for partly wasting work force and opportunity cost of capital are not included in ***surplus value added*** as a new category that really means newly created value in an organization. Surplus value added presents a value that has to be distributed to stakeholders that contribute to organization's risk management.

* * *

Surplus value added, as the most important outcome of an organization, requires its particular accounting statement. The surplus value-added statement shows creation and distribution of surplus value added and takes into account the equality of stakeholders. It is an integral part of an integral reporting and presents a basis for analyzing of organization's performance and its economics with new data and indicators.

* * *

A new general model for value-added-based management is offered. It is directed to achieve triple bottom line and sustainable development through creating the volume and the structure of surplus value added for organization's stakeholders. It includes ethics, risk management and quality management. All elements of intellectual capital should be considered. Employees, as the owners of human capital, are bearers of the intellectual capital (they revive it through their work), which the company must maintain and increase. They are also holders of long-term interests and legitimate contributors to an organization's monitoring and controlling system including the role of trade union.

* * *

Organization's financial policy is important mostly in decisions regarding long-term investments, and establishing and maintaining an adequate structure for financing the operations (capital adequacy of the organization). A model of a comprehensive financial policy is offered. It uses ethical principles in value-added law instead of trade-off theory and alike.

* * *

Ethical dilemmas in accountancy are deeply discussed. Firstly, there is no place for the shy treatment of value-added statement in accounting standards. In this direction, the responsibility of the accounting profession and accounting professionals is not negligible. Second task is to achieve changes in tax legislation regarding the elimination of interest as a deductible item from the organization's tax base. Next ethical task is to achieve better quality of accounting information through higher efficiency and the effectiveness of reporting. A comprehensive model of ethics in the management of accountancy is offered as well. There are not several *types* of ethics, but there is always only one type of ethics: ***personal ethics***. Therefore, business and professional ethics represent two partial systems (and not subsystems) of personal ethics, where a social well-being is a fundamental criterion of ethical conduct. The ethical aspect is closely linked to the notion of accountability. Therefore, a comprehensive meaning of accountability is emphasized and shown in a table.

* * *

Drivers of accounting process development are information needs and information technology. In this framework a development of accounting department and its tasks are discussed.

* * *

There are several discussions about accounting theory and its development. Based on the shortcomings of recent theories and on the implementation of better understanding of accountancy, the concept of comprehensive accountancy theory is offered. It is based on a surplus value added as a common denominator for all objectives in all organizations. It includes three basic areas: principles and rules of accounting process, principles and rules of management in accountancy, and accountancy system, regarding its tangible and intangible resources. It is emphasized that the right way for accountancy development is its social responsibility.

* * *

Several critical remarks on recent social responsibility theory and practice are emphasized. Among them are: slower development of social responsibility in other areas of society comparing corporate area, a relatively small effect in practice, wrong direction of accounting standards (in profit and not in value added), lack of system about the distribution of value added, etc. On a value-added basis, a broader definition of social responsibility is offered: the responsibility of individuals and organizational systems of all forms and levels in the creation and distribution of added value that is, in increasing the welfare of the whole society.

* * *

Special attention is given to the role of individual person in overall social responsibility. The main conclusion is that the behavior of an individual depends on the individual's ability of feeling the risk and its response to that feeling. This response could be regarded from biological, sociological, psychological and economic points of view. The social responsibility of an individual is a reflection of his personal maturity. It is at the same time an obligation to behave properly and the right to cooperate in society. Therefore, social responsibility is a fundamental criterion for the proper response of the individual person. It is shown also through a proposal of individual's accounting statements that could be transformed also to higher levels of society.

* * *

The notion of sustainable development is developed to the notion of sustainable future and finally to the notion of sustainable society. The main role and the position of accountancy theory and practice are found and depicted in the sustainability triangle among sustainable society, social responsibility and information system. The sustainability triangle is defined as a foundation of sustainability pyramid with the society well-being as a main goal at the top.

Accountancy as the main part of information system should support socially responsible decisions to become a precondition for achieving and maintained sustainable society. Recognizing accountancy role in sustainability triangle is the first important stage in further development of accountancy into a relevant, socially engaged science.

Such recognition would have important consequences on the development in other social sciences and on the socio-economic system as a whole. In this way, the humankind could make an important step toward the sustainable society. It confirms the role of accountancy that is discussed through this work.

> It is not enough to be reasonable
> if people are unreasonable.

CHAPTER 12

Who Should Do What?

The biggest challenge, without a doubt, lies in the academic sphere and education system. This is called first of all to a unified view on accountancy theory, which should also be the basis for changing the general perception of relations in society. This may seem like an illusion today, but an important argument is available. It is a recognition of the operation of the general value-added law, which does not depend on ideological assumptions or individual interests. We can see the consequences of its actions today and in the entire history of mankind. It is not difficult to identify dissatisfaction with the situation around the world. This is also reflected in the search for a new world order (e.g. Block 2018, p. 167) and appeals for "a decent life for all" (e.g. Stiglitz 2019, p. 209). To date, no declarations and calls for fairness have helped. Only the value-added law shows an alternative: either we will consider it or not. The latter means further growth of entropy in the world and the worst future for the next generations. This, of course, also means socially irresponsible behavior.

It follows from the above that politicians and politics have a great responsibility to take science and the profession into account in moving toward a sustainable society and to protect future generations. Policy change is always (or should be) the result of changes in people's expectations and demands. These changes can only be realized by a changed education system, for which, again, the academic sphere is responsible.

Ž. Bergant, *Accountancy and Social Responsibility*,
Palgrave Studies in Impact Finance,
https://doi.org/10.1007/978-3-030-77928-3_12

Academics need to shake off their possible apologetic roles and expose their independent thinking and suggestions.

Nevertheless, the most important factor in implementing changes is the state (in its broadest sense), since it defines the fundamental legal order and, in this context, also the basic conditions for the operation of business systems. This has a decisive influence on the manifestations of the general operation of the value-added law in business systems.

The most important task of the state is to ensure the safeness and well-being of citizens in the broadest sense. To perform this task, the state collects taxes and therefore provides appropriate services. By drafting the legal order, the state creates opportunities for the formation of different types of groups, with the fundamental purpose of achieving the safety and well-being of individuals from their perspective.

The success of every state in carrying out its fundamental task is reflected in the relative reduction of the number of poor people and people at the border of their chances of survival. From this point of view, we cannot generally speak of the success of states, which needs not even be mentioned, as statistics and surveys show, to confirm this fact. This confirms the growing need for increased operating range of charitable organizations. Therefore, in their own way they act to mitigate the negative effects of malfunctioning of the state. However, they must not become a cover for the poor functioning of the state on long-term.

One of the often forgotten stakeholders that could require changes in information system are trade unions. They should be ultimate bearers of long-term interests and control in organizations. However, they often forget about their power and still more often do not direct it properly. They should be better aware of their social responsibilities and become an important driver of changes.

There are of course enormous obstacles at all levels of the society. Mason has emphasized one of them: "What characterizes the present moment of history is a pervasive sense of unrealism among elites" (Mason 2019). I am afraid that this is not a disease only among elites. I believe only in one thing: we will go to our own funeral, if we do nothing.

12.1 Invitation

Živko Bergant.
(Inspired by Slovenian poet Oton Župančič, 1878–1949).

Man, do you know your debt?
Have you anything said?
Why are you quiet?
Give something to all.
Give us something new,
All of us will follow you.

Yes, I know my debt.
Yes, I know my mind.
Yes, I have my words.
I will tell them loudly
From the top of the mountain.
The whole world to know.

What about you, my friend?
Will you come with me?
Are you still afraid?
Don't hide yourself in comfort,
Don't be shy and silent.
Come and climb up with me,
We shall shout and sing together.
Because we have something to say.

References

Block, L. Fred (2018). *Capitalism: The Future India Illusion*. Oakland: University of California Press.

Mason, Paul (2019). The Unbearable Unrealism of the Present. (Retrieved: July, 2020). https://www.socialeurope.eu/postcaptalism-unbearable-unrealism.

Stiglitz, E. Joseph (2019). *People, Power, and Profits. Progressive Capitalism for an Age of Discontent*. New York: Norton & Company.

References

Adizes, Ichak (2020). *Why We Are NOT Socially Responsible*. Adizes blogs. Adizes Institute: July 3, 2020. https://www.ichakadizes.com/post/why-we-are-not-socially-responsible.

Agwuezie, O. Remi (2019). *The Concept of Corporate Social Responsibility*. (Retrieved: July, 2020). https://www.academia.edu/38797711/THE_CONCEPT_OF_CORPORATE_SOCIAL_RESPONSIBILITY.

AICPA (2015). *Introduction to Accounting*. American Institute of certified Accountants. (Retrieved: December, 2019). http://www.ncert.nic.in/ncerts/l/keac101.pdf.

Al-Adeem, K. Rasheed (2010). *Accounting Theory: A Neglected Topic in Academic Accounting Research*. Doctoral dissertation. Cleveland: Case Western Reserve University.

Anderson, Elisabeth (2000). Beyond Homo Economicus: New Developments in Theories of Social Norms. *Philosophy & public Affairs*, Vol. 29, No. 2, pp. 170–200.

Andriessen, Daniel (2004). IC Valuation and Measurement: Classifying the State of the Art. *Journal of Intellectual capital*, Vol. 5, No. 2, pp. 230–242.

Arangies, G., Mlambo, C., Hamman, W. D., Steyn-Bruwer, B. W. (2008). The Value Added Statement: An Appeal for Standardization. (Retrieved: April, 2020). *Management Dynamics*, Vol. 17, No. 1/2008, pp. 31–43. https://mpra.ub.uni-muenchen.de/25970/1/MPRA_paper_25970.pdf.

Arnold, Glen (1998). *Corporate Financial Management*. London: Pitman Publishing.

Ž. Bergant, *Accountancy and Social Responsibility*, Palgrave Studies in Impact Finance,
https://doi.org/10.1007/978-3-030-77928-3

Artur, Victoria (2018). Business Ethics. (Retrieved: May, 2020). https://www.researchgate.net/publication/328789262_Business_Ethics.

Aruwa, A. S. Suleiman (2008). The Worth of Disclosures in the Value-added statements and Pattern of Value Added Distribution. *Journal of Finance and Accounting Research*, No 1/2009. (Retrieved: April, 2020). http://www.academia.edu/222418/THE_WORTH_OF_DISCLOSURES_IN_THE_VALUE_ADDED_STATEMENT_AND_PATTERN_OF_VALUE_ADDED_DISTRIBUTION.

Arvidson, Susanne (2019). *Challenges in Managing Sustainable Business*. Cham: Springer Nature.

ASSC-Accounting Standard Steering Committee (1975). *The Corporate Report*. (Retrieved: January, 2016). http://www.ion.icaew.com/clientfiles/6f45ef7e-1eff-41ff-909e-24eeb6e9ed15/the%20corporate%20report2.pdf.

Al-Hudhaif, A. Sulaiman (2010). Measuring Quality of Information System Services in Manufacturing Organizations in Riyadh. *JKAU*, Vol. 24, No 1, pp. 24–171. (Retrieved: April, 2020). https://www.kau.edu.sa/Files/320/Researches/55327_25670.pdf.

Baba, Hideaki, Ishida, Yu, Aoki, Takahiro (2015). Social Accounting for Nonprofit Organizations: Visualizing the Invisible Value of Social Impacts. *Kansai University Review of Business and Commerce*, No. 16/2015, pp. 1–22). (Retrieved: June, 2020). http://baba-hi72.up.seesaa.net/image/Kandai Review2015_baba_etal.pdf.

Bajo, C. Sanchez, Roelants, bruno (2015). *Kapital in past zadovževanja*. Capital and the trap of borrowing) (In Slovene). Ljubljana: Modrijan.

Balthazard, Claude (2015). *Are Professional and Business Ethics the Same Thing?* (Retrieved: May, 2020). https://www.hrpa.ca/Documents/Designations/Job-Ready-Program/Are-professional-ethics-and-business-ethics-the-same-thing.pdf.

Barloworld Limited (2017). Integrated Report 2017. (Retrieved: March, 2020). http://www.barloworld-reports.co.za/integrated-reports/ir-2017/value-added-statement-and-highlights.php.

Baumüller, Josef, Schaffhauser-Linzatti, Michaela-Maria (2018). In Search of Materiality for Nonfinancial Information-Reporting Requirements of the Directive 2014/95/EU. (Retrieved: July, 2020). https://www.researchgate.net/publication/326997551_In_search_of_materiality_for_nonfinancial_information-reporting_requirements_of_the_Directive_201495EU.

Beck, Ulrich (1992). *Risk Society*. London: Sage.

Benabou, Roland, Tirole, Jean (2010). Individual and Corporate Social Responsibility. (Retrieved: July, 2020). https://www.researchgate.net/publication/48264162_Individual_and_Corporate_Social_Responsibility.

Bentham, Jeremy (1780). *An Introduction to the Principles of Morals and Legislation*. (Retrieved: December, 2018). http://www.utilitarianphilosophy.com/jeremybentham.eng.html.

Bergant, Živko (2015). Social Responsibility and Corporate's Solvency. The 10th International Conference About Social Responsibility in Maribor, 2015. (Retrieved: July, 2020). http://www.irdo.si/skupni-cd/cdji/cd-irdo-2015/referati/37-zivko-bergant-paper-final-(.pdf.

Bergant, Živko (2017). Appropriate Consideration of Value-Added Law as a Precondition of Social Responsibility. 12th International conference about social responsibility in Maribor. (Retrieved: December, 2019). http://www.irdo.si/irdo2017/referati/plenarna-bergant.pdf.

Bergant, Živko (2019a). A New Approach to the Capital Adequacy Assessment of Companies. *Journal of Accounting and Management*, Vol. 9, No. 1, pp. 1–14. (Retrieved: March, 2020). https://hrcak.srce.hr/file/327727.

Bergant, Živko (2019b). The Quality of Accounting Information and User's Social Responsibility: Social Aspect. *International Journal of Advances in Management and Economics*. (Retrieved: December, 2019). http://www.managementjournal.info/index.Php/IJAME/article/view/617/514.

Bergant, Živko (2020). Starting Points to Comprehensive Treatment of Social Responsibility. *International Journal of Advances in Management and Economics*, Vol. 9. No. 1, pp. 1–7.

Bergant, Živko, Manohin, Igor (2020). Methods for an Accounting Estimation of Company's Capital Adequacy. Poreč: International conference: Accounting and management. June, 2020.

Bergant, Živko (2021). Accountancy Information System for Sustainable Future. *International Journal of Latest Research in Humanities and Social Science (IJLRHSS)*, Vol. 4, No. 1, pp. 01–07.

Bermuda Stock Exchange (2018). (Retrieved: December, 2020). https://www.google.com/search?q=Bermuda+Stock+Exchange+(2018).&oq=Bermuda+Stock+Exchange+(2018).&aqs=chrome..69i57.3092j0j15&sourceid=chrome&ie=UTF-8.

Bessler, Wolfgang, Drobetz, Wolfgang, Grüninge, C. Matthias (2011). Information Asymmetry and Financing Decisions. *International Review of Finance* No 1/2011, pp. 123–154.

Bidvest. (2012). Value-Added Statement. (Retrieved: January, 2016). http://bidvest.com/ar/bidvest_ar2011/value_added_statement.php.

Bierman H. Jr., Drebin R. A. (1978). *Financial Accounting*. 3rd Edition. Philadelphia: W. B. Saunders Company.

Blakburn, Simon (2001). *Ethics: A Very Short Introduction*. Oxford university Press.

Block, L. Fred (2018). *Capitalism: The Future India Illusion*. Oakland: University of California Press.

Blue Label Telecoms (2018). Annual Report 2018. (Retrieved: March, 2020). https://www.bluelabeltelecoms.co.za/online_reports/ar2018/value-added-statement.php.

Boatright, J. John (2000). *Ethics and the Conduct of Business.* Hoboken, NJ: Prentice-Hall Inc.

Brennan, M. Niamh (2001). Reporting Intellectual Capital in Annual reports: Evidence from Ireland. *I Accounting and Accountability Journal*, Vol. 14, No. 4, pp. 423–436.

Brennan, M. Niamh (2008). Corporate Governance, Accountability and Mechanisms of Accountability: Overview. *Accounting, Auditing & Accountability Journal*, Vol. 21, No. 7, pp. 885–906.

Brigham, F. Eugene, Gapenski, C. Louis, Daves, R. Phillip (1999). *Intermediate Financial Management*. 6th Edition. Orlando: The Dryden Press.

Brooks, J. Leonard, Dunn, Paul (2018). *Business and Professional Ethics for Directors, Executives & Accountants.* 8th Edition. Bosron: Cangage Learning.

BSI (2020). British Standard Institution. *ISO* 26000 *Guidance on Social Responsibility.* (Retrieved: April, 2020). https://www.bsigroup.com/en-GB/ISO-26000-Social-Responsibility/.

Busati, Greg (2014). *Accountability*. New York: McGraw-Hill Education.

Business Dictionary (2015). *Total Net Value*. (Retrieved: January, 2016). http://www.businessdictionary.com/definition/total-net-value-added-TNVA.html.

Bustin, Greg (2014). *You Can Count On Me*. Mc Graw-Hill Education.

Byars, M. Stephen, Stanberry, Kurt (2018). *Business Ethics*. Houston, Openstax.

Carrington, Donley (2013). An Empirical Study on the Impact of the Process of measuring *IC* on Performance. *The Electronic Journal of Knowledge Management*, Vol. 11, No. 4/2013, pp. 282–294. (Retrieved: February, 2017). https://www.google.si/?gws_rd=ssl#q=Carrington+Donley+An+Empirical+Study+pdf&*&spf=64.

Cabrita Maria do Rosario, Vaz Jorge Landeiro (2006). Intellectual capital and value Creation: Evidence from the Portuguese Banking Industry. *The Electronic Journal of Knowledge Management* No. 1/2006, pp. 11–22. (Retrieved: January, 2017). http://www.ejkm.com/front/search/index.html.

Centenary Bank (2018). Annual Report 2018. (Retrieved: April, 2020). https://www.centenarybank.co.ug/uploads/page/Annual_report_2019.pdf.

CGAP Glossary English to French (2007). (Retrieved: December, 2019). https://www.cgap.org/sites/default/files/CGAP-Glossary-English-to-French-Jan-2007.pdf.

Chow Hoi Hee (2007) Aholistic Approach to Business Management. *Singapore management Review*, Vol. 29, No. 1, pp. 73–84.

Cipolla, M. C. (1988). *Allegro ma non troppo.* Bologna: Societá editrice il Mulino.

Chen, Jin, Zhu, Zhaohui, Xie, Y. Hong (2004) Measuring Intellectual Capital: A New Model and Empirical Study. *Journal of Intellectual capital* No 1/2004, pp. 195–212. (Retrieved: January, 2017). http://citeseerx.ist.psu.edu/viewdoc/download?doi=10.1.1.195.4946&rep=rep1&type=pdf.

Coutinho de Arruda Maria Cecilia, Rok, Boleslaw (2016). *Ethics and Responsibilities. In: Understanding Ethics and Responsibilities in a Globalizing World.* (Retrieved: February, 2021). https://www.academia.edu/21950107/Economic_Inequality_as_an_Obstacle_to_Development?auto=download&email_work_card=download-paper.

Cohen, Elie (1990). *Analyse Financière.* Paris: Economica.

Communities Scotland (2006). Making the Case: Social Added Value Guide. (Retrieved: May, 2020). http://www.forthsectordevelopment.org.uk/documents/Making%20the%20case%20-%20SAV%20guide.pdf.

Coper D. J., Sherer M. J. (1984). The Value of Corporate Accounting Reports: Arguments for a Political Economy of Accounting. *Accounting, Organizations and Society*, No 3–4/1984, pp. 207–232.

Crouch, Colin (2020). *Social Europe: A Manifesto.* Berlin: Social Europe Publishing.

Crossan, Kenny (2004). The Theory of the Firm and Alternative Theories of Firm Behaviour: A Critique. *International Journal of Applied Institutional Governance*, Vol. 1, No 1. (Retrieved: April, 2020). http://www.managementjournals.com/journals/ig/vol1/21-1-1-2.pdf.

D'Amato, Alessia, Henderson, Sybil, Florence, Sue (2009). *Corporate Social responsibility and Sustainable Business.* Greensboro: Center for Creative Leadership.

Del Castillo, A. Ponce (2020). Labour in the Age of AI: Why Regulation Is Needed to Protect Workers. *Forsight Brief*, *No 8.* The European Trade Union Institute, Brussels. (Retrieved: May, 2020). https://www.etui.org/Publications2/Foresight-briefs/Labour-in-the-age-of-AI-why-regulation-is-needed-to-protect-workers.

Democratizingwork (2020). Work: Democratize, Decomodify, Remediate. (Retrieved: July, 2020). https://democratizingwork.org/.

Dethier, Fanny, Defourny, Jacques (2015). *The Effects of Workers' Participation in Governance, Ownership and Profit on the Economic Performance of Worker Cooperatives.* (Retrieved: January, 2017). https://orbi.ulg.ac.be/bitstream/2268/194594/3/Article%20SCOP.engl.final.150621.pdf

Donleavy, D. Gabriel (1994). *Cash Flow Accounting.* London: Routlege.

Donleavy, D. Gabriel (2015). Usefulness Unfulfilled: A Performance Review of Value-Added Statements. *International Journal of Critical Accounting* No. 4/2015, pp. 315–334.

Drayson, Paul (2009). The 2009 Value Added Scoreboard. The Top 800 and 750 European Companies by Value Added. BIS, Department for innovation & Skills, UK. http://webarchive.Nationalarchives.gov.uk/20100908131539/http://innovation.gov.uk/value_added/downloads/2009_ValueAdded_Analysis.pdf.

Dubnick, J. Melvin (2002). Seeking Salvation for Accountability. (Retrieved: July, 2020). http://mjdubnick.dubnick.net/papersrw/2002/salv2002.pdf.

Dumay, John, Guthrie, James, Rooney, Jim (2020). Being Critical About Intellectual Capital Accounting in 2020: An Overview. *Critical perspectives on Accounting*, Vol. 70, July, 2020.

Dyck, G. Robert, Mulej, Matjaž, Knez-Riedl, Jožica, Jurše, Karin, Lutar-Skerbinjek, Andreja, Potočan, Vojko (1998). *Self-Transformation of the Forgotten Four-Fifths.* New York: Kendall/Hunt Publishing Company.

Elkington, John, Hailes, Julia, Makower, Joel (1998). *Triple Bottom Line.* Appendix 11. (Retrieved: April, 2020). http://archive.babymilkaction.org/pdfs/spinpdfs/appendices/triplebl.pdf.

Eller, Helene (2013). Volunteers within an Organizational Context-One Term Is Not Enough. *Journal of Business and Economics*, Vol. 4, No. 9, pp. 895–904.

Epstein, Marc, McFarlan, F. Warren (2011). Nonprofit vs. For-profit Boards. *Strategic Finance*, No. 3/2011, pp. 28–35.

EU (2003). *Directive EU2003/51.* (Retrieved: January, 2016). http://www.kapitalmarktrecht-im-internet.eu/en/Areas%20of%20Law/Company_Law/European_Law/9033/Directive_2003_51_EG.htm.

EU (2008). *Commission Regulation No 1126/2008*: Adopting Certain International Standards in Accordance with Regulation (EC) No 1606/2002 of the European Parliament and of the Council. *Uradni list Evropske unije*, 29. 11. 2008. Appendix: International accounting standards (*IAS*). (Retrieved: March, 2020). http://eur-lex.europa.eu/legal-content/SL/TXT/PDF/?uri=CELEX:32008R1126&from=EN.

First National Bank Ghana Limited (2018). Financial Report 2018. (Retrieved: April, 2020). https://www.firstnationalbank.com.gh/downloads/Ghana/financial-reports/Annual_Report_and_Financial_Statements_31December2018.pdf.

Eurodiaconia (2016). *Measuring Social Value.* (Retrieved: July, 2020). https://cmsimpact.org/wp-content/uploads/2016/01/Eurodiaconia-Measuring-Social-Value.pdf.

FNB Botswana (2019). Annual Report: 30 June 2019. (Retrieved: March, 2020). https://www.fnbbotswana.co.bw/downloads/fnbBotswana/annual/FNBAnnualReport2019.pdf.

Frampton, Paul (1987). Measuring and Evaluating the Benefits of an In-House Bank. *5th International Cash Management Conference.* London.

Freeman, R. Edward, Harrison, Jeffrey, Hicks, Andrew, Parmar, Bidhan, Simone de Cole (2010). *Stakeholder Theory: The State of the Art.* Cambridge: Cambridge University Press.

Friedlob, T. George, Schleifer, Lydia L. F. (2003). *Essentials of Financial Analysis.* New York: Wiley.

Friedman, Milton (1970). The Social Responsibility of Business Is to Increase Its Profits. *New York Times*, September 13, p. 33.

Gaffikin, Michael (2007). Accounting Theory and Practice: The Ethical Dimension. (Retrieved: May, 2020). https://www.researchgate.net/publication/30386402_Accounting_Theory_and_Practice_the_Ethical_Dimension.

Galtung, Johan (1978). The Basic Needs Approach. (Retrieved: May, 2020). https://www.transcend.org/galtung/papers/The%20Basic%20Needs%20Approach.pdf.

Garben, Sacha (2019). Tackling Precarity in the Platform Economy-and Beyond. Social Europe. (Retrieved: May, 2020). https://www.socialeurope.eu/tackling-precarity-in-the-platform-economy-and-beyond.

Gill, W. David (2006). The Triple Bottom Line by Andrew Sawitz with Karl Weber. (Retrieved: April, 2020). https://static1.squarespace.com/static/57b0be1c579fb3136382b62d/t/57c8e87037c5815308cb0bb7/1472784496702/Savitz-A.-Triple-Bottom-Line.pdf.

Gholami, Sajad, et al. (2012). Social Responsibility Accounting: From Theory to Practice. *Journal of Basis and Applied Scientific Research*, Vol. 2, No. 10.

Gleim, N. Irvin, Delaney, R. Patrick (1989). *CPA Examination Review*, Vol. 1. 16th Edition. New York: Wiley.

Godfrey, Jayne, Hodgson, Allan, Tarca, Ann, Hamilton, Jane, Holmes, Scott (2019). *Accounting Theory.* 7th Edition. Milton: Willey.

Gostiša, Mato (2014). *Teorija ekonomske demokracije kot nove sistemske paradigme kapitalizma*. The Theory of Economic Democracy as a New Paradigm of the Capitalist System. (In Slovene). Kranj: *ŠCID.*

Gould, Stathis (2019). *Building Data Science and Analytics Capabilities in Finance and Accounting.* (Retrieved: July, 2020). https://www.ifac.org/knowledge-gateway/preparing-future-ready-professionals/discussion/building-data-science-and-analytics-capabilities-finance-and-accounting (*IFAC* Knowledge Gateway).

Granof, H. Michael, Zeff, A. Stephen (2008). Research on Accounting Should Learn from the Past. *The Chronicle of Higher Education*, Vol. 54, No. 28, p. A34.

Gray, Rob, Bebbington, Jan (2000). Environmental Accounting, Managerialism and Sustainability: Is the Planet Safe in the Hands of Business and Accounting? (Retrieved: October, 2020). https://www.st-andrews.ac.uk/media/csear/discussion-papers/CSEAR_dps-sustain-envaccman.pdf.

Gray, Rob, Milne, J. Markus (2002). Sustainability Reporting: Who's Kidding Whom? (Retrieved: October, 2020). https://cgi.st-andrews.ac.uk/media/csear/discussion-papers/CSEAR_dps-sustain-whoskidding.pdf.

Greene, Robert (2018). *The Laws of Human Nature.* New York: Penguin Random House LLC.

GRI (2015). Global Reporting Initiative. Informing Decisions, Driving Change: The Role of Data in a Sustainable Future. (Retrieved: June, 2020). https://www.globalreporting.org/resourcelibrary/Informing-decisions,-driving-change-The-role-of-data-in-a-sustainable-future.pdf.

GRI Standards (2016). Consolidated Set of *GRI* Sustainability Reporting Standards 2016. (Retrieved: May, 2020). http://www.ekvilib.org/wp-content/uploads/2018/03/GRI-standardi-2016.pdf.

GRI (2016, Discloser 201-1). *GRI* 201: Economic Performance. (Retrieved: July, 2020). http://www.ekvilib.org/wp-content/uploads/2018/03/GRI-standardi-2016.pdf#page=90&zoom=100,0,0.

Groenendijk, Lisa (2003). *Planning and Management Tools.* Enschede: The International Institute for Geo-Information Science and Earth. (Retrieved: May, 2020). https://webapps.itc.utwente.nl/librarywww/papers_2003/tech_rep/groenendijk.pdf.

Grupo Carrefour Brasil (2020). Financial Statements 2019. (Retrieved: April, 2020). https://www.grupocarrefourbrasil.com.br/wp-content/uploads/sites/174/2019/09/Grupo-Carrefour-Brasil-Financial-Statements-31.12.2018_final.pdf.

Guthrie, James (2001). The Management, Measurement and the Reporting of Intellectual Capital. *Journal of Intellectual Capital*, Vol. 2, No. 1, pp. 27–41.

Haller, Axel, Stolowy, Hervé (1999). *Value Added in Financial Accounting:* A Comparative Study of Germany and France. (Retrieved: January, 2016). https://www.researchgate.net/publication/29865542_Value_Added_in_Financial_Accounting_A_Comparative_Study_of_Germany_and_France.

Hadi, U. Noor. (2013). *Comprehensive Guide & Key to Modern Accountancy.* Peshavar: Nadeem Trade Center. (Retrieved: December, 2019). https://www.researchgate.net/publication/280597660_Comprehensive_Guide_Key_to_Modern_Accountancy.

Head, H. Joel (2009): Building an Accountable Workplace. (Retrieved: June, 2020). https://www.envisionexcellence.net/elements/uploads/files/Building-Workplace-Accountability-Whitepaper.pdf.

Hendriksen, Eldon (1965). *Accounting Theory.* Homewood: Richard D. Irwin, Inc.

Hines, D. Ruth (1988). Financial Accounting: in Communicating Reality, We Construct Reality. *Accounting, Organization and Society*, Vol. 13, No. 3, pp. 251–261.

Hines, D. Ruth (1989). Financial Accounting Knowledge, Conceptual Framework Projects and the Social Construction of the Accounting Profession. *Accounting & Auditing Journal*, Vol. 2, No. 2.

Hines, D. Ruth (1992). *Accounting: In Communicating a World, We Create a World.* Doctoral dissertation. Lancaster University, 1992.

Hodgson, M. Geoffrey (2012). On the Limits of Rational Choice Theory. *Economic Thought* No. 1/2012, pp. 94–108.

Hoffer, Frank (2020). *Beyond "Green Growth".* Social Europe. (Retrieved: July, 2020). https://www.socialeurope.eu/beyond-green-growth.

Hopwood, G. Anthony (1987). The Archaeology of Accounting Systems. *Accounting, Organizations and Society*, Vol. 12, No. 3, pp. 207–234.

Hopwood, G Anthony (2009). Accounting and the Environment. *Accounting, Organization and Society*, Vol. 34, No. 3–4, pp. 433–439.

Hulten, R. Charles (2009). Growth Accounting. *Working Paper* No. 15341. (Retrieved: May, 2020). http://www.nber.org/papers/w15341.

Hutchens, David (2001). *The Tip of the Iceberg*. Waltham: Pegasus Communications, Inc.

Ianniello, Giuseppe (2010). *The Voluntary Disclosure of the Value-Added Statement in Annual Reports of Italian Listed Companies.* (Retrieved: March, 2016). http://www.agriculturejournals.cz/publicFiles/25300.pdf.

IAS-International Accounting Standard 7. EU Commission (2008). (Retrieved: March, 2020). https://eur-lex.europa.eu/legal-content/EN/TXT/PDF/?uri=CELEX :02008R1126–20200101&qid=1408602215971&from=EN.

ICA-The Institute of Chartered Accountants of India (2014). *Developments in Financial Reporting*. Chapter 10. Unit 1: Value-Added Statement. (Retrieved: January, 2016). http://www.icaiknowledgegateway.org/littledms/folder1/Chapter-10-developments-in-financial-reporting.pdf.

ICCA (2006). *The ICCA Handbook on Corporate Social Responsibility*. Chichester: Wiley.

ICCA (2010). *The A to Z of Corporate Social Responsibility*. Chichester: Wiley.

Idowu, O. Samuel, Louche, Céline, Edit. (2011). *Theory and Practice of Corporate Social Responsibility.* Heidelberg: Springer.

IFRS—International Accounting Standards Board (2018). *Conceptual Framework for Financial Reporting*. (Retrieved: June, 2020). https://www.ifrs.org/-/media/project/conceptual-framework/fact-sheet-project-summary-and-feedback-statement/conceptual-framework-project-summary.pdf.

Ionel, C. Vatasoiu, Alina, Cornescu, Dumitru, I. Motoniu (2020). Human Resources Accounting – Accounting for the Most Valuable Asset of an Enterprise. (Retrieved: May, 2020). https://www.researchgate.net/publication/49615448_HUMAN_RESOURCES_ACCOUNTING_FOR_THE_MOST_VALUABLE_ASSET_OF_AN_ENTERPRISE/link/0f3196273829de2216413960/download.

Islam, Fakhrul (2019). The Voluntary Disclosure of Value-Added Statement in Financial Reporting-A Study on Listed Companies of Bangladesh. (Retrieved: April, 2020). https://www.researchgate.net/publication/330497717_The_voluntary_Disclosure_of_Value_Added_Statement_in_Financial_Reporting-A_Study_on_listed_Companies_of_Bangladesh.

Jamali, Dima (2008). A Stakeholder Approach to Corporate Social Responsibility: Afresh Perspective into Theory and Practice. *Journal of Business Ethics*, Springer, Vol. 82, No. 1, pp. 213–231. (Retrieved: July, 2020). https://www.academia.edu/15824941/A_Stakeholder_Approach_to_Corporate_Social_Responsibility_A_Fresh_Perspective_into_Theory_and_Practice.

Joannides, Vassili (2012). *Critical Perspectives on Accounting*, Vol. 23, No. 3, pp. 244–257.

Joia, L. Antonio (2000). Measuring Intangible Corporate Assets. *Journal of Intellectual Capital* No. 1/2000, pp. 68–84. (Retrieved: December, 2016). http://app.ebape.fgv.br/comum/arq/JIC.pdf.

Johnson, Carol (2019). Is the Crisis of Social Democracy a Crisis of Equality? https://www.socialeurope.eu/crisis-of-equality.

Jones, Stewart (2015). *The Routledge Companion to Financial Accounting Theory*. New York: Routledge.

Joseph, Augustine (2014). The Need of Personal Responsibility and Integrity in Corporate Social Responsibility Theories. *International Journal of Recent Advances in Organizational Behavior and Decision Sciences*, Vol. 1, No. 1, pp. 45–67.

Juthani, Toral, Urvi Mehta. Book. Keeping & Accountancy. STD. XI. Mumbai: Target Publications Pvt. Ltd. (Retrieved: December, 2019). https://www.targetpublications.org/download/11-commerce/std-11-book-keeping-and-accountancy.pdf.

Kállay, Bálazs (2002). Ktheory of the Firm. *Economics & Sociology*, Vol. 5, No. 1, pp. 39–50.

Kaur, Prabhjot (2020). Value-Added Statement (VAS). (Retrieved: April, 2020). http://www.yourarticlelibrary.com/accounting/financial-reporting/value-added-statement-vas/57379.

Kaye, Leon (2012). Time to Start Valuing Human Capital as an Asset on the Balance Sheet. (Retrieved: May, 2020). https://www.theguardian.com/sustainable-business/valuing-human-capital-asset-balance-sheet.

Kazmi, B. Ali, Leca, Bernard, Naccachew, Philippe (2015). Is Corporate Social Responsibility a New Spirit of Capitalism? *Organization*, Vol. 23, No. 5, pp. 742–762. (Retrieved: June, 2020). https://www.researchgate.net/publication/288021009_Is_corporate_social_responsibility_a_new_spirit_of_capitalism.

Kempner, J. Jack (1968). The Basic Concepts of Accounting. *Montana Law Review*, Vol. 30, No.1, pp. 1–17.

Keynes, J. Maynard (1936). *The General Theory of Employment, Interest and Money*. London: Macmillan.

Khan, T. Muhammad, et. al. (2012). Corporate Social responsibility (CSR) – Definition, Concepts and Scope (A Review). *Universal Journal of Management and Social Sciences*, Vol. 2, No. 7, pp. 41–51.

Khan, Majid, Majid, Abdul (2013). The Effect of Corporate Social Responsibility on Profitability and Market Share: A Case of Cement Industry of Pakistan. *Academic Journal of Management Sciences*, Vol. 2, No. 1, pp. 44–62.

Khoshkho Omid Imani, Fahim, Seyed Reza Seyed Nezhad, Mokhtari, Masoud (2013). The Impact of Net Value Added on Predicting the Earnings and

Operating Cash Flow: An Empirical Study Base on Tehran Stock Exchange. *Management Science Letters* No 3/2013, pp. 2923–2932. (Retrieved: April, 2020). https://pdfs.semanticscholar.org/c5ed/237265d3caaf1061a96d082e57a9cc4050aa.pdf?_ga=2.147408817.784419649.1587388447-1321762634.1587388447.

Kianto, Aino, Ritala, Paavo, Vanhala, Mika, Hussinki, Henri (2020). Reflections on the Criteria Indian Sound Measurement of Intellectual Capital: A Knowledge-Based Perspective. Critical Perspectives on Accounting, Vol. 70, July, 2020.

Kinney, W. R. (1986). Empirical Accounting Research Design for Ph.D. Students. *The Accounting Review*, Vol. 61. No. 2, pp. 338–350.

Kilig, Levent (2006). *Compta Finance*. Paris: Groupe Eyrolle.

Kilpi, Jukka (1998). *The Ethics of Bankruptcy*. London: Routledge.

Knoflacher, Markus (2002). *A Conceptual Model for Integrated Assessment*. Seibersdorf: Austrian Research Center. (Retrieved: May, 2020). https://pdfs.semanticscholar.org/3c56/6be91c590506c382e14a280ed92a6cd84e8a.pdf?_ga=2.104776320.1440620216.1588506548-1321762634.1587388447.

Knowledge (2003). *Intellectual Capital Statements – The New Guideline*. Copenhagen: Danish Ministry of Science, Technology and Innovation. (Retrieved: May, 2020). http://pure.au.dk/portal/files/32340329/guideline_uk.pdf.

Koster, E. G. Jan (2017). Human Capital as a Part of the Financial Balance Sheet. (Retrieved: May, 2020). https://www.eapm.org/human-capital-part-financial-balance-sheet/.

KPMG. (2020). *The Social Contact in the 21st Century*. McKinsey Global Institute. (Retrieved: June, 2020). https://www.mckinsey.com/~/media/McKinsey/Industries/Social%20Sector/Our%20Insights/The%20social%20contract%20in%20the%2021st%20century/MGI-The-social-contract-in-the-21st-century-Executive-summary-final.pdf.

Kraaijenbrink, Jeroen, Spender, J. C. (2011). *Theories of the Firm and Their Value Creation Assumptions*. 31st Strategic Management Society international Conference. (Retrieved: May, 2020). https://www.researchgate.net/publication/42243920_The_Resource-Based_View_A_Review_and_Assessment_of_Its_Critiques.

Kukoleća, Stevan (1972). *Osnovi teorije organizacionih Sistema. Fundamental Theory of Organizational Systems*. (In Slovene). Beograd: privredno finansijski vodič.

Lagouarde-Segot, Thomas, Paranque, bernard (2018). Finance and Sustainability: From Idea to Utopia. *International Review of Financial Analysis*, Vol. 55, January, pp. 80–92.

Lee, P. Min-Dong (2008). A Review of the Theories of Corporate Social Responsibility: Its Evolutionary Path and the Road Ahead. *International Journal of Management Reviews*, Vol. 10, No. 1, pp. 53–73.

Liebowitz, Jay, Suen, Y. Ching (2000). Developing Knowledge Management Metrics for Measuring Intellectual Capital. *Journal of Intellectual Capital* No. 1/2000, pp. 54–67. (Retrieved: January, 2017). http://cos.ufrj.br/~jano/LinkedDocuments/_papers/aula05/Developing%20Knowledge%20Management%20Metrics%20for%20Measuring%20Intellectual%20Capital.pdf.

López Davis, S., et al., (2017). Introducing Personal Social Responsibility as a Key Element to Upgrade CSR. *Spanish Journal of Marketing – ESIC*, Vol. 21, No. 2, pp. 146–163.

Lynch, David (1994). *Quality in Finance Function.* London: Kogan Page.

Machado, A.V. Márcio, Macedo, M. A. da Silva, Machado, R. Márcia (2016). Analysis of the Relevance of Information Content of the Value-Added Statement in the Brazilian Capital Markets. (Retrieved: October, 2016). http://papers.ssrn.com/sol3/papers.cfm?abstract_id=2601211.

Mandal Niranjan, Goswami, Suvarun (2008). Value-Added Statement (VAS) – A Critical Analysis. *Great Lakes Herald*, No. 2 (2008). (Retrieved: May, 2015). http://www.greatlakes.edu.in/pdf/Herald/Vol2/Value%20Added%20Statement%20-%20A%20Critical%20Analysis.pdf.

Marr, Bernard, Schiuma, Gianni, Neely, Andy (2004). Intellectual Capital – Defining Key Performance Indicators for Organizational Knowledge Assets. *Business Process Management Journal* No 5/2004, pp. 551–569. (Retrieved: January, 2017). https://pdfs.semanticscholar.org/be99/efdcf4dffc95763e175616928d63974e661a.pdf.

Mason, Paul (2019a). Time for Postcapitalism. (Retrieved: may, 2020). https://www.socialeurope.eu/time-for-postcapitalism.

Mason, Paul (2019b). The Unbearable Unrealism of the Present. (Retrieved: July, 2020). https://www.socialeurope.eu/postcaptalism-unbearable-unrealism.

Matsa, A. David (2018). Capital Structure and a Firm's Workforce. *Annual Review of Financial Economics*, Vol. 10, No. 1, pp. 387–412.

Max-Neef, A. Manfred (1991). *Human Scale Development: Conception, Application and Further Reflections.* New York: The Apex Press.

Mazzucato, Mariana (2020). *Capitalism's Triple Crisis.* Social Europe. (Retrieved: April, 2020). https://www.socialeurope.eu/capitalisms-triple-crisis.

MBN – Market Business News. Accounting – Definition and Meaning. (Retrieved: October. 2019). https://marketbusinessnews.com/financial-glossary/accounting-definition-meaning/.

McCredie, Helen (1957). The Theory and Practice of Accounting. *The Accounting Review*, Vol. 32, No. 2, pp. 216–223.

McLeay, Stuart (1983). Value Added: A Comparative Study. *Accounting, Organizations and Society*, Vol. 8, No. 1/1983, pp. 31–56. (Retrieved: April, 2020). https://www.researchgate.net/profile/Stuart_McLeay/publication/221953528_Value_Added_A_Comparative_Study/links/00b495264ab1aea7aa000000.pdf.

McLure, B. (2004). *The Small Business Handbook*. Melbourne: Bas Publishing.

McPhail, Ken, Walters, Diane (2009). *Accounting and Business Ethics*. London: Routledge.

Meihami, Bahram, Varmaghani, Zeinab, Meihami Hussein (2014). Role of Intellectual Capital on Firm Performance (Evidence from Iranian Companies). *International Letters of Social and Humanistic Sciences*, Vol. 12, pp. 43–50.

Migros Group (2018). Annual Report 2018. (Retrieved: March, 2020). https://report.migros.ch/2017/en/overview-of-migros/environment-commitment/value-added-statement/.

Milost, Franko (2012). Accounting for Invisible Business Assets of an Organization. Računovodsko obravnavanje nevidnih poslovnih prvin organizacije (In Slovene). *2nd Conference About Internal Reporting*, pp. 128–139. Ljubljana: ZES, ZRFRS, IPR.

Miller, Peter (1998). The Margins of Accounting. *European Accounting Review*, Vol. 7, No. 4, pp. 605–621.

Miller, B. W., Paul, Bahnson, R. Paul (2002). *Quality Financial Reporting*. New York: McGraw-Hill.

Mínguez, Norberto (2002). Business Ethics and Corporate Image. (Retrieved: May, 2020). https://www.researchgate.net/publication/27590734_Business_ethics_and_corporate_image.

Miltiadis, D. Lytras, Edvinsson, Leif, Ordóñez de Pablos, Patricia (2008). The Intellectual Capital Statements: Evolution and How to Get Started. (Retrieved: May, 2020). https://www.researchgate.net/publication/267301892_The_intellectual_capital_statements_Evolution_and_how_to_get_started.

Montagna, Paul (1991). Accounting Elites and Accounting Theory. *Accounting, Organizations and Society*, Vol. 16, No. 1, pp. 93–99.

Mook, L. Ingrid (2003). *A Social Accounting Framework for Cooperatives: The Expanded Value-added statement*. (Retrieved: January, 2016). http://www.ace.coop/portals/0/institute/03/mook.pdf.

Mook L. Ingrid, Richmond, B. Jane, Quarter, Jack (2003a). Calculating the Value of Volunteer Contributions for Financial Statements. *The Philanthropist*, Vol. 18, No. 1, pp. 71–83.

Mook, L. Ingrid, Quarter, Jack (2004). *Estimating and Reporting the Value of Volunteer Contributions*. (Retrieved: May, 2016). http://sectorsource.ca/sites/default/files/resources/files/Quarter_Estimating_Reporting_Final.pdf.

Mook, L. Ingrid (2007). *The Expanded Value-Added Statement*. Doctoral dissertation, University of Toronto. (Retrieved: January, 2016). http://home.oise.utoronto.ca/~lschugurensky/Mook_Thesis.pdf.

Morley, F. Michael (1979). The Value-Added Statement in Britain. *The Accounting Review* No. 3/1979, pp. 618–629.

Mostafei, Parasto (2015). An Empirical Investigation of Relationship Between Intellectual Capital and Different Dimensions of Company's Performance.

Science International No. 3/2015, pp. 2899–2909. (Retrieved: January, 2017). http://www.sci-int.com/pdf/115352362899-2909%205+++.pdf.

Mouritsen, J., Larsen, H. T., Bukh, P. N. (2001). Valuing the Future: Intellectual Capital Supplements at Skandia. *Accounting, Auditing & Accountability Journal*, Vol. 14, No. 4, pp. 399–422. (Retrieved: December, 2020). https://www.researchgate.net/profile/Per-Bukh/publication/235295483_Valuing_the_future_Intellectual_capital_supplements_at_Skandia/links/02e7e52dff67e9c034000000/Valuing-the-future-Intellectual-capital-supplements-at-Skandia.pdf?origin=publication_detail.

MPRA (2016). Corporate Social Responsibility: A Review on Definitions, Core Characteristics and Theoretical Perspectives. *Mediterranean Journal of Social Science*, Vol. 6, No. 4, pp. 63–95.

Mulej, Matjaž (2020). *Sustainable Future Concept vs. Sustainable Development After 15 years (Remembering Timi Ečimović, 1941–2018)*. (Retrieved: June, 2020). 15th IRDO International Science and Business Conference. June, 2020, Maribor. http://www.irdo.si/irdo2020/referati.html.

Munasinghe, Mohan (2007). Sustainable Development Triangle. (Retrieved: May, 2020). https://editors.eol.org/eoearth/wiki/Sustainomics_and_sustainable_development.

Netcare Limited (2017). Annual Integrated Report 2017. (Retrieved: March, 2020). https://www.netcare.co.za/InvestorReport/netcare_annual-2017/downloads/Netcare_IAR_2017_Value-added_statement.pdf.

Neves, Catarina, Merrill, Roberto (2020). Encouraging European Solidarity: An Unconditional Basic Income. Social Europe. (Retrieved: May, 2020). https://www.socialeurope.eu/encouraging-european-solidarity-an-unconditional-basic-income.

Noufe, Daniel (2016). Corporate Social Responsibility and Financial Performance: A Literature Review. (Retrieved: July, 2020). https://www.academia.edu/32452298/Corporate_Social_Responsibility_and_profitability.

Nuhu, Mohammed (2014). Role of Ratio Analysis in Business Decisions: A Case Study NBC Maiduguri Plant. *Journal of Educational and Social Research*, Vol. 4, No. 3, pp. 105–118.

Nuttall, Douglas, Young, Lay (2017). Building the Framework for Absolute Sustainability. *OIDA International Journal of Sustainable Development, Canada*, Vol. 10, No. 11, pp. 11–32.

OANDO Plc (2018). Oando Energy and Trading. Annual Reports 2018. https://www.oandoplc.com/wp-content/uploads/2019/04/FinancialStatementFull.pdf.

Obama, Barack (2012). Remarks by the President at the Associated Press Luncheon. (Retrieved: Julij, 2020). https://obamawhitehouse.archives.gov/the-press-office/2012/04/03/remarks-president-associated-press-luncheon.

OECD Manual (2001). Measuring Productivity. (Pridobljeno: May, 2020). https://www.oecd.org/std/productivity-stats/2352458.pdf.

Ogu, I. Michael (2013). Rational Choice Theory: Assumptions, Strengths, and Greatest Weaknesses in Application outside the Western Milieu Context. *Arabian Journal of Business and Management Review* (*Nigerian Chapter*), Vol. 1, No. 3, pp. 90–99.

O'Hare, J. (2013). *Analyzing Financial Statements for Non-Specialists*. New York: Routledge.

Okeke, C. John (2016). Human Capital Accounting: A Literature Review. (Retrieved: May, 2020). https://www.researchgate.net/publication/288872492_Human_capital_accounting_A_literature_review.

Oldroyd, David, Tyson, N. Thomas, Fleischman, K. Richard (2015). American Ideology, Socialism and Financial Accounting Theory: A Counter View. *Critical Perspectives on Accounting*, Vol. 27, March 2015, pp. 209–218.

O'Reagan, P. (2002). *Financial Information Analysis*. London: Wiley.

Organicsoul (2020). Understanding the Triple Bottom Line, Its Shortcomings, and the Solution. (Retrieved: May, 2020). http://www.organicsoul.com/understanding-the-triple-bottom-line-its-shortcomings-and-the-solution/.

Oshika, Tomoki, Saka, Chika (2015). Created Value as Sustainability KPI for Integrated Reporting. (Retrieved: January, 2016). http://www.insead.edu/facultyresearch/areas/accounting/events/documents/OshikaandSaka-2015.pdf.

Perera, L. Aldama, Zicari, Adrián (2012) Value-Added Reporting as a Tool for Sustainability: A Latin American Experience. *Corporate Governance*, Vol. 12, No. 4/2012, pp. 485–498. (Retrieved: January, 2016). http://live.v1.udesa.edu.ar/files/MBA/Papers/Value_added_reporting_Zicari_2012.pdf.

Perrot, Pascal (2006). Définition et mesure de la »valeur ajoutée sociale« dans les associations. RECMA – *Revue internationale de l'economie sociale*, No. 301/2006, pp. 42–60. (Retrieved: April, 2020). http://www.recma.org/sites/default/files/301-042060.pdf.

Petty, William (1690). *Political Arithmetic*. (Retrieved: January, 2016). https://www.marxists.org/reference/subject/economics/petty/index.htm.

Pierleoni, M. Rita: The Analysis of Inequalities: The Review of Economic Approach and Policies. *Journal of Business and Economics*, Vol. 9, No 2, pp. 123–136.

Piketty, Thomas (2014). *Capital in the Twenty-First Century*. USA: Amazon.

Pojman, P. Louis, Fieser, James (2011). *Ethical Theory*. Boston: Wadsworth.

Pong, Chris, Mitchell, Falconer (2014). Accounting for a Disappearance: A Contribution to the History of the Value-Added Statement in the UK. *Accounting Historians Journal*, No 2/2014. (Retrieved: January, 2016). http://www.accountingin.com/accounting-historians-journal/volume-32-number-2/accounting-for-a-disappearance-a-contribution-to-the-history-of-the-value-added-statement-in-the-uk/.

Prasad, Suresh (2015). *Preparation of Gross/Net Value-Added Statement for Companies*. (Retrieved: April, 2020). https://www.scribd.com/document/370437728/Preparation-of-Gross-Net-Value-Added-Statement-for-Companies.

Prindl, R. Andreas, Prodhan, Bimal (1994). *Ethical Conflicts in Finance*. Oxford: Blackwell Publishers.

Proudhon, Pierre-Joseph (1868). *Solution du problème social*. Paris: Librairie Internationale.

Radhakrishnan, G. T., Kumaran, T. S. S., Moorthy, T. N., Rama, N. (2017). *Accountancy*. Government of Tamil Nadu, India, Tamilnadu Textbook and Educational Services Corporation, Chennai, 2017. (Retrieved: December, 2019). https://www.academia.edu/34412465/ACCOUNTANCY_HigHer_SeCONdArY_FirST_YeAr.

Rahim, Azlina, Atan, Ruhaya, Kamaluddin, Amrizah (2011). Intellectual Capital Reporting in Malaysian Technology Industry. *Asian Journal of Accounting and Governance*, No. 2/2011 Intellectual Capital Reporting in Malaysian Technology Industry Intellectual Capital Reporting in Malaysian Technology Industry, pp. 51–59.

Rao, K. S. Ramesh (1987). *Financial Management*. London: MacMillan Publishing Company.

Ratnatunga, Janek, Alam, Manzurul (2011). Strategic Governance and Management Accounting: Evidence from a Case Study. *ABACUS, Journal of Accounting, Finance and Business Studies*, Vol. 47, No. 3, pp. 343–382.

Rawls, John (1917). *A Theory of Justice*. Cambridge MA, Harvard University Press.

Rawls, John (2001). *Justice as Fairness. A Restatement*. Harvard University Press.

Reichmann, Thomas, Lange, Christoph (1981). The Value-Added Statement as Part of Corporate Social Reporting. *Management International Review* No 4/1981, p. 17–22.

Riahi-Belkaoui, Ahmed (1998). *The Coming Crisis in Accounting*. Westport, CT: Quorum Books.

Riahi-Belkaoui, Ahmed (2003). Intellectual Capital and Firm Performance of U.S. Multinational Firms: A Study of the Resource-Based and Stakeholder Views. *Journal of Intellectual Capital* No 4/2003, pp. 215–226. (Retrieved: April, 2020). https://papers.ssrn.com/sol3/papers.cfm?abstract_id=365580&rec=1&srcabs=1152892&alg=1&pos=6.

Riahi-Belkaoui, Ahmed (2010). *Wealth and Value Added: Reporting, Analysis, Prediction, and Taxation*, April, 2020. Pridobljeno. https://www.researchgate.net/publication/247621754_Usefulness_of_value_added_reporting_A_review_and_synthesis_of_the_literature.

Riahi-Belkaoui, Ahmed (2012). *Accounting Theory*. 5th Edition. Hampshire: Cengage Learning.

Richard, Jacques (2014). The Dangerous Dynamics of Modern Capitalism (from static to IFRS' Futuristic Accounting. *Critical perspectives on Accounting*, Elsevier, Vol. 30, pp. 9–34.

Riddle, Stewart, Honan, Eileen, Bright, David (2018). *Writing with Deleuze in the Academy: Creating Monsters*. Singapore: Springer Pte Ltd.

Roberts, John, Scapens, Robert (1985). Accounting Systems and Systems of Accountability – Understanding Accounting Practices in Their Organisational Contexts. *Accounting, Organizations and Society*, Vol. 10, No. 4. pp. 443–456.

Roos, Göran, Bainbridge, Alan, Jacobsen, Kristine (2001). Intellectual Capital Analyses As a Strategic Tool. *Strategy and Leadership Journal* No 4/2001, pp. 21–26. (Retrieved: January, 2017). https://pdfs.semanticscholar.org/2201/b9ec8834062d6cef991b76448262856e2e05.pdf.

Rus, V. (1976). *Etika in Socializem* (In Slovene). Ljubljana: Mladinska knjiga.

Samuels, M. J., Wilkes, F. M., Brayshaw, R. E. (1995). *Management of Company Finance*. London: Chapman & Hall.

Sarkar, R. Chitta, Nandi, C. Kartik (2011). Corporate Social Performance Through Value Added Reporting – A Case Study of Hindustan Petroleum Corporation Ltd. *International Journal of Research in Commerce and Management*, št. 6/2011, pp. 89–95. (Retrieved: January, 2017). http://ijrcm.org.in/article_info.php?article_id=914.

Schaltegger, Stefan, Bennet, Martin, Burrit, Roger (2006). *Sustainability Accounting and Reporting*. Dordrecht: Springer.

Shodhganga (2017). *Analysis of Value Added Ratios*. (Retrieved: May, 2020). https://shodhganga.inflibnet.ac.in/bitstream/10603/144387/17/17_Chapter-5.pdf.

Scott, R. William, O'Brien, C. Patricia (2019). *Financial Accounting Theory*. Toronto, ON: Pearson Canada Inc.

Singh, Pooja (2013). *A Critical Analysis of Value Added Reporting Practices in Selected Indian Companies*. Doctoral dissertation, Faculty of Commerce, Dayalbagh, AGRA. (Retrieved: January, 2016) http://shodh.inflibnet.ac.in:8080/jspui/bitstream/123456789/2045/1/synopsis.pdf.

Singtel (2019). Annual Report 2019. (Retrieved: 2020). https://cdn.aws.singtel.com/annualreport/2019/files/Group_Value_Added_Statements.pdf.

Smart, B. S., Megginson, W. L., Gitman, L. J. (2004). *Corporate Finance*. Mason, OH: Thomson, South-Western.

Soonawalla, Kazbi (2006). *Contemporary Issues in Management Accounting*. Oxford: Oxford University Press.

Stanko B. Brian, Zeller, L. Thomas, Melena F. Matthew (2014). Human Asset Accounting and Measurement: Moving Forward. *Lornal of Business & Economic Research*, Vol. 12, No. 2, pp. 93–104.

Stanton, B. F., Jinkins, E. John, Ahearn, C. Mary, Hanson, D. Gregory (1992). Perspective on Farm Size and Structure Provided by Value-Added Measures. *The Journal of Agricultural Economics Research*, Vol. 44, No. 2/1992, pp. 36–44. (Retrieved: April, 2020). http://ageconsearch.umn.edu/bitstream/138012/2/5Stanton_44_2.pdf.

Stiglitz, E. Joseph, Fitoussi, Jean-Paul, Durand, Martine (2018). *For Good Measure: Advancing Research on Well-being Metrics Beyond GDP.* Paris: *OECD* Publishing.

Stiglitz, E. Joseph (2019). *People, Power, and profits. Progressive Capitalism for an Age of Discontent.* New York: Norton & Company.

Stulz, René (1996). Rethinking Risk Management. *Journal of Applied Corporate Finance*, Vol. 9. No. 3, pp. 8–24.

Sumner, N. Levine (1988). *The Financial Analyst's Handbook.* Homewood, IL: Dow Jones Irwin.

Suojanen, W. W. (1954). Accounting Theory and the Large Corporation. *The Accounting Review*, Julij, 1954, pp. 618–629.

Sustainability & Impact Investor Forum (2020). *Driving Value with Value.* (Retrieved: May, 2020). https://informaconnect.com/sustainability-and-impact-investor-forum/?vip_code=FKN2742GOOGLE&gclid=EAIaIQobChMIw_TU7_Oe6QIVhOJ3Ch0grABIEAAYASAAEgLI2_D_BwE.

SPAR Group Limited—Online (2020). (Retrieved: March, 2020). https://investor-relations.spar.co.za/ir2017/reports-from-our-leaders/value-added-statement/.

Smyth, Danielle (2018). What Are the Basic Accounting Theories? (Retrieved: January. 2020). https://bizfluent.com/about-5121481-basic-accounting-theories.html.

Straub, Richard (2018). Socially Responsible Business Can Only Succeed If It Becomes a Movement. *Harvard Business Review*, March, 2018. (Retrieved: July, 2020). https://hbr.org/2018/03/socially-responsible-business-can-only-succeed-if-it-becomes-a-movement.

Šarotar Žižek, Simona, Mulej, Matjaž (2020). Society & Welfare. (Retrieved: July, 2020). http://www.irdo.si/irdo2020/referati/a2-1-sarotarzizek&mulej.pdf.

Širovnik, David (2016). Sinthesis of Sustainable Systems by Maximizing Sustainable Net Present Value. (In Slovene). *Sinteza sistemov z maksimiranjem trajnostne neto sedanje vrednosti.* Master's Thesis. Maribor. (Retrieved: April, 2020). https://dk.um.si/Dokument.php?id=105690.

Taleb, N. Nicholas (2009). Errors, Robustness, and the Fourth Quadrant. *International Journal of Forecasting*, Vol. 25, pp. 744–759.

Taleb, N., Goldstein, G. D., Spitznagel, W. M. (2009). The Six Mistakes Executives Make in Risk Management. *Harvard Business Review*, October 2009, pp. 78–81.

Taleb, N. Nicholas (2010). *The Bed of Procrustes: Philosophical and Practical Aphorisms*. New York: Random House.
Taleb, N. Nassim (2012). *Antifragile*. London: Penguin Books.
Taleb, N. Nassim (2018). *Skin in the Game: Hidden Asymmetries in Daily Life*. New York: Random House.
Tinker, T., Puxty T. (1995). *Policing Accounting Knowledge: The Market for Excuses Affair*. New York: Markus Weiner Publishers.
Tomescu, M. Ada, Romania, Oradea, Bodog, S. Aurelia (2015). *Business management and Business Ethics – Two Paradigms and Their Relationship*. (Retrieved: May, 2020). https://www.researchgate.net/publication/285381076_Business_Management_and_Business_Ethics_-Two_Paradigms_and_Their_Relationship.
Tsoutsoura, Margarita (2004). Corporate Social Responsibility and Financial Performance. (Retrieved: July, 2020). https://escholarship.org/uc/item/111799p2.
Turk, Ivan (1978). *Podatki in informacije v poslovnem sistemu*. (In Slovene). Ljubljana: ZRFS.
UN (2015). *Sustainable Development Goals*. (Retrieved: June, 2020). https://www.sightsavers.org/policy-and-advocacy/global-goals/?gclid=EAIaIQobChMI3MHO0vCh6gIVrIBQBh2A5wANEAAYASAAEgI9FfD_BwE.
Unegbu, O. Angus (2014). Theories of Accounting: Evolution & Developments, Income-Determination and Diversities in Use. *Research Journal of Finance and Accounting*, Vol. 5, No. 19, 2014. (Retrieved: January, 2020). https://arxiv.org/abs/1411.4633.
Unilever Nigeria Plc (2018). Annual Report. (Retrieved: March, 2020). https://www.unilever-ewa.com/Images/unilever-audited-financial-statements-ye-31-december—2018_tcm1283-535769_1_en.pdf.
Valvassori, Antonella, Vaccari, Vittorio (2009). Sustainability Report: Present Status and Future. (Retrieved: may, 2020). https://www.researchgate.net/publication/265676522_SUSTAINABILITY_REPORT_PRESENT_STATUS_AND_FUTURE
Van Parijs, Phillippe (2020). Finland's Final Verdict. (Retrieved: May, 2020). https://www.socialeurope.eu/basic-income-positive-results-from-finland.
Van Staden, Chris (2000). *The Value-Added Statement: Bastion of Social Reporting or Dinosaur of Financial Reporting?* (Retrieved: January, 2016). http://poseidon01.ssrn.com/delivery.php?ID=364085089029103082121125101025126110062049053076063030120001106113095066076064105069032124000100104011004099125064081002024107015062036037082105104113015000025066080052110082122017094127000064113028095078086069016099103089073101064088079094016085&EXT=pdf.

Van Staden, J. Chris (2001). *Aspects of the Motivation for Voluntary Disclosures: Evidence from the Publication of Value-added statements in an Emerging Economy.* (Retrieved: January, 2016). http://www.massey.ac.nz/massey/fms/Colleges/College%20of%20Business/School%20of%20Accountancy/Documents/Discussion%20Papers/206.pdf.

Van Staden Chris, Haller Axel, Landis Cristina (2013). Value Added Information as Part of Sustainability Reporting – Initial International Insights. (Retrieved: January, 2016). http://www.apira2013.org/proceedings/pdfs/K248.pdf.

Villiers, Charl, Sharma, Umesh (2020). A Critical Reflection on the Future of Financial, Intellectual Capital, Sustainability and Integrating Reporting. *Critical Perspectives on Accounting*, Vol. 70, July, 2020.

Volkswagen Group (2017). Annual Report 2017. (Retrieved: March, 2020) https://annualreport2017.volkswagenag.

Vovk Korže, ana (2020). Understanding Sustainability Today. 15th IRDO International Science and Business Conference. June, 2020, Maribor. (Retrieved: June, 2020). http://www.irdo.si/irdo2020/referati.html.

Yogesha, B. S., Mahadevappa, B. (2014). Analysis of Value Added Ratios of Indian Oil Corporation. *Journal of Humanities and Social Science*, Vol. 19, No. 11, pp. 18–25). (Retrieved: December, 2016). http://iosrjournals.org/iosr-jhss/papers/Vol19-issue11/Version-5/E0191151825.pdf.

Zakari, Murtala (2017). The Relationship Between Corporate Social Responsibility and Profitability: The Case of Dangote Cement Plc. *Journal of Finance and Accounting*, Vol. 5, No. 4, pp. 171–176.

Zeng, Tao (2013). Corporate Social Responsibility, Tax Aggressiveness, and Firm Market Value. (Retrieved: May, 2016). https://doi.org/10.1111/1911-3838.12090/epdf.

Walsh, C. (1996). *Key Management Ratios.* London: Pitman Publishing.

Wan-Jan, W. Saitfuk (2006). Defining Corporate Social Responsibility. *Journal of Public Affairs*, Vol. 6, August–November, 2006.

Watts, L. Ross, Zimmerman, L. Jerold (1979). The Demand for and Supply of Accounting Theories. *The Accounting Review*, Vol. 54, No. 2, pp. 273–305.

Westwick, C. A. (1989). *How to Use Management Ratios.* 2nd Edition. Aldershot: A Grower Workbook.

Zingales, L. (2000). In Search of New Foundations. *Journal of Finance*, Vol. 55, No. 4, pp. 1623–1653.

Index

Ž. Bergant, *Accountancy and Social Responsibility*, Palgrave Studies in Impact Finance,
https://doi.org/10.1007/978-3-030-77928-3